BELSEN IN HISTORY AN͏

To the Memory of Hugo Gryn (1930–1986)

BELSEN IN HISTORY AND MEMORY

edited by

JO REILLY
DAVID CESARANI
TONY KUSHNER
COLIN RICHMOND

FRANK CASS
LONDON • PORTLAND, OR

First published in 1997 in Great Britain by
FRANK CASS & CO. LTD.
Newbury House, 900 Eastern Avenue,
London IG2 7HH

and in the United States of America by
FRANK CASS
c/o ISBS, 5804 N.E. Hassalo Street,
Portland, Oregon 97213-3644

Copyright © 1997 Frank Cass & Co. Ltd.

British Library Cataloguing in Publication Data

A catalogue record for this book is available
from the British Library

ISBN 0 7146 4767 5 (cloth)
0 7146 4323 8 (paperback)

Library of Congress Cataloging-in-Publication Data

A catalog record for this book is available
from the Library of Congress

Printed in Great Britain by
Antony Rowe Ltd., Chippenham, Wilts.

Contents

List of Illustrations

Acknowledgements

This volume grew out of a conference on 'The Liberation of Belsen' held in London on 9–10 April 1995. The conference was organised jointly by Dr David Cesarani, Director of the Institute of Contemporary History and Wiener Library, London and Dr Tony Kushner, Marcus Sieff Lecturer in the Department of History and Parkes Library, University of Southampton. The administrative arrangements were ably handled by Anne Beale and Gerta Regensburger of the Wiener Library. The conference was sponsored by the Lord Ashdown Settlement; The R.M. Burton Charitable Settlement; Mr Ernst Fraenkel; Friends of the Parkes Library; Mr Jack Goldhill; The Sue Hammerson Foundation; The Hartley Institute and the School of Research and Graduate Studies, University of Southampton; Sir Sigmund Sterberg Charitable Foundation. The editors of this volume wish to tank these sponsors for making possible the event and the publication based on it. They also wish to thank Frank Cass who maintained his patient support for the project and Sybil Lunn who worked on the index. Rabbi Hugo Gryn, who died in 1996, closed the conference. This volume is intended as a small memorial and tribute to his courage and wisdom, and the inspiration he provided to all those concerned to increase knowledge and awareness of the Holocaust.

PART I: INTRODUCTION

Approaching Belsen: An Introduction

I

In a century that has witnessed ever-increasing opportunities for voyeurism, the liberation of Bergen-Belsen concentration camp by British forces in April 1945 has special significance.[1] Although Nazi camps of a far more murderous nature were liberated before Belsen, the scenes recorded at Belsen by the soldiers, journalists, photographers, broadcasters and film crews were perhaps the most gruesome of all images relating to Nazi atrocities. The impact on those carrying out the liberation of Belsen, as will be stressed throughout this volume, was traumatic. Yet even those in the comfort of the cinemas, front rooms and libraries of the Home Front exposed to the newsreels, press and radio reports were left in a state of emotional shock by the attempts to communicate the horror of Belsen. Susan Sontag relates how in a Santa Monica bookstore she came across photographs from Bergen-Belsen and Dachau in July 1945:

> Nothing I have seen – in photographs or in real life – ever cut me as sharply, deeply, instantaneously. Indeed, it seems plausible to me to divide my life into two parts, before I saw those photographs (I was twelve) and after, *though it was several years before I understood fully what they were about* [editors' emphasis].

As a young child growing up in the United States, Sontag's lack of wider context in which to place these photographed atrocities is neither surprising nor unusual. But her simplistic comment as late as

All four editors contributed to this Introduction: the preliminary section was written by Tony Kushner; section II by David Cesarani; section III by Jo Reilly; and the conclusion by Colin Richmond.

1979 that these were 'the first photographs of the Nazi camps' (rather than the first such images of two idiosyncratic western concentration camps with very different histories at the time of their liberation) indicates that even for a culturally aware individual, such as Sontag, the process of understanding 'what they were about' was ongoing well after the end of the Second World War. Indeed, the 50th anniversary commemorations of the war revealed that this working out was still far from complete. Moreover, the intervention of memory and myth had further confused and obscured the meaning of those images with regard to the specific function of Belsen and its place in the history of the Holocaust.[2]

From the last months of 1994 through to the 'VE Day' celebrations in May 1995, brief film clips and photographs from Belsen frequently framed media representations of the Second World War in its last stages and the Holocaust as a whole. The lack of sensitivity in the use of such images (and in particular specific scenes such as the bulldozing of dead bodies into the mass graves of Belsen) was indicative of the failure to understand, or in any way to confront, the complexity of what was actually being portrayed. The feelings, for example, of survivors in relation to these images was overshadowed by the desire to communicate other messages. The repugnant figures were being reproduced to show the nature of Nazism (and therefore, the reflected decency of the western Allies), rather than the immeasurable damage caused to the Jewish people and others in Europe.

Such representation echoed that of 50 years earlier when the horror images were shown as part of a formal and informal attempt against collective amnesia. Thus *LEST WE FORGET: THE HORROR OF NAZI CONCENTRATION CAMPS REVEALED FOR ALL TIME IN THE MOST TERRIBLE PHOTOGRAPHS EVER PUBLISHED*, compiled by the *Daily Mail* and mass-circulated in the early summer of 1945 reproduced image after image so as to 'maintain the loathing for all that Hitler and the Nazis represented'. The book was 'a constant reminder to the British people of the menace they have beaten'. The hundreds of photographs of the victims were accompanied by captions such as 'Wrecks of Humanity'. The survivors were contrasted with the demonic SS men and women of the camp and were represented as merely 'an example of their brutality'. Even the penultimate page of photographs, which was accompanied with the question 'CAN *THEY* FORGET?', presented two survivors looking terrified and without any hint of individuality.[3]

Who were these victims? In *LEST WE FORGET*, as in so much else of the instant atrocity material of 1945, they were simply identified through the concentration camp in which they had been liberated – there are no names, personal histories or anything else that would undermine their use merely as illustrators of the true nature of Nazism. In 1958, the French government attempted to remove the remains of its 'own' nationals from Belsen with the intention of re-interring them in France. The response of Brigadier Glyn Hughes, Chief British Medical Officer at Belsen was clear:

> It was I who gave the order to dig the mass graves. Even at the time there was no possibility whatsoever to identify any of the victims. I was, therefore, astonished to hear in Paris a French minister say that it was still possible to sort out and remove the Frenchmen from the mass graves. Medically speaking it is, of course, an absurdity; morally there seems no reason for such an attempt.'[4]

If the dead of Belsen remained understandably unidentifiable, much the same was true (though with far less justification) for attitudes towards the survivors. Problems of communication, which went way beyond the basic problem of different languages, hindered a general comprehension that most of the victims had come from other camps from across Europe designed to exterminate every last Jew. More critically in coming to terms with the common humanity of the liberators and survivors, was a lack of awareness relating to the diverse lives of the latter before the war. There was a sense, even amongst the most sympathetic of observers and relief workers, that the victims would never be able to recover either physically or mentally. It would be hard to conceive, for example, of the sheer *ordinariness* of a London youth football team of 1948 represented on the cover of *The Journal of Holocaust Education* (Winter 1995) made up of child survivors of the camps.[5]

In turn, this lack of faith in them having any future was mirrored by a lack of concern about their past. The victims' grotesque state in April 1945 thus dominated overall consideration of them as human

beings at the time of their liberation. In addition, in countries with
such diverse war histories as Britain, the United States and France,
there was little consideration of the fact that most of those liberated
at Belsen were Jewish. This tendency in large part reflected a refusal
to accept the uniqueness of the Jewish plight in the war under the
Nazi onslaught. Although increasingly detailed information became
available to the western allies about the 'Final Solution' from the
summer of 1941 onwards, the material was rarely assimilated either
by the state or public.[6]

It was frequently said during the 1995 commemorations that the
camp liberation's in spring 1945 'brought home the reality of the
Holocaust'. In fact, neither the specifically anti-Semitic nature of
Nazi atrocities nor the particular role of the western camps was
understood at the time. *LEST WE FORGET* was actually unusual in
mentioning, if only in one sentence, Auschwitz 'where it is reported
[though inaccurately as we now know; the figure was closer to
1,500,000], at least 4,000,000 people were done to death in
circumstances of peculiar horror'. It was typical, however, in mixing
together indiscriminately a whole list of Nazi camps. The booklet's
suggestion that 'The butcher's hooks, the ovens, the gas-chambers
were common to all the camps' represented another common
misconception, although it was equally believed in 1945 that the
western camps, without the apparatus of mass murder, were by far
the worst in the Nazi system.[7]

How far were contemporary distortions of Belsen and the other
western concentration camps corrected in the 50-year
commemorations? In one crucial respect, the events and reflections
of 1995 did restore a sense of proportion missing in the last six
months of the war: Auschwitz, whose liberation by Soviet troops was
hardly noticed in the western world in January 1945, became the
focal point of Holocaust remembrance. At the time of its liberation
anniversary, the events and visits to this most murderous of camps
received world-wide and sustained coverage in which the Jewishness
of up to 90 per cent of its victims was generally acknowledged – in
spite of renewed Polish–Jewish conflict over the site. Moreover, the
voices of those who had survived were, at long last, given
prominence in media coverage allowing them the individuality so
lacking 50 years earlier. Indeed, the attention given to Belsen,

Dachau and Buchenwald in April/May 1945 rather than stimulating an interest in camps of mass, systematic murder, had the reverse effect.[8]

It has taken a long time in post-war consciousness to even out the imbalance in the awareness of eastern as opposed to western camps and to recognise the centrality of Auschwitz within the implementation of the 'Final Solution'. It is significant, therefore, with regard to the future memory of the Holocaust, that subsequent to the Auschwitz commemorations in 1995, the German parliament has designated 27 January as 'National Memorial Day for victims of Nazism and genocide'. Indeed, the danger is now that Auschwitz has become so dominant as a metaphor for the 'Final Solution' (and evil more generally), that other sites and experiences relating to the Holocaust will be neglected in the popular imagination. That the anniversaries in spring 1995 of the western camps' liberations received less attention than Auschwitz was thus not in itself a major cause for concern. More dangerous, however, were the ongoing tendencies to distort the histories of the western camps and to fail to contextualise their liberation other than as part of the Allied war narrative.[9]

Although the history of Belsen, with its changing functions within the Nazi state and its constantly fluctuating population, was complex in the extreme, there is little excuse 50 years later for the continuing inability of those inside and outside the media to understand its true nature. This is especially the case in an area of very popular misunderstanding about Belsen – that gas chambers were used to exterminate its victims. Confusion that the presence of crematoria in Belsen implied the existence and use of gas chambers, as well as a more general belief that all Nazi camps were designed to murder Jews in such a manner, probably explain why so many still make this fundamental error. It is one which Nazi apologists in the form of Holocaust deniers have been quick to seize upon.[10]

It was thus particularly regrettable that the major international documentary on the camp liberation's to emerge from the fiftieth anniversary commemorations (Rex Bloomstein's *Liberation*) unwittingly added to the popular mythology. Captain Robert Daniell, a British army veteran, was interviewed in Bloomstein's film shown on 22 January 1995 and also in a national British quality Sunday newspaper a week earlier. Daniell recounted how he was the first British soldier to go into Belsen and how he 'saw the gas ovens, which had been cleaned out because there was no fuel to run them. This was why there were so many corpses lying around ... It was pathetic. There were worn paths to each of the gas chambers and on the side a pile of spectacles at least 6ft high.'

Daniell's recollections ('It is as clear to me now as it was then') at the time of the 1995 anniversaries was a classic example of the role of myth in the construction of personal testimony. But that it should be used so unthinkingly in an area where memory has become so blatantly politicised for neo-Nazi/anti-Semitic purposes was unforgivable. Belsen, for the sake of convenience and a good story, had become indistinguishable from Auschwitz. History was being re-written. The most horrible images available of Nazi atrocities, or what the *Daily Telegraph* at the time of VE Day Commemorations called 'the exemplar of Nazi evil', had to be connected to the by now most infamous symbol of the extermination programme, the gas chamber.[11]

A similar distorting process can be seen at work in the film version of Robert Harris' important novel, *Fatherland* (1992). A thriller based on the January 1942 Wannsee conference, Harris carried out careful research to make sure that his account of the 'Final Solution' up to 1942 (after that date the history provided is counter-factual) was accurate. The work is based on a post-war Europe which is still dominated by National Socialist Germany, although the war in the east continues to be fought with the USA backing the USSR. The 'Final Solution' has been carried out but its existence concealed. The possibility of a new relationship between the Americans and Germans is threatened, however, by the seeping out of information concerning the fate of the Jews. In the far inferior film version of the book, which was released just before the Auschwitz commemorations, those seeking to convince the Americans and themselves of the 'Final Solution' use the standard horror images from the western camps. Faced with the obscure nature of Nazi euphemisms in documents relating to the extermination campaign, the photographs convey to the film audience 'the reality' of what had taken place. The dialogue between the heroine (an American journalist) and the hero (a renegade SS officer) at a time of high tension within the film is dramatic but dangerously misleading:

'They killed all the Jews.'

'What happened at Auschwitz and Belsen? What was Zyklon B?'

'They killed them with gas.'[12]

Harris, a history graduate of Cambridge, had done his homework (appropriately enough in the context of this volume at the Wiener Library). If anything, his book has a pedagogic mission to explain the details of the 'Final Solution' as his characters discover the secrets of the Nazi racial new order:

'I don't understand ... Here, for example – what is "Zyklon B"?'

'Crystallised hydrogen cyanide. Before that, they used carbon monoxide. Before that bullets.'

'And here – "Auschwitz/Birkenau". "Kulmhof [Chelmno]". "Belzec". "Treblinka". "Majdanek". "Sobibor".'

'The killing grounds.'

'These figures: eight thousand a day ... '.

'That's the total they could destroy at Auschwitz/Birkenau using the four gas chambers and crematoria.'

Harris's list of camps – later the hero shouts them out defiantly as he is tortured – is not without possible criticism. The 'Operation Reinhard' camps, which exclude Chelmno, were designed specifically to murder the Jews of the General Government and are mixed together by Harris with Auschwitz and Majdanek with their more complex functions. Nevertheless, nowhere in his text does the author refer to Belsen. In the film version it is more than possible that the camp of Belzec, which has little popular resonance even though it was the first purpose built camp with gassing facilities, is transmogrified into the more infamous Belsen with its related images. It should also be mentioned that the failure in the film to retain reference to Belzec is an example of the dangers referred to earlier of an overly Auschwitz-centred Holocaust remembrance.[13]

The efforts, however, of historians and others who have fought hard to get the differences between concentration camp and extermination camp within the Nazi system recognised did not go unrewarded in the spring of 1995. Although fatigue had set in with regard to reporting camp liberation commemorations, some were particularly anxious to get the history of Belsen 'right'. Thus the BBC's chief religious programme carried out a feature on the liberation of Belsen in mid-April 1995 with a commentary which stressed at the start the fundamental differences between Auschwitz and Belsen (indicating that inmates at the latter died because of hunger and disease). It is, however, likely that the future memory of Belsen will be influenced more by the distortions of the Anglo-American films *Fatherland* and *Liberation* rather than the sober presentations in 1995 of the camp's history. Indeed, the well-meaning comments of *The Times* at the time of the German memorial meeting in April 1995 that 'Belsen soon became a concentration camp, albeit without gas chambers' was indicative that its typicality in that respect is still to be grasped.[14]

Belsen has a massively important place in the collective memory of the Germans, British and Jews with regard to the Second World War. In each case (and none is mutually exclusive) its role has a different significance which has evolved in the years following 1945. In April 1995, ownership of Belsen's memory in competing narratives of the war continued to be contested within and between these national/ethnic groups, although there was, perhaps, greater harmony in this respect than at any time since the end of the war. In Germany itself, consideration of Jewish sensitivities was uppermost. The remembrance service was delayed until the end of April so that it did not coincide with Passover and in fact it took place on *Yom Ha'Shoah* (Holocaust Remembrance Day). President Herzog called upon Germans 'to never forget their crimes or sublimate their guilt'. He stressed the responsibility of those in the Nazi era who ignored the plight of their Jewish compatriots and who lived thoughtlessly in and profited from an anti-Semitic society. At a time when Chancellor Kohl and others to his right were attempting to normalise recent German history (taken to the extreme by the 'Against Forgetting' movement which emerged in 1995 and avoided mention of the Holocaust and instead concerned itself with post-war German suffering), Herzog stressed both German responsibility *and* the rootedness of Jews in German life before the Nazi era. The presence of Chaim Herzog, former President of Israel, and hundreds of survivors with their families, including Sam Bloch, President of the Bergen-Belsen Survivors' Association, further highlighted that the underlying purpose of the event was to remember and to pay respect to the camp's victims.[15]

In marked contrast to the reporting of the camp's horrors in April 1945, the presence of survivors 50 years on allowed the victims to be seen as individuals. Such personalisation was enabled further by reference to the life of Anne Frank, who died with her sister Margot in Belsen in its final weeks as a concentration camp. Anne Frank had become a world-wide cultural icon by the late 1950s and awareness of her gave a new meaning to the piles of corpses and mass graves of Belsen. Indeed, President Herzog was one of many who referred to Anne Frank at the time of the 1995 Belsen commemorations.[16]

Anne Frank has been increasingly used as a symbol for all the Jews killed in the Holocaust. The accessibility of her diary has no doubt facilitated such a process but it is not without its problems. Even within the distinct history of Belsen, the experiences of the Frank sisters cannot be regarded as representative. One feature that emerged strongly in the conference from which this volume evolved was the multiplicity of contrasting experiences and memories of Belsen amongst its survivors. In particular, those who were in the Belsen in its earlier stages as the 'Star Camp' for 'exchange Jews' have been marginalised in contrast to those who arrived from the east in the last six months of its existence. Many of the former were removed from the camp just before its liberation and have subsequently been neglected by historians and others. Age, gender, nationality and politics add further complexity to the many layers of Jewish memory relating to Belsen. At least in the German example, respect and the focus of attention was paid to the Jews and other victims of Belsen. Sam Bloch's speech reinforced the strong motif running through the German Belsen commemoration – to remember those millions of victims who were left even without a grave. He implored on their behalf 'Do not forget us! Carry in your hearts our memory!'. But in sharp contrast to Germany, during April 1995 the memory of Belsen in Britain as a camp of particular *Jewish* tragedy was far less recognised.[17]

The images coming to Britain from Belsen at the time of its liberation were frequently used to illustrate the justification of the *British* war effort. After 1945 a popular mythology started to develop that Britain had actually fought the war to end Nazi atrocities and even to save the Jews. This re-invention of the Second World War (which is an utter distortion of British responses to the Jewish plight) continued in the spring of 1995. It was perhaps most dangerously represented in a Department for Education document: *The End of the Second World War* for use in British secondary schools. In the section 'What were the Allies fighting for?', a heading 'The Holocaust' is added. In a later passage on 'The significance of the Holocaust', the very worthy comment is made that 'We cannot undo the past, but we can at least honour the victims of this depraved tyranny by remembering their fate'. Its sincerity, however, is called into question by the totally erroneous statement that

> One aspect of the Nazi tyranny against which the Allies fought was its obsessive concern to 'cleanse' society by removal of elements deemed injurious to its health. 'Harmful' groups included, among others, political opponents, the 'asocial', the mentally or physically handicapped, homosexuals, Jehovah's Witnesses, gypsies and Jews.[18]

In general, the Holocaust occupied only a minor place in British war commemorations in 1994 and 1995. But reference to the British army's liberation of Belsen enabled attention to be drawn to Nazi atrocities without in any way confusing matters by considering Jewish death and suffering during the war. Indeed, as in 1945, the liberation of Belsen could be used to concentrate further on the moral righteousness of the British war effort. The tendency to view the liberation of Belsen as *British* rather than Jewish/victim-centred, was dominant in Britain during April 1995. Media reports did utilise the testimony of Belsen survivors, but their experiences were heard infrequently and less extensively than the British soldiers who liberated the camp.[19]

This was most noticeable in what was the major national event to recall Belsen's liberation, 'Belsen Fifty Years On', organised by the Imperial War Museum. The large majority of those attending were British military personnel and only one of the 13 major addresses came from a survivor, Mrs Anita Lasker-Wallfisch, who was sent to Belsen from Auschwitz. In many respects, this event was an extension of the approach adopted by the Imperial War Museum in its permanent exhibition, 'Belsen 1945', which ironically was reduced in size in 1995. The exhibition's approach is summarised in its opening statement: 'The Nazi concentration camp at Bergen-Belsen was liberated by British troops on 15 April 1945'. Most of the descriptions of the camp comes from British soldiers, reporters and medical workers. When survivors are represented, it is often to refer back to the reflected decency of the liberators. Thus Zdenka Ehrlich, a former inmate, tells how she managed to crawl from a hut at the time of liberation and how her life was then saved by a British officer. Similarly, one of the brief clips from the liberation film focusing on those still alive (in fact most of the images concentrate on the dead on the ground or in mass pits), which is shown as part of the exhibition, illustrates a pathetic figure gratefully kissing the hand of a British soldier. The Imperial War Museum's commemoration on 12 April 1995 in no way corrected past imbalances and in fact reconfirmed its use of Belsen as part of the British war story.[20]

It is against this general background that the Wiener Library/ Parkes Library conference, 'The Liberation of Belsen', which took place in London on 9 and 10 April 1995, has to be placed. The biographies of Alfred Wiener (1885–1964) and James Parkes (1896–1981), and the histories of their respective libraries, deserve to be better known. This is not the place to provide a detailed account of their life work, but it is important to stress that these two men, with their very different backgrounds (Wiener was Jewish and born in Germany. He came to Britain in 1939 having emigrated to Holland when the Nazis came to power. Parkes was a Channel Islander who became a Church of England clergyman). Both were marginal figures in their own communities from the late 1920s onwards, devoted their whole lives to researching and documenting Nazism and anti-Semitism. Providing information and understanding about the dangers of anti-Semitic prejudice and practice was central to their careers. Their libraries (the Wiener remains in London and the Parkes is located in the University of Southampton), with their own particular focus – Nazism, the Holocaust and the German Jewish experience in the case of the Wiener; anti-Semitism, Christian–Jewish relations and Jewish history in the case of Parkes – continued to expand after their founders' death. Each one is now an internationally important research institution. It was therefore appropriate that the two libraries combined to organise the only sustained event in 1995 reflecting on the fiftieth anniversary of Belsen's liberation.[21]

This was not the first such venture undertaken by these institutions with regard to Second World War/Holocaust commemoration. The Wiener Library particularly, often in conjunction with the Parkes Library, had created through a series of conferences a parallel but challenging narrative of war memory to that offered in general culture and society in Britain. Alien internment in Britain, the 'Final Solution', the Warsaw ghetto uprising, and the Holocaust in Hungary had all been marked by major anniversary conferences in many of which survivors and other witnesses joined with historians from a range of countries and backgrounds. The use of personal testimony alongside the presentations of professional historians has, on the whole, been remarkably successful in these events. It does not follow, however, that the combination of history and memory is an unproblematic one. Indeed, there has sometimes been tensions between historians and survivors as well as difficulties within these groups as the specific aspects of the Holocaust have been reflected upon. Nevertheless, the conferences have provided important bridges and forms of communications between the groups and have fulfilled the diverse roles as important educational events in addition to acts of remembrance. 'The Liberation of Belsen' was very much within this tradition.[22]

'The Liberation of Belsen' conference was, as Paul Oppenheimer, a survivor of Westerbork and Bergen-Belsen, has suggested, the first time that survivors, eyewitnesses and historians have been brought together to discuss the camp. Half the conference was devoted to the testimony of survivors (including Alfred Garwood from the 'Star Camp' as well as those such as Esther Brunstein and Anita Lasker-Wallfisch who arrived later in Belsen from the death camps in the east), liberators and those involved in helping the survivors in the weeks that followed. Their testimony is included in the Appendix to this volume. In addition, the audience included many survivors and liberators who added their testimony in the discussion periods. The students and others who attended, as well as the historians who presented their specific papers which form the basis of this volume, learned and understood much from these testimonies. It reinforced the sense of humility that most of those who work in the field of Holocaust studies (but were born well after the war) experience when trying to communicate the history of Belsen and its victims. In particular, the need to be aware of the sensitivities of survivors (and also the liberators) was forced home in the two days of the conference. Indeed, the danger, as Yehuda Bauer and others have stressed, of the attempted destruction of European Jewry becoming dry as dust history 'that turns the event into a vast sea of footnotes and rationalistic analyses ... avoiding the abyss that was the Holocaust', will become greater as we lose the survivor generation.[23]

Similarly, the horror images of Belsen and other camps, whilst on the one hand impressive in the impact they make for post-war generations not aware of the true nature of Nazism, on the other hand are fraught with dangers with regard to the image of survivors that they represent. They can, at worst, de-humanise the victims as much as they demonise the perpetrators. We still have not learnt to listen with enough care and attention to the myriad voices of the survivors. As Paul Oppenheimer later wrote of the three formal presentations by survivors of their individual experiences: 'their quite different emotional stories were the highlights of the Conference for me'. Although the near-total marginalisation of survivors at the Imperial War Museum commemoration was avoided, 'The Liberation of Belsen' only began the process of acknowledging the importance of their testimony.[24]

Nevertheless, the conference did include eight testimonies as well as ten presentations by historians. If the comments of the many survivors and eye witnesses indicated the potential limitations of history in this area, it also revealed the complexity of individual/ group memory. In the case of Belsen, the memories of all those involved have to a lesser or greater extent been neglected. For example, a poignant letter from Dr M.R. Sheridan appeared in the *Jewish Chronicle* at the end of April 1995 relating to the paper's coverage of Belsen in the preceding weeks. It was from a former London medical student recruited by the Red Cross to work in Europe towards the end of the war. These students ended up carrying out the shattering work of dealing with the medical needs of Belsen survivors in the days following the liberation. Sheridan wrote: 'Of the 12 in our University College Hospital group, four died within two years from illnesses contracted in the camp. We asked for no "thank yous", but we did receive the France and Germany Star. We would, however, like to be remembered.'[25]

It is unfortunate but perhaps inevitable that those that have been particularly marginalised in the memory of Belsen have felt some sense of resentment against those who, relatively, have received more attention. In this respect, 'The Liberation of Belsen' conference, was, perhaps, the first relating to the subject matter in Britain which concentrated on the importance of Belsen in *Jewish* history and memory – even though it also addressed many other themes and included many non-Jews involved in the camp's liberation.

Ultimately, however, its bringing together of so many different types of witnesses emphasised the intricate, multi-layered nature of personal testimony. In addition, it illustrated the potential dangers of generalising about the experience of any particular group associated with Belsen. Memory, as well as history, is, by nature, politicised containing the possibility of conflict as well as harmony. Survivors and liberators are bound to have different perceptions of the camp and its memory. Moreover, every survivor testimony of the camp or eyewitness account of its liberation is unique. Indeed, the conference, and this volume that emerges from it, could not and cannot be complete in its coverage. Thus, for example, the history of Belsen as a brutal and murderous camp for Soviet prisoners of war has only just begun. 'The Liberation of Belsen', however, at least made an important start in bringing together for the first time many of the various strands of the camp's history and memory.[26]

II

The 'Final Solution' seems to defy the normal canons of historical scholarship and pushes interpretation to its limits. Saul Friedlander and Omer Bartov, amongst others, have remarked on the 'unease in historical interpretation': the disturbing effect when cold analysis and scholarly apparatus is applied to this subject.[27] It certainly feels churlish to evaluate the liberators, and the very notion of liberation, in less than reverential tones. Yet this volume is both a commemorative venture and an attempt at a critical, historical approach. Hopefully it will manage to be both. When the Holocaust is 'just history', as it inevitably will be in 50 or 100 years' time, the monuments and sites will be as banal or mute as are Nelson's Column and the Tower of London in reference to the events and eras they represent. But a living tradition of argument and interpretation will truly keep alive the memory of the victims and the survivors, and engage future generations with the actions of the perpetrators, bystanders, and liberators.

Five decades after the liberation of Bergen-Belsen it is possible and necessary to question some of the myths surrounding the event and the triumphalist narrative which has marginalised discordant voices and sidelined those whose experiences do not accord with it. Both Annette Wieviorka and Hagit Lavsky reinstate accounts that have traditionally been occluded, partly because they reflect less than glowingly some elements of the behaviour of the liberators. Both illustrate the manner in which specificities amongst the survivors, based on gender, nationality, religiosity, and politics inflected their experience of the liberation. From these particular points of view liberation was somewhat less than the term suggests.

Wieviorka begins by noting that Belsen is privileged in British national memory because British forces liberated the camp. The liberation gave rise to a single, monolithic and heroic narrative embedded in popular memory and official accounts. By contrast the inmates were disparate, as well as desperate, and it was hard for any unified, collective memory of the camp to coalesce amongst those who lived through the liberation. There were prisoners who had built the camp and lived miserably (if they lived at all) separated by barbed wire from 'privileged' inmates who were there as bargaining counters for the SS. Other prisoners from various labour and concentration camps were sent to the camp to 'convalesce' (that is, to die), while the majority were 'veterans' who had experienced several camps in their deadly trek through the Nazis' shrinking exterminatory empire.

Nationality further separated these groups. Wieviorka provides disturbing evidence that the inmates were afforded less attention by the British than the inhabitants of a nearby POW camp while, within Belsen, the French fared less well than some others. At least that is how they perceived their treatment. Highly compartmentalised and differentiated experiences gave rise to wildly varying testimonies. So Wieviorka notes that the historian is faced with conflicting sources and will perhaps never be able to offer a definitive version of events. With great sensitivity she describes the transition from euphoria to disillusionment amongst the French prisoners, a bitter sense of neglect that included an indictment of the French authorities in Paris. Her chapter is a compelling demonstration of the necessity of balancing conventional, heroic accounts of the liberation, usually based on British sources, with a more chequered perspective from the periphery of the camp population.

Here, too, there are noble stories. One cannot but be moved by the efforts of POWs who stole food and clothing to supply their compatriots in the camp, or stirred by the redoubtable Dr Fréjafon and the solidarity of the French inmates who bribed German orderlies with cigarettes so that the Francophones could lie together in one of the makeshift hospital wards. It is only by shifting the gaze from the traditional actors in the saga, and departing from the familiar testimonies, that these personalities and occurrences come into sight. A critical approach is not necessarily a debunking one: new heroes emerge from what were formerly the shadows. The old ones are not diminished by this, but their ranks are augmented.

The largest single group was, of course, Jewish and its memory of liberation was deeply marked by the post-war conflict between Zionists and the British. For them, Hagit Lavsky remarks, liberation 'would not be complete until a new homeland was found for all those uprooted by the war who refused to go back to their former countries of residence'. In this sense, Belsen is the immediate post-war history of the Jews in microcosm and a quite separate narrative from that which conventionally ends with the incineration of the camp.

As well as containing a massive Jewish population at the time of liberation, Belsen became the collection point for thousands of Jewish survivors in the British Zone of Germany. The percentage of Jews in the adjacent camp where survivors were rehoused and rehabilitated grew as members of other nationalities were repatriated. The Jews were further augmented by waves of refugees from Poland, Hungary and Romania in 1946–47. Since most Jewish refugees and survivors preferred the US Zone and moved southwards to this more congenial administration, the importance of the cluster of Jews at

Belsen increased. They became virtually synonymous with the Jews in the British Zone and took a leadership role.

The result was a collision with the British Zonal authorities and a full-scale challenge to Britain's policy in Palestine. Conditions in the DP camp were poor, with most inmates unable or unwilling to work. Crime, blackmarketeering and corruption ran at worrying levels. British handling of the camp accentuated these trends by penning the inmates in and treating them as if their Jewish identity was an incidental addition to their ostensible nationality, a matter of choice. Relief efforts by external Jewish organisations were obstructed rather than risk the acknowledgement that the Jews were a distinct group with any special claims. On the contrary, such requests were treated as favouritism. Rebuffed and ignored, the Jews united in anger. Zionism was the natural vehicle for discontent.

Yet Lavsky acknowledges that Jewish nationalism and the clamour for 'aliyah', emigration to Palestine, was conditional. 'Zionism was the name of the game as long as the survivors remained homeless.' Given a variety of destinations to chose from, Israel was only one of many. 'The fact is, when Bergen-Belsen was liquidated in 1950, many of its former inmates found their future in Israel. However, this was not true for all, or even most of them.' In other words, whereas all but the ultra-Orthodox Hungarians had been vociferous Zionists from 1945 to 1950, only a minority of Jewish DPs went to Israel when they had the chance. Most notably, Yossele Rosensaft, who was an inspiring Zionist leader and a thorn in the side of the British authorities, migrated to New York.

Rosensaft and Norbert Wollheim presided over an astounding renaissance of Jewish life in the camp, which became the seed corn for the revival of Jewry in the West German Republic. They promoted educational and cultural work, wisely seeing them as 'the main channels to recovery'. Youth work was vital since there were so many youngsters in the camp and because of the baby-boom that followed the liberation. This astonishing affirmation of life and the will to overcome the horror of the past is rendered invisible in accounts which end in 1945. In a deeper sense procreation was a kind of liberation, too. It marked an emancipation from the hopelessness of the months and years in captivity when thoughts of the future were fantasy or mere consolation. The DP camp inverts the years of the concentration camp and its precursors. Death gave way to life, despair to hope. Lavsky's chapter is organised around an explicit Zionist interpretation; but she assembles a rich variety of evidence that illuminates the powers of recovery of the survivors and the quality of regeneration that occurred in the camp, for which Zionism was a vehicle as well as a direct expression.

III

Zionist readings of Belsen have stressed Jewish self-determination in the camp, especially after the liberation. In contrast, representations of the camp's history in British culture have downplayed its Jewishness, concentrating largely on the moment of its liberation. It is partly for this reason that although Belsen has featured prominently in the British narrative of the Second World War, there has never been a widely available account in English of the history of the camp during the war years. In the opening article of this volume, Christine Lattek, building on the path-breaking work of historian Eberhard Kolb, presents us with a moving, detailed history of the Belsen camp and the experience of the various categories of prisoners who were incarcerated there.

Lattek describes the awful scenes that met the liberators and were to become for many around the world the damning evidence of Nazi Germany's policy of terror against sections of its population. Despite (or because of) the impact of the images the public in 1945 showed little interest in specifics, namely who the victims were, how they had arrived at the camp or how the camp had come to exist. Fifty years on, when interest in the Nazi camps has reached a new peak, the public have largely come to appreciate that the majority of people liberated in Belsen were Jewish and the camp now stands in the public consciousness, in Lattek's words, as 'a metaphor besides Auschwitz and Dachau for the entire Holocaust'. Yet this development in understanding about the role of Belsen in the Nazi scheme of persecution has not been accompanied by a necessary examination of the history of this unique camp.

Lattek outlines the development of the Nazi concentration camp system in general, providing a backdrop to developments that led to the relatively late establishment of the Belsen camp in 1943. We learn that the camp was set up as a response to an initiative agreed by the German Foreign Office and the SS leadership which meant that certain prominent Jews still in the hands of the Nazis would be exempted from the death transports – by this time in Spring 1943 millions of Jews in the occupied territories had already met their death – with a view to offering them in exchange deals with the Allies who were holding German nationals. The first exchange prisoners arrived at the new 'detention' camp in July 1943 and a year later there were more than 4,000, though it is important to note that some of the first Belsen prisoners were sent to Auschwitz regardless of their initial designation by the Germans as 'privileged'. In the event only a small number of the Belsen internees were ever exchanged, the majority remained in the camp, enduring increasingly worse conditions and despairing of their fate.

An impressive diversity of national communities was represented in Belsen, including Jews from North Africa and Albania, but, by the spring of 1944, the overwhelming majority were Dutch. Various groups of Jews depending on their background and status were housed in sealed compounds or sub-camps of the main camp, presumably to prevent communication between the different groups. Thus, there was a 'Neutral's camp', a camp for Poles and the 'Star camp', where the Dutch exchange Jews were held. Lattek uses the available survivor testimony effectively to describe the daily life and concerns of those in the 'Star camp' as far as possible. Although, relative to the treatment of Jews elsewhere in the Reich-controlled territories, life in Belsen was initially bearable, it was never privileged. We should be under no illusions; these 'valuable' Jews lived in a confined, unsanitary world where food was scarce and SS brutality real, the kind of world where a small boy could expect to receive only an extra taste of sweetness with his bread for his birthday.

We are fortunate to have eyewitness descriptions of the camp, in the form of both contemporary diaries and some written reports produced by those 200 or so people who were actually exchanged and reached Palestine in 1944. Through these accounts presented by Lattek we are able to marvel at the tenacity and integrity of people who, despite the heavy 'psychological burden of … [their] existence', despite their 'lack of freedom and permanent humiliation', were able to motivate themselves to educate even the orphaned children in clandestine assemblies and continue to observe religious rites. Yet, we cannot help but feel saddened that the testimonies of other groups held in the camp – the Greeks, the Spanish and the North Africans – appear to have been lost to us.

In reading about the 'Star camp' in Belsen we are struck by the realisation that, in contrast, there are so many aspects of the camp that we know little of; but then in this respect Belsen is a microcosm of the *Shoah* as a whole. Nevertheless, these glimpses of some of the Belsen internees functioning as individuals are an important and necessary antidote to the characterisations of Belsen victims, emanating from the liberators' descriptions, that we have become so familiar with. We are reminded again of the dignity and culture of individuals that was stolen from them by the Nazis and, unwittingly again, by the liberator's shell-shocked and limited use of vocabulary and the sensationalist, intrusive newsreel cameras.

The descent of the Belsen camp into the abyss that the British found is described by Latteks: its new and cruel designation as a 'recuperation camp' despite the complete lack of any caring facilities, and its incorporation into the concentration camp system; the arrival of 1,000 men with TB in March 1944 left to die; the dumping of more and more sick and exhausted prisoners marched from other camps, including thousands of women from Auschwitz, housed in appalling accommodation increasingly unable to cope with the numbers; the starvation, the thirst, the disease; 18,000 deaths in March 1945 alone.

Richard Breitman's article complements the opening contribution, also examining the origins and development of the Belsen camp, although this time from the perspective of the perpetrator, namely Heinrich Himmler. Breitman gives us a further justification, if we need one, for investigating this camp's history more closely: the very fact that the Bergen-Belsen camp was established, its aim unquestionably to keep Jews alive and away from the transports sits uneasily with the predominant view of the Nazi policy against the Jews and what we know about the persistence and conviction with which the 'Final Solution' was implemented. Further work on the role of the Belsen camp during the war, challenging the view that it was a peripheral camp in the Nazi system before that system began to collapse, could help us to further deepen our understanding of the 'Final Solution' policy and the less than clear-cut attitudes of the Nazi leaders and the Nazi regime in general to the Jewish question.

Breitman's concern is with Himmler's role in attempts to sell or exchange Jews. He admits that 'the documentary evidence on Himmler is by no means complete or ideal'; in this article he pieces together a jigsaw of interrupted correspondence, minutes and notes and questionable testimony. Indeed, Breitman's contribution raises as many questions as it attempts to answer about the role of Himmler in determining the fate of the Belsen internees, particularly in the final phase of the war. Breitman agrees with Yehuda Bauer's analysis, put forward most recently in his *Jews for Sale?*, that though fully committed to the 'Final Solution' at all times, Himmler saw no contradiction in keeping a small number of Jews back from the transports if he thought they could be used to tactical advantage, that is, be utilised as pawns in fruitful negotiations with the Allies.[28] If these negotiations came to naught, then nothing would be lost and the Jews could be disposed of eventually.

Breitman fleshes out what we know about the moves that led to the establishment of the Belsen camp and makes it clear that the camp emerged out of a number of initiatives suggested by different departments at different times throughout 1942 and early 1943. The crucial points to note about Belsen are that it was set up with the knowledge and acquiescence of Hitler and it was set up on Reich soil, in the heart of Germany, despite the fact of the Nazis' decision that the Reich should be *Judenfrei*.

Once we have accepted that the Nazi leaders were willing to negotiate with the Allies – hoping to exchange individuals under Nazi control for either German nationals, goods or money – some consideration must be given to the responses of the British and American governments to this kind of suggestion. Breitman chooses the example of the proposed rescue of 5,000 Jewish children from eastern Europe, an incident not widely documented in the current literature (and highlighted as significant by *The Guardian* newspaper at the time of the Belsen conference in 1995), to illustrate the relationship between the German and British governments in this regard.[29]

When the British government made the offer to allow 5,000

children into Palestine in May 1943, Himmler and Ribbentrop at the Foreign Office both gave it their consideration. Instead, they eventually developed a suggestion for an exchange scheme that the British were to find unacceptable. Although Breitman does not mention this, successful exchanges had been negotiated between the British and German governments earlier in the war, for example, when Palestinians trapped in Europe by the onset of hostilities were allowed to return home in 1941 and 1942 in exchange for German nationals living in Palestine.[30] In 1943 the British were not prepared to countenance ceding to German demands and, Breitman tells us, replied 'that Germans can only be exchanged against subjects of the British Empire'. Such diplomatic negotiations would surely be an area for further research.

We are made aware that Himmler was far more flexible on the question of the fate of Jews than Hitler, and this tendency increased as the war neared its end. Himmler's aim appears to have been to use the Jews remaining under Nazi control, including those in Bergen-Belsen, in negotiating deals designed to gain him favour with the Allies. Hitler was against the release of Jews and Himmler seems to have been careful not to antagonise him by disobeying orders. Yet there is evidence that in March 1945 he made limited moves to ensure that the death rate of the Jews in Belsen was not further accelerated, either by disease or forced evacuation, while at the same time putting out 'peace feelers to the Western Allies'. His efforts had little impact; in Belsen people were dying in their thousands in the final weeks before the liberation. Himmler has been dubbed by Breitman elsewhere as 'the architect of genocide'.[31] Yet the fact that Himmler 'managed to refrain from ordering the evacuation of Bergen-Belsen and consented to the military turnover of the camp', and thereby spared the fatal humiliation of a final death march can give us little comfort.

Paul Kemp picks up the theme of the negotiated surrender of the Belsen camp before delivering a detailed descriptive account of the liberation by British army units and their immediate crucial relief efforts. In doing so he utilises the Imperial War Museum's growing collection of reports, letters and memoirs written by liberators from or about the Belsen camp. Thus, using the words of the liberators themselves, Kemp describes the scene that met the unprepared British troops when Bergen-Belsen fell into their line of advance. Not since the Falaise Gap had one officer seen such desolation and carnage. For another Belsen camp 'was just a barren wilderness' except 'corpses lay everywhere'.

The immense difficulty of the task faced by a pitifully inadequate number of personnel is made clear. Basic priorities were quickly established but intensive care was impossible under the circumstances. Those who could be moved safely were evacuated to newly improvised hospital camps in the German Panzer school a mile and a half away from the main camp. Meanwhile, kitchens were organised and corpses were buried quickly and, in the first weeks, without ceremony.

We know from interviews that many of these liberators were profoundly affected by what they witnessed in Belsen. The soldiers who liberated Belsen had immense difficulties finding the appropriate words at the time. Echoing Lieutenant Gonin, so many of the written testimonies contain such words as 'I can give no adequate description ... '. Although Kemp does not explore this human angle, we know that the soldiers who documented their experience so determinedly at the time would be haunted by the memory of Belsen for the rest of their lives. The work involved one 'heartbreaking' task after another: how could one choose only scores of individuals to be evacuated from the hundreds of equally deserving cases lying in the huts, knowing that those who stayed in the filthy, lice-infested surroundings for one more day might not make it to see any real kind of liberation?

Eventually the daily death rate began to fall and more medical units were free to aid the relief effort. Among them were 96 medical students from London who arrived in early May and were the first personnel to work intensively with the patients still lying hopelessly in Camp I. Kemp tells us that they worked for long hours with very little equipment and medicine. They tried to ensure that each patient received something approaching a suitable diet and lived long enough to be moved to the hospital camp where they stood a better chance of survival and recovery.

Kemp's article, reflecting as it does the Imperial War Museum's testimony collection, presents us with a largely male-dominated perspective of this period of British history. Jo Reilly also takes the rehabilitation effort as her subject, but attempts to uncover the role played by women relief workers in Belsen and to examine gender relations in the camp, a perspective so far missing from the historiography. Reilly documents the work that women – nurses and volunteers – did in the camp, and, using the limited testimony given by women that has been uncovered, attempts to give voice to their experiences.

The historiography of the liberation of Belsen in Britain has bound the event very closely to the victorious British war effort; the liberation of the faceless 'victims of Nazism' in Belsen has been portrayed as an act of British righteousness. It has become one of a series of important markers in the history of Britain and the Second World War, between the Battle of Britain and the final occupation of Berlin. Whereas the history of the Holocaust as a whole was undeveloped in Britain until recent years, the history of the liberation of Belsen has been told as a chapter in the general story of the fight against fascism that was the Second World War. Thus Reilly maintains, the liberation of Belsen, reflecting most mainstream written histories of war, has been presented by men, as a wholly male experience.

Reilly acknowledges that the number of men among the liberators was far greater than the number of women but, nevertheless, it seems the women who were there and fulfilled crucial roles in the relief effort have all but disappeared from the history and official (if not private) memory. This may be due, in part, to the fact that women were banned from entering the main camp (an interesting reflection of gender relations at the time), where the majority of the photographs and newsreels that we know so well as documenting the horror of Belsen were taken. These images feature only the British soldier as liberator, the intermediary between Nazi-inflicted horror and redemption. The women were involved in the task of setting up hospital camps and receiving the first patients from the main camp.

Reilly describes the routine of the nursing staff who, like the 96 medical students described by Paul Kemp, worked intensively with the survivors and were faced with innumerable problems; as one nurse put it: 'It seemed to us sometimes that we were living on another planet.' Through descriptions of the work conducted by women, we are also given an insight into the emotional state of many of the survivors; after all, very often, it was to the medical staff that they first attempted to relate their experiences in the camps. The simple human contact between liberator and liberated was frequently as important as nutritional and medical care and a sympathetic ear could mean an enormous amount to a patient. Reilly reports that one nurse was given a treasured necklace by a survivor with the words: 'I want you to have it because you have listened to me when I unburdened myself for the first time about the worst period of my life.' Clearly, a nurse could not hope to understand the depth of pain endured by a patient in Belsen or help to ease it significantly, but the human contact and compassion that they could offer seemingly helped the internees to feel more positive about the future.

IV

The only way to conclude an introduction to a collection of this kind is open-endedly. Or un-endingly. Because for those who survived it the Holocaust has not ended. Historians find it hard to tell when the Holocaust began; the survivors, however, know that it has no closure. In the last paragraph of his account of the Warsaw Ghetto and the Ghetto Uprising, *The Stars Bear Witness*, Bernard Goldstein wrote, 'Those of us who survived that holocaust are freaks of nature … If there is any purpose in our survival, perhaps it is to give testimony.'[32] Not all survivors think of themselves as freaks (and why 'of nature': was the Holocaust natural?); most of them, none the less, want to give testimony. Historians need to listen to every nuance in every narrative. That was a lesson we learned once again at the 'Liberation of Belsen' conference. The one thing all and every narrative has in common is suffering. It is easy to overlook suffering. It was easy then. It is easy now. The suffering of those caught up by the Holocaust was limitless, or rather it was limited only by death itself. We cannot imagine another's suffering. That does not mean we cannot recognise it, acknowledge it, cannot put it into (and at the heart of) every historical discourse. We must.

How to do so is a dilemma for historians. Survivors wring our souls, wrench our minds. Does Theo Richmond's *Konin* do that? I think it does. Why does it? Is it because it goes as far as one can go in recovering a lost people of a lost place in a lost time? For me it is the place that makes the difference. I do not mean that the time and people do not. Of course not. It is the distinctiveness of the Jewish community in Konin which counts. That community was like any other Jewish community in Poland, yet it was not any other community; it was not the community of Bochnia or Bodzentyn, Pruszków or Piaseczno, Otwock or Oswiecim.

The historian has to distinguish as well as generalise. Belzec was not Buchenwald; neither was Bergen-Belsen. The poet David Jones loved what he called the blessed differences (of locality, of local custom, of local lore); they were lively, they nourished life, they were life itself. Those differences he contrasted with the levelling stride of Imperial Rome. The Nazi Empire was more obliterating than levelling and Bochnia, Bodzentyn and the rest are no more what they were, but the imperious thrust was just the same. Destroy the differences, iron out the anomalies, diminish the discrepancies. The historian has always to be an anti-imperialist. He has to record the distinctiveness. His task is to distinguish between Konin and Kutno, between Belzec and Buchenwald. As the survivors of more than one camp tell us: every camp, like every community, was different.[33]

Hence the need for historians to ask questions of detail, as relentlessly as Claude Lanzmann asked them about the gas vans at Chelmno in his film *Shoah*: What were the vans like? What colour were they? What was the make? Who were the drivers? How many were there? Did the driver sit in the cab of the van? Did he race the motor? Was it a loud noise? Was the van stationary while the motor ran? How fast did the vans go? Were the people already dead? To that sort of question there is an answer. That is because, as Raul Hilberg has told us, historians have to begin (and perhaps to end?) with questions of detail, so that if nothing else is achieved a description can be made, a description, an inventory even, of suffering.

It is, of course, a description made from the outside. Mrs Michelsohn, a German witness to the suffering at Chelmno, reminds us of that. Did you see the gas vans, Lanzmann asked her. No, she replies; then she hesitates, Yes, she goes on, from the outside. Apart from those who cleaned it out after each deadly journey, all those who saw the inside of a gas van were murdered in it. There are no complete 'insider' accounts of the Holocaust, because no one can answer the question: How long did it take you to choke to death? Nor did it matter to the murdered that the gas van they died an agonising death in was coloured green and was made by the Saurer Company, still van-makers to the German nation. It matters to historians. Why green? It was the colour the Germans used: green, ordinary. Ordinary, yes ordinary. Why the Saurer company? Because that was an ordinary van manufacturer going about its ordinary business of making vans. It is the ordinariness of the Holocaust which comes as the Big Answer to all those small questions. Every death was different, the suffering of each man, woman, and child was different. The Holocaust was extraordinary; it was not extra-ordinary. And that is how modern mass murder was done.[34]

Not that the perpetrators always knew what they were doing. Listen to Mrs Michelsohn again. Why do you call them Poles and not Jews, Lanzmann asked this woman with a pioneering spirit. Sometimes I get them mixed up, she answered. As Himmler told one of his subordinates in the occupied Eastern Territories, no decree concerning the definition of 'a Jew' should be published. We only tie our hands with these stupid commitments. Mixed-up murderers? Only in that they were attempting to exterminate an idea, an idea (it goes without saying) of which they had the wrong idea, by destroying people. However many millions of men, women, and children ideologues kill, the idea they want rid of will persist. If Germany had won the war Auschwitz would have consumed anyone whom the Nazis decided was looking at them askance – to paraphrase Hitler.

The persistence of the idea is best exemplified in Thomas Rahe's contribution. The idea, we might note, is bigger even than God, as there seem no recorded instances at Belsen (or elsewhere) of conversions *to* religion. There are, however, in that piece numerous examples of the differences between, on one hand, *echt* men and women and, on the other, their tormentors, whom one is tempted to call *untermenschen*. I am reminded of Mrs Michelsohn again, of the nerve-jangling moment when Lanzmann asks her what her first impression of Poland was. It was primitive, worse than primitive, she tells him. And why was that? The sanitary facilities were disastrous, she says; there were only privies, no water closets except one in Kolo townhall. Mrs Michelsohn, the schoolteacher's wife, had no difficulty with Jews in chains hobbling past her front door every day. That was not primitive? Presumably not: that was simply (simply?) an outcome of the civilising mission of pioneering Germans like Mr and Mrs Michelsohn.

The Holocaust stood language on its head, turned words into their opposites. Mrs Michelsohn's mistaking the water closet for civilisation makes one wonder about the primitive sanitary facilities at Bergen-Belsen (or Auschwitz, or Stutthof, or anywhere else in the German camp system). They were primitive presumably not because the managers of the system strove to keep costs to a minimum though, like all modern managers, that is what they did strive to do, in their case coming close to the perfect managerial achievement (where sanitary facilities were concerned) of zero costs, but because they wished to (had to?) de-civilise those whom they killed. Many refused to become that sort of victim, many whom we shall never know about. Some, those who remained religious, Thomas Rahe tells us about, like the so-called 'primitive' North Africans, or those illiterate Albanian women who worked in the SS kitchen and who, despite being beaten, stopped working whenever a funeral procession passed. Were they not truly *zaddikim*?

Thomas Rahe's contribution, like every other one in the collection, like the Holocaust itself, makes us confront, in the end and as a consequence of asking questions about *minutiae*, the *echt* nature of modern culture, of contemporary civilisation. After all, it is commonplace to assert that it was the most cultured, or at any rate *kultured*, people on earth who perpetrated the greatest barbarity on earth. In the movie *Shoah* Raul Hilberg relates a story Czerniakow recorded in his diary:

> There was a lady somewhere in Warsaw in love with a man, and the man was hit, grievously wounded, with his insides coming out. This woman stuffed the insides back with her own hands. She carried the man to a first-aid station. He died. He was buried in a mass grave. She disinterred him and buried him. This, to Czerniakow – this simple episode – was the ultimate of virtue.[35]

As it was for Sophocles. As it is for us. As, presumably, it would not have been for Mr and Mrs Michelsohn. It is that Warsaw Jew who was cultured; she it was who was civilised.

There is one other matter. That of memory. Of memory and the purloining of memories. If for no other reason, and there are countless other reasons, historians need the memories of survivors in order to combat those, and they are too many, who seek to deny such recollections of suffering or endeavour to misuse them. Tony Kushner demonstrates how readily the English (British?) have anglicised Bergen-Belsen. Its liberation by the British Army has become another excuse for them to celebrate themselves. Was there ever so self-congratulatory a people as the English? Yet, do they ever ask, does the Imperial War Museum ever think: if only the camp had been liberated two months, a month, a fortnight earlier? How many lives would have been saved? How much suffering would have been alleviated? What of those reconnaissance photographs taken by the RAF in September 1944? Could something have been done before 15 April 1945? The 50th anniversary of the liberation of the camp (but hardly the 'liberation' of its Jewish inmates) should not have been a time of celebration. It ought to have been an occasion for repentance.

The Holocaust was perpetrated by Germans. They had enthusiastic accomplices in too many places; if they had got to England in 1940 they undoubtedly would have had collaborators there too. That said, the Holocaust was wholly of German design and was almost entirely managed by Germans. That does not mean that theirs was the only responsibility for what happened, when what happened happened, and the ways in which what happened happened. Little was done by the British government, even to draw attention to Jewish suffering, because ultimately that suffering did not matter enough (did not count for enough) with that government, even with Winston Churchill, whose sympathy was never translated into action. In time of war a government does what it thinks it has to do. The British government did not think it had to do anything for European Jewry. It is of that failure of perception, if it is not anything worse (and it almost certainly is) that we, the English, need to be reminded, and the reminding has to include repentance. What, for the sake of civilisation, for the survival of (English) culture, is not needed is complacency.

NOTES

1. Norman Denzin, *The Cinematic Society: The Voyeur's Gaze* (London: Sage Publications, 1995) is one of the only studies on voyeurism but it fails to deal with the genre of Holocaust film or even horror films.
2. Susan Sontag, *On Photography* (Harmondsworth: Penguin, 1979; originally published 1967), pp.18–21. The most thorough analysis of the 1945 images is to be found in

Marie-Anne Matard-Bonucci and Edouard Lynch (eds.), *La Liberation des camps et le retour des deportes: l'histoire en souffrance* (Paris: Editions Complexe, 1995).

3. Daily Mail, *LEST WE FORGET* (London: Daily Mail, 1945), pp.4–5, 35, 43, 79. The booklet was produced in a limited first edition within days of the liberation and then in a mass-circulated form in the weeks following.

4. *LEST WE FORGET*, pp.17–79; Hughes in *Jewish Chronicle*, 10 July 1959 and more generally Menachem Rosensaft, 'The Mass-Graves of Bergen-Belsen: Focus for Confrontation', *Jewish Social Studies*, Vol.41 (1979), pp.155–81.

5. This was one of the Primrose Club football clubs whose young members had come from the concentration camps to recuperate in Britain at the end of 1945. See the cover from *The Journal of Holocaust Education*, Vol.4, No.2 (Winter 1995): 'Family/History: Survivors and Their Children'. In contrast, see the caption to the first photograph in *LEST WE FORGET*, p.17: 'All Hope Abandon, Ye Who Enter Here ... Belsen'.

6. See Matard-Bonucci and Lynch, *La Liberation des camps* and Tony Kushner, *The Holocaust and the Liberal Imagination: A Social and Cultural History* (Oxford: Blackwell, 1994), Chs.4 and 7.

7. ITV News, 27 Jan. 1995; Jonathan Dimbleby in 'Richard Dimbleby at Belsen', BBC 2, 9 Jan. 1995; *LEST WE FORGET*, pp.4–5.

8. See Tony Kushner, ''It's a Bastard When You Come to Think of It': Anglo-America and the End of Auschwitz', *The Jewish Quarterly*, No.156 (Winter 1994/95), pp.10–14; *Jewish Chronicle*, 13 and 27 Jan. 1995 for Polish–Jewish conflict.

9. Regine Wosnitza, 'Germans Decide to Observe Holocaust Memorial Day', *Jewish Chronicle*, 16 June 1995.

10. See, for example, 'Holocaust Lies: Bergen-Belsen Gassings', *The Journal of Historical Review*, Vol.13, No.6 (Nov./Dec. 1993), p.24.

11. Bloomstein's *Liberation* was shown on Channel 4, 22 Jan. 1995; Brian Cathcart, 'The Man Who Found Belsen', *Independent on Sunday*, 15 Jan. 1995; Trevor Fishlock, 'Belsen: The Exemplar of Nazi Evil', *Daily Telegraph*, 2 May 1995.

12. Robert Harris, *Fatherland* (London: Arrow Book, 1993, originally published 1992); *Fatherland*, 1994 (Home Box Office films).

13. Harris, *Fatherland*, pp.356, 364; Yizhak Arad, *Belzec, Sobibor, Treblinka: The Operation Reinhard Death Camps* (Bloomington, IN: Indiana University Press, 1987).

14. Reverend Colin Morris on 'Sunday', Radio 4, 16 April 1995; *The Times*, 28 April 1995.

15. *The Times*, 28 April 1995; *Daily Telegraph*, 28 April 1995; *The Independent*, 28 April 1995 and *Jewish Chronicle*, 28 April 1995 for detailed coverage of the memorial at Belsen. See also Paul Oppenheimer, 'The 50th Anniversary of the Liberation of Belsen', unpublished typescript, pp.1–2, 7–8 for a personal reaction to the event from a Belsen survivor; for Kohl see *Jewish Chronicle*, 12 May 1995. The manifesto 'May 8, 1945 – Against Forgetting' was launched in *Franfurter Allgemeine Zeitung*. See *Jewish Chronicle*, 21 April 1995 and *The Guardian*, 9 May 1995.

16. For references to Anne Frank, see *The Times*, 28 April 1995. A report in *Jewish Chronicle*, 3 March 1995 suggested that 'March 1995 is the 50th anniversary of the tragic death of Anne Frank, in Auschwitz', but this was an unusual mistake in the commemorations. A unique service of remembrance for Anne Frank took place in St Paul's Cathedral on 25 April 1995.

17. Alvin Rosenfeld, 'Popularization and Memory: The Case of Anne Frank', in Peter Hayes (ed.), *Lessons and Legacies: The Meaning of the Holocaust in a Changing World* (Evanston, IL: Northwestern University Press, 1991), pp.243–78; Bloch's speech is reported in Oppenheimer, 'The 50th Anniversary', p.8.

18. Department for Education, *The End of the Second World War: The commemoration of VE Day and VJ Day* (London: DFE, 1995), pp.12–14, 39–40.

19. For passing comments on the Holocaust see, for example, Michael Dewer (ed.), *The Official Government Programme to Mark the 50th Anniversary of the End of World War II* (London: Whitehall Publications, 1995), p.11; Geoffrey Elliot (ed.), *VE Day: It's All Over* (Portsmouth: Portsmouth News and Hampshire County Council, 1995), p.11 includes images of Belsen alongside the testimony of two British soldiers in a feature on 'Courage amid the wreckage of hell'. See also *Daily Telegraph*, 2 May 1995 for the exclusive use of testimony from *British* Belsen survivors, echoing a trend started at the British-organised Belsen Trial in 1945.

20. Oppenheimer, 'The 50th Anniversary', pp.2–3 for a more generous review of the Imperial War Museum event. 'Belsen 1945' was installed in 1991 and given less space in 1995.

21. Ben Barkow, *Alfred Wiener and the Making of the Holocaust Library* (London: Vallentine, Mitchell, forthcoming); Nicholas de Lange, 'James Parkes' in Lord Blake and C.S. Nicholls (eds.), *The Dictionary of National Biography 1981–1985* (Oxford: Oxford University Press, 1990), pp.307–8.

22. Publications emerging from these conferences include David Cesarani (ed.), *The Final Solution* (London: Routledge, 1994) and David Cesarani and Tony Kushner (eds.), *The Internment of Aliens In Britain During the Twentieth Century* (London: Frank Cass, 1993). A volume, *Genocide and Rescue in Hungary, 1944* (Oxford: Berg), also edited by David Cesarani, is forthcoming.

23. Oppenheimer, 'The 50th Anniversary', p.3. For the conference as a whole see *Hampstead and Highgate Express*, 14 April 1995; *The Guardian*, 10 April 1995 and *Jewish Chronicle*, 14 April 1995; Yehuda Bauer, *The Holocaust in Historical Perspective* (London: Sheldon Press, 1978), pp.43–4.

24. Oppenheimer, 'The 50th Anniversary', p.5. See more generally Annette Wieviorka, 'On Testimony', in Geoffrey Hartman (ed.), *Holocaust Remembrance: The Shapes of Memory* (Oxford: Blackwell, 1994), pp.23–32.

25. 'Doctor Remembers Belsen's liberation', *Jewish Chronicle*, 28 April 1995.

26. James Fentress and Chris Wickham, *Social Memory* (Oxford: Blackwell, 1992), Chs. 1–3; Paul Connerton, *How Societies Remember* (Cambridge: Cambridge University Press, 1992), Ch.1 and Jonathan Boyarin, *Storm from Paradise: The Politics of Jewish Memory* (Minneapolis, MN: University of Minnesota Press, 1992). On Soviet prisoners, see *Sowjetische Kriegsgefangene 1941–1945. Leiden und Sterben in den Lagern Bergen-Belsen, Fallingboostel, Oerbke, Wietzendorf* (Niedersächsischen Landeszentrale für poolitishe Bildung, 1991).

27. Omer Bartov, *Murder in Our Midst: The Holocaust, Industrial Killing and Representation* (New York: Oxford University Press, 1996); Saul Friedlander, *Probing the Limits of Representation, Nazism and the 'Final Solution'* (Cambridge, MA: Harvard University Press, 1992).

28. Yehuda Bauer, *Jews For Sale?: Nazi-Jewish negotiations, 1933–1945* (New Haven, CT and London: Yale University Press, 1994).

29. *The Guardian*, 10 April 1995.

30. See Bernard Wasserstein, *Britain and the Jews of Europe 1939–1945* (Oxford: Oxford University Press, 1979), pp.223–8.

31. Richard Breitman, *The Architect of Genocide: Himmler and the Final Solution* (New York: Knopf, 1991).

32. Bernard Goldstein, *The Stars Bear Witness* (translated and edited by Leonard Shatzkin) (London: Gollancz, 1950), p.295.

33. Theo Richmond, *Konin: A Quest* (New York: Pantheon Books, 1995).

34. Claude Lanzmann, *Shoah: An Oral History of the Holocaust: The Complete Text of the Film* (New York: Pantheon Books, 1985).

35. Lanzmann, *Shoah*, p.180.

PART II: THE HISTORY OF BERGEN-BELSEN

Bergen-Belsen:
From 'Privileged' Camp
to Death Camp

CHRISTINE LATTEK

The Notoriety of Belsen

British troops liberated the Bergen-Belsen concentration camp on 15 April 1945. Some 37,000 prisoners had perished there, almost all Jews; some 13,000 more died within the following ten weeks, that is over 20 per cent of the roughly 60,000 who were liberated. It is hard to imagine the degree of exhaustion, starvation and sickness which led to such atrocious death rates, which so weakened one in five survivors of the camp regime that they could not recover.

Yet Bergen-Belsen was not conceived as an extermination camp, and occupies an unusual place in the history of the Nazi camp system both in its origins, purpose and internal history and in the notoriety and symbolism that the name of 'Bergen-Belsen' has gained since April 1945. This notoriety is almost entirely due to the scene that presented itself to the Allies; the liberation of the camp's inmates was a cathartic moment not only for those to whom the camp had meant starvation, torture and permanent threat of imminent death, but also for the world's public at large. Bergen-Belsen was among the first such camps liberated by Western Allies and, as such, instantly infamous. It contained some of the most squalid and fetid living conditions of any of the German camps. The ground was strewn with thousands of naked and decomposing corpses; men and women, clad in rags, were barely able to move, often simply incapable of greeting the liberators; the starved and desperately sick survivors were crowded in miserable huts; food and medicine were non-existent; hygenic conditions were appalling, the emaciated bodies of dead and dying lay on stinking straw bunks in every state of filth and degradation; typhus raged and the dying continued for weeks; people collapsed as they walked and fell dead; bodies were eventually bulldozed into mass graves.

One doctor, himself a former inmate, testified as to the conditions: 'As every day the number of people who died was over 1,000 the result was that every day several thousand bodies were lying about in the camp in a terrific state, green and swollen through the heat, some of them stinking.'[1]

The British medical officer Brigadier Glyn Hughes was scarcely able to describe the atrocious scenes:

> ... no description nor photograph could really bring home the horrors that were there outside the huts, and the frightful scenes inside were much worse. There were various sizes of piles of corpses lying all over the camp, some outside the wire and some in between the huts. The compounds themselves had bodies lying about in them. The gutters were full and within the huts there were uncountable numbers of bodies, some even in the same bunks as the living. Near the crematorium were signs of filled-in mass graves, and outside to the left of the bottom compound was an open pit half-full of corpses ... .

> There were no bunks in a hut in the women's compound which contained the typhus patients. They were lying on the floor and were so weak they could hardly move. There was practically no bedding.

Asked about sanitation, he specified:

> There was none. The conditions were indescribable because most of the internees were suffering from some form of gastro-enteritis and they were too weak to leave the hut ... The compounds were absolutely one mass of human excreta. In the huts themselves the floors were covered, and the people in the top bunks who could not get out just poured it on to the bunks below.[2]

The news of these atrocities was sent immediately around the world. Derrick Sington, a captain in an intelligence corps and a journalist, who entered the camp with the first loudspeaker van announcing the takeover, described his impressions on entering the camp on 15 April and his very gradual process of comprehending what he saw of the overcrowding, starvation and dying among the inmates. Many other journalists followed and reported immediately in all British newspapers; Richard Dimbleby made his famous radio broadcast of 19 April, audibly still in a state of shock at the scenes he had encountered. The wide circulation of photos and film material taken by the British Army contributed to the public sense of shock and now preserve the images of horror for future generations.[3]

Somewhat later, the Belsen trial of some 40 SS camp staff – most notoriously Irma Grese and Josef Kramer – from September to November 1945 in Lüneburg revealed many details of sadism and cruelties by individual SS personnel, as well as the systematic brutality of the camp regime. Also, accounts of survivors were published in the immediate aftermath: in 1944 conditions in the camp became public when one former inmate published his story after having been exchanged to Palestine.[4] More eyewitness testimonies appeared later. Finally, but perhaps most importantly, Anne Frank's diaries of her life in hiding before her discovery and deportation to Auschwitz and Bergen-Belsen gained international fame, and today for many schoolchildren remain the most easily accessible introduction to Nazi persecution of Jews throughout Europe.

Thus, Belsen became a symbol to the world public, and the name of a small town in a northern German heath became a metaphor besides Auschwitz and Dachau for the entire Holocaust, even though far fewer victims died in Belsen than in, for example, Treblinka or Chelmno. Belsen retained this symbolic function also in the long run, as evidenced, for example, by Ronald Reagan's visit there in the 1980s. Today, the name of Belsen still evokes ideas of a system of annihilation, of incredible suffering, of the utterly pitiless neglect of human values, of anti-Semitic brutalities, and of the 'Final Solution of the Jewish Question'.

None the less, it has been argued that in many ways the liberation of Bergen-Belsen was more a British than a Jewish event. While the impact of the liberation on British public opinion was enormous, the suffering of the Belsen inmates represented only a part of the immense killings of the Jewish people and misery of the entire

Holocaust. Most subsequent historical studies of the Nazi system of concentration camps or of the extermination of Jews do not give a great deal of space to an analysis of Bergen-Belsen. Yet in April 1945, and for British eyes, the situation appeared different. The gruesome sights were not initially seen as a specifically Jewish tragedy.[5] But the psychological moment at which previously suspected cruelties and terror became visible realities, and the fact that the discovery of the camp came unexpectedly to the liberators, both contributed to their shock.

It was British troops who freed the survivors of Belsen, and who set up the most amazing organisation of immediate help under extremely difficult conditions. The war was nearly won, and people began to think about the society they encountered in Germany and about its future possibilities. The name of 'Belsen' became synonymous with the atrocities and terror that Britain had been fighting for almost six years, as one observer pointed out in 1949:

> All these matters were the subject of sensational accounts in the newspapers, and Belsen became the symbol of all that had been told (and scarcely credited) of the vileness and rottenness of the Nazi system. Other camps were unearthed as the Allied armies moved forward, and some of them were worse than Belsen, at least with regard to their calculated savagery and cruelty. But Belsen, because it was the first of which an impartial account was available, became the archetype of the rest; and a proof that it was not an imaginary evil which the Allies had been fighting for almost six years.[6]

To understand, thus, what gave Belsen its unique position within the vast system of imprisonment and extermination, the camp's history must be viewed in the context of the Nazis' concentration camp system and anti-Jewish policies.

Concentration Camps and the 'Final Solution'

The background for the horrendous catastrophe in Belsen was provided by the vast German camp system. Both violent anti-Semitism and the creation of concentration camps had characterised the Nazi regime from its beginnings in 1933 and were well established ten years later when the first Jewish prisoners arrived in Bergen-Belsen. Set up immediately after the National Socialist 'seizure of power' in January 1933, the concentration camps quickly became the uncontested domain of the SS under Heinrich Himmler and remained an integral part of the terror system against political enemies until 1945.[7] The first camp in Dachau, near Munich, set the pattern for internal administration and the punishment (including executions) of prisoners. Esterwegen, Oranienburg, Fuhlsbüttel and other camps followed quickly; and the concentration camps had about 25,000 inmates by the beginning of the war.

With war preparations, however, economic considerations began to play a decisive role in the recruitment of new prisoners. 'Habitual criminals' and 'anti-social elements' (gays, Jehovah's Witnesses, gypsies and others) were sent into the camps and used as cheap labour in quarries and brickworks, especially in Buchenwald and Sachsenhausen.[8] The number of prisoners in Buchenwald had risen to 13,000 by November 1939, of whom almost 20 per cent died within the following five months.[9] The SS founded their own building materials company in early 1938 and used the camps' production to support various Nazi building projects; the SS economic empire later culminated in weapons' production at Dora-Nordhausen, but they also rented out prisoners to private sector companies, most notoriously to IG Farben for their buna (rubber) productions at Auschwitz.[10] To co-ordinate these economic activities the SS-WVHA (SS Main Office of Economic Administration) in early 1942 took over the camps holding nearly 100,000 prisoners.

During the war, it was mainly nationals of the occupied countries who were sent to the camps: Poles, French, Dutch, later Russians and many others. Treatment became crueller, and executions abounded. Above all, Jews now became victims of the camps, as with the invasion of Poland some 2,000,000 Jews had fallen into German hands. Beyond the original narrow function of imprisoning political opponents, the concentration camps became linked to a vast system of various other camps – labour, transit, prisoner of war camps, ghettos, and finally extermination camps – all of which increasingly overlapped in their role.[11] In Neuengamme, for example, work in the quarries was more or less intended to eventually kill the prisoners, a policy aptly described as 'extermination through labour'.[12]

Starvation, exhaustion, but also mass shootings, particularly of Soviet prisoners of war, took a huge toll on life.

The camps now also became the main instrument of the National Socialist racist policy. Anti-Semitism had been a central tenet of Nazi ideology from its onset, but policies against the Jews had undergone a variety of changes between 1933 and 1941. Social and legal segregation, plunder and pauperisation, humiliation and harassment, culminated in the organised brutalities of the November pogrom of 1938 (the so-called 'Kristallnacht'), when about 35,000 Jews were sent to the camps and singled out for cruel treatment there. The expulsion and emigration of all Jews from Germany as the overriding goal of Nazi policy towards Jews, however, gave way in 1941 to the new aim of total physical annihilation, the mass murder of all Jews within German reach.[13] In July 1941 Heydrich was commanded to organise the mass killings, and in October emigration from the Reich was stopped and systematic deportations began. In occupied Poland deportations, ghettos, brutalities, pogroms, starvation, and forced labour became merely the prologue to extermination in specially constructed death camps.

Thus, simultaneously with the territorial annexation programme, the Nazis began to realise their second ideological aim of creating 'racial purity' by eliminating all Jews. Although some Jews were temporarily exempt for various reasons, the overall ideological aim remained the murder of the entire Jewish population. When German armies invaded the Soviet Union, they were followed by special units (Einsatzgruppen) whose purpose was to kill the Jewish population. They murdered a total of about 1,000,000 Russian Jews.[14] For 'efficiency' reasons, the SS then switched from mass shootings to murder by poison gas, based on methods developed to kill the mentally ill and others in the 'euthanasia' programme. Beginning in Chelmno in October 1941, and continuing in the specially constructed extermination camps at Belzec, Sobibor, and Treblinka in Eastern Poland, approximately 1,500,000 Jews were killed up to the end of 1942. Here genocide was committed with the 'deliberate use of state power, totally systematic, factory-like, and supported by auxiliary bureaucracies'.[15] Despite attempts to keep the atrocities secret, knowledge spread among intended future victims in the Polish ghettos and camps as well as among Germans in the Reich.[16]

While this so-called 'Final Solution' had begun outside the concentration camps, they soon became its principal instrument. Auschwitz (established as a concentration camp in May 1940) was to become the main centre for the extermination of Jews. Unlike the camps of Belzec, Sobibor and Treblinka, Auschwitz-Birkenau and the Lublin-Majdanek camp served a double function, being also integrated into the system of concentration camps and exploiting forced labour for German industry.[17] The first group of prisoners (some 800 Russian prisoners of war and others) was gassed in Auschwitz in September 1941. In the following year more effective gas chambers and crematoria were built, and their operation did not stop until November 1944, after the horrendous, industrialised murder of over 1,000,000 people. Here the infamous 'selections' took place, separating on arrival those who were to be gassed immediately, and those who were deemed fit enough to withstand some months of slave labour for German munitions companies or the chemical company of IG Farben. Jews from all over Europe were murdered here, notoriously 400,000 deportees from Hungary, in addition to gypsies, Poles, Soviet prisoners of war and many others.

All remaining labour and extermination camps were evacuated before advancing Allied troops, but this did not yet mean an end to the massive killing of Jews. In the final chaos during the last months of the war, in the freezing winter, prisoners were marched or transported, without sufficient food, clothing or shoes, to other camps further from the front line, under conditions so wretched that vast numbers of evacuees died of starvation, exposure, exhaustion or were shot by their SS escorts – in effect this was another phase of the National Socialist mass murder.[18] The reception camps, into which these evacuees were herded, finally became so overcrowded that conditions there continued to kill prisoners by the thousands. Bergen-Belsen became the worst of these camps. Including these victims of the last hour, the Holocaust had thus claimed some 6,000,000 Jewish lives by the end of the war.[19]

The Origins of Bergen-Belsen, 1943

The horrors of the Bergen-Belsen concentration camp were mostly created in this last phase of the Holocaust. By that time, however, the camp had been in existence for two years and had passed through several quite different phases.[20]

The origins of Belsen lie outside the system of concentration camps and form a part of the history of that small minority of Jews whom the Nazis for one reason or another exempted from immediate annihilation. By the spring of 1943, millions of Jews had already been deported and murdered. At that point, the Foreign Office and the SS leadership worked out an agreement to hold back from the transports Jews who might be exchanged for Germans interned by the British or the Americans. The Foreign Office envisaged that 30,000 mainly Dutch, Belgian, French and Norwegian Jews with family, friends, or business partners in enemy states, might be held back, especially if they also held British or American papers. Revealingly, the Foreign Office added that 'in case the above-mentioned exchange negotiations come to nothing the deportation of these Jews can still take place later'.[21] This idea met with similar projects suggested by the SS leadership to concentrate perhaps 10,000 Jews as hostages, held in order to apply economic or political pressure abroad, in a special camp where – again in revealing language – 'they are to work but in conditions which will keep them healthy and alive'.[22] It should be emphasised here that neither Himmler nor the RSHA nor the Foreign Office wavered in their determination to expedite the 'Final Solution'; they merely found it temporarily more opportune to exempt from the deportations a small group of Jews whom they 'credited with having a certain value on the international market in human beings'.[23]

In spring 1943 a suitable location was found to house this special group. This was an isolated compound at Bergen-Belsen in the Lüneburg Heath in northern Germany, which had originally been established as a military training area and was designated in 1941 as 'Stalag 311' to receive Soviet prisoners of war. In Bergen-Belsen, and three other camps in the immediate vicinity, desperate prisoners of war ate the bark from trees and dug small earth hovels as their only shelter in winter. Thousands died from exhaustion, starvation, epidemics and systematic cruelties. An outbreak of typhoid fever in the winter of 1941–42 killed more than 50,000 Soviet prisoners in these four camps (perhaps 18,000 in Bergen-Belsen alone), and only one in ten inmates survived. From 1942, Bergen-Belsen was used as a hospital for Soviet and other prisoners of war, sent there, most to die, when they had become too exhausted to work.[24] Even before the beginning of our story, Bergen-Belsen had thus seen another harrowing tragedy, which had left the camp virtually empty – a miserable and little known prologue to the camp that became infamous to the world.

While the prisoner of war hospital camp continued to exist until January 1945, the then vacant section of the compound was chosen in April 1943 to house the 'exchange Jews' in what was euphemistically called a 'privileged', or 'detention' camp (Vorzugslager, Aufenthaltslager). An important, and indeed fateful, decision was made at the foundation of the camp, which set the course towards the catastrophe of spring 1945. This planned detention camp could have had the status of a civilian internment camp, but instead, it was immediately integrated into the concentration camp system run by the SS Economic Administration. There were two main reasons for this: a civilian camp would have been open to inspection by the International Red Cross, and placing the camp within the concentration camp system left open the option to deport the inmates at any time to one of the extermination camps.[25] As it was, both the SS Economic Administration, concerned with war production, and the Reich Security Main Office, organising the 'Final Solution', largely ignored Bergen-Belsen because its isolated position and its special function made it unsuitable for mobilisation in armament production and marginal in the extermination programme. This strange and exceptional position between the governing SS bodies of WVHA and RSHA had grave consequences. Both organisations neglected the camp. Its buildings remained dilapidated and its sanitary installations remained primitive, despite the efforts of a building squad sent there in May 1943.

The first 'exchange Jews' arrived in Bergen-Belsen in July 1943. They were two transports totalling 2,400 Polish Jews with Latin American passports or 'promesas', papers promising a passport. By this time, however, the Germans had already decided not to recognise these 'promesas', and deported most of their holders to Auschwitz within a few months.[26]

Further transports arrived in the summer and autumn. Among

them were some 360 Sephardic Jews from Salonika, who had retained their Spanish nationality and thus fell into the Nazi category of *Heimkehrer*, citizens of neutral or satellite countries who were to be repatriated at the request of their government. After lengthy negotiations this group was actually sent to Palestine via Spain in February 1944. About 200 Jews from North Africa who held British passports, and several hundred French, Yugoslav and Albanian Jews also arrived in Belsen during the first half of 1944.

From early 1944, the largest group of inmates in Bergen-Belsen consisted of 3,670 Dutch 'exchange Jews'. They had been held back from the otherwise ruthless extermination of Dutch Jews mostly because they had previously been listed as emigrants, had dual citizenship or connections to enemy states, or were highly skilled diamond workers. About 110,000 Dutch Jews were deported during the German occupation of the Netherlands; only some 5,500 survived the deportations and of these, most were interned in Bergen-Belsen.[27]

By July 1944, over 4,000 'exchange Jews' of different nationalities were thus detained in Belsen, but only 358 among them were ever genuinely 'exchanged'.[28] These were 222 out of approximately 1,300 holders of Palestine certificates, who eventually arrived in Haifa in July 1944, and 136 inmates with South and Central American papers who reached Switzerland in January 1945.[29] A very small number of other inmates also left Bergen-Belsen for safer places: several hundred nationals of neutral states were sent abroad, and another several hundred to internment camps with better living conditions.

Life in the 'Detention Camp', 1943–44: Hunger, Work, Deprivation and 'Privileges'

For the vast majority of the Bergen-Belsen 'exchange Jews', exchange proved not to be an option. They remained in the camp, which was increasingly filled, under continuously worsening conditions. The main part of the camp, by July 1944 housing some 4,000 'exchange Jews', was called 'Star camp' (after the Star of David the inmates had to wear). They lived in some 18 barracks, two of which were set aside as an 'old people's home', but the accommodation was inadequate and hard to endure. In May 1944, for example, hot weather turned one typical hut into 'an oven. A hundred and eighty people, one single toilet – without a door on top of that – open chamber pots and buckets under the beds, laundry, clothes and other items hang in the narrow space between the three-layered bunk beds and from the ceiling. Dust, dirt, heat and stench.'[30]

All inmates of the Star camp were forced to work in very unpleasant conditions under considerable harassment from the SS. One work squad was occupied with cutting out usable pieces of leather from worn-out shoes for 14 hours a day, ending so late that some women never saw their children.[31] Others dug out tree stumps to use as firewood, or worked for camp sanitation or in 'youth care'. To many internees, helping in the kitchen seemed desirable because of the extra food that could be 'organised' there, but that was really little compensation for the long hours and hard work in the kitchen: 'After two days I ate only one slice of bread with butter and drank a little coffee. It was too much for me, the exhausting work and the all too short night's rest made me too tired to breakfast properly.' Renata Laqueur, a Dutch 'exchange Jew' in the Star camp from March 1944, concluded 'I do not think that I will go back to the kitchen squad. I use up more of my strength there than I can gain from additional food.'[32]

Food was becoming the main concern even in the summer of 1944. Herbert Kruskal, who was among those exchanged to Palestine in June 1944, listed the rations: 325 grams of bread and one litre of turnip broth daily, plus a weekly ration of 75 grams of margarine, a tablespoon of jam, occasionally some cottage cheese, unsweetened coffee substitute and twice weekly some water broth with groats. Infants up to nine months received a cup of skimmed milk a day.[33] Renata Laqueur described a scene when raw swedes were brought into the camp, and people 'pounced on them and fought for them. And the SS Lance Sergeant stood by, clapped his thighs and laughed because people were eating such things: "Really, I have never seen anything like that … "'.[34]

Besides hunger and hard work, it was SS cruelty that inmates found hardest to bear. Many cases of psychopathic savagery occurred, for example, when a man with a stubble had his beard singed off, when a SS woman crushed a child's hand into a potato fire with her jackboot and when a roll-call NCO shot two men because they did not get up quickly enough. Kicking and thrashing was so common that many victims had to be kept in hospital with their injuries.[35] In one sub-camp a woman was sent to a hospital in Celle to give birth, but was caught smuggling letters out:

> Commandant Haas was furious. He said that we were ungrateful and had abused his trust. The woman and her infant were exhibited up front during the daily roll-call. The Gestapo men kicked the woman, demanding the names of those who gave her the letters. She remained silent and clutched her baby. The Gestapo man drew his gun. At this point the camp commandant intervened. He waved the Gestapo man away and ordered us to spend the rest of the day standing on the parade ground.[36]

Yet on the whole personal sadism was a relatively minor cause of suffering compared to other camps and compared to the institutional sadism of the Bergen-Belsen system itself. The SS derived 'satanic pleasure' from putting ill-clad, hungry and sick people through interminable roll-calls in mud and sleet.[37] Another real torture were the sudden moves to other, usually more inferior huts. When the 'old people's home' was moved, for example, 325 frail people had to be evacuated within the hour into huts without chairs, tables or light, where the upper tier of the beds was too high for old people to climb up. The weakest of them arrived too late to get a bed at all, and meanwhile their blankets got soaked and bread was stolen in the chaos of the transfer.[38] Hut inspections were not held to combat infections and dirt; their sole aim was 'to intimidate, persecute and humiliate'.[39] One inmate concluded:

> What they did, the Nazis … , they did with joy and with lust. There was no question of the slightest wavering or doubt, let alone recoiling from the ultimate and the worst. There was not even any question of unconcern or indifference. They went the whole way. Their ruthless cruelty kept growing, it gave them a sense of well-being. Always and everywhere there was the bitter sneer of malicious pleasure at the wretched misery beneath them, under their impeccably polished boots.[40]

Mistreatment, food and work were, however, not the only

preoccupation of the inmates. The SS had categorised the 'Star camp' as a *'Vorzugslager'*, a camp with 'privileges', which for one Dutch inmate, the lawyer Abel Herzberg, was 'a relative but far from fictitious concept, despite the fact that the camp was in many repects, especially towards the end, far worse than other camps'.[41] In the 'Star camp', families could get together at least during the day – a crucial feature as the norm in the camps was to wrench husbands, wives and children apart. On 12 December 1944, 684 children and 100 pregnant women and nursing mothers were living in the 'Star camp', so childcare played an important role.[42] Prams were bitterly fought over, and it spelled disaster when an order suddenly forbade the hanging of nappies and children's laundry to dry inside the huts.[43] The children's situation can be gauged from the birthday presents that one little boy, alone in the camp except for his sister, received: a slice of bread with jam, another slice of bread with a little sugar, a biscuit and a lump of sugar, and '[a]ccording to the custom here, he also gets an extra ration of soup.'[44]

Although education and assemblies of youngsters were strictly forbidden, a school was set up under disguise, without materials and among the noise and overcrowding. It became a lifeline for many of the 110 children in the hut of a teacher and communist partisan from Sarajevo, Hanna Lévy-Hass, who wrote:

> I devote myself regularly to the children. I feel very clearly that our 'school' has become an indispensable part of their existence, the only influence that keeps their spiritual lives cheerful and refreshed. The great majority of them are enthusiastic to learn and have the will to make up for the time they have lost. When I call them to come, they respond with shouts of joy and shout 'Hurrah!' Then the ablest among them clear a corner in the hut so that we can start, and they gather round me, their wonderful faces filled with delight but also with attentiveness and concentration.[45]

For the many children robbed of their parents, inmates even set up an 'orphanage'. One transport from Westerbork included 35 children under five years of age with a sign around their necks saying 'Unbekanntes Kind' ('unknown child').[46] Other orphans, too, were looked after by camp inmates with heroic devotion. In particular

Luba Tryszynska and Hermina Krantz, nurses sent from Auschwitz in the autumn of 1944, succeeded in saving a group of 90 orphans aged between one month and 12 years.[47] Liberators later were astounded that 'these wretched internees had taken good care of the 700 children in the camp. There were many babies in arms among them, and children of all ages. They were alive, they did not stagger as they walked.'[48] But care in the camp did not alter Nazi policies, and the Westerbork orphanage later went on transport, while other children were ruthlessly separated from their mothers, such as the children of the diamond workers' group – on St. Nicholas Day, a traditional festivity for Dutch children.[49]

Besides this (permanently threatened) contact between family members, the 'privileges' of the Star camp included a degree of self-administration. While this was essentially fictitious and largely meant carrying out orders by the SS, some harshness could be mitigated. The 'Jewish Elder' of the Star camp, the Greek Jacques Albala, was empowered to mete out punishment in the Star camp, but he was regarded as corrupt. In dealing with theft (mostly of bread) he was advised by the so-called 'judicial commission', led by lawyers amongst the prisoners, whose objectivity and integrity was widely trusted.[50] The *Ältestenrat* ('council of elders') negotiated and formed working parties, and despite some corruption saved hundreds from total exhaustion.[51] Self-administration also allowed for grouping inmates in huts together according to their nationality, which most preferred, and setting aside two huts for the elderly.[52] 'Privileges' of the 'Star camp' also included the receipt of occasional parcels and postcards from Holland, the American Jewish Joint Distribution Committee, or the Red Cross.

The psychological burden of this kind of existence is indescribable. Lack of freedom and permanent humiliation weighed on people's minds, as one inmate put it: 'that was the worst of all: the oppression. Worse than the long working day and worse than punishment, worse than roll-call, was the endless oppression, the constant shouting, snarling, hounding, from early morning till late at night.'[53]

Without news from relatives or of events of the war, people felt abandoned, angry and afraid. They were hungry, exhausted, disgusted with their surroundings, with the behaviour of the SS and tired of their fellow-inmates in the involuntary close community.

Daily routines and self-esteem collapsed, and aggression and fear mounted:

> Our hut is like a madhouse. Only a few are capable of controlling themselves. The slightest incident leads to vicious arguments, threats, insults and abuse. Everyone is irritable, on edge, waiting to be provoked, ready to assume a personal animosity on the part of the next person. Everyone's mind is full of distrust, suspicion, and deceitfulness. It makes one shudder.[54]

Squabbling and loathing increased as conditions worsened, and theft and 'organising' were seen as proof of social and moral breakdown, which for many was accompanied by religious doubts. Increasingly, fear of beating, pain, hunger and imminent death dominated everybody's personality: 'As the days passed, during March, each one of us lost more and more of his individuality, until finally we became one mass of misery and suffering.'[55]

None the less, in this 'enforced community' of the Star camp, inmates tried to keep their spirits up in different ways. Intellectual activity, observation of religious rites and expression of Zionist aspirations, for instance, provided a sense of identity, moral fortitude and defiance, even for non-Zionists and atheists.[56] Hope for the end of the Third Reich, according to Herzberg,

> strengthens our resistance. And anyone who wants to know how that manifests itself should go into hut 12 on Sunday evenings when the French, Albanian and Serbian Jews are the guests of the Greeks, and there is singing. Then there is excitement and life in the group. A freedom song, and the rhythm is accompanied by hand clapping and stamping of feet. The SS finally leaves us in peace. They are out of sight. Only the sentry in the tower can hear us and is probably getting annoyed and may report us. But the song wells up and the full vitality, the stubborn power of the Jewish nation breaks through. French and Greek, Serbian and Russian songs are sung, most are incomprehensible, but everyone knows their meaning: 'Il faut se tenir.' They are not going to beat us. Then at the end the Greek national anthem is sung and after that ... Hebrew, Ha-Tikvah.[57]

Living conditions in the Star camp are fairly well documented, but Bergen-Belsen also had smaller sub-camps for other groups of 'detained' Jews about whom less is known.[58] A separate 'Neutrals' camp' housed some 250 citizens of Spain, Portugal, Argentina and Turkey in somewhat better conditions without forced labour. Also separated in a special compound lived some 350 Poles, who were isolated presumably because of their knowledge of the atrocities in the East. A larger 'Hungarians' camp' was opened in July 1944 for about 1,700 Jews who travelled through Bergen-Belsen as part of their odyssey to Palestine in the Becher-Kastner exchange operation. They were relatively well treated, and after their departure in August and December 1944 this section of the camp remained to receive new transports. Besides these sections, an appalling 'Prisoners' camp' existed, originally to house a squad of some 500 Poles and Russians brought in to build the Belsen camp in 1943. No 'privileges' were granted here, as this had from the start a regular concentration camp regime with hard labour, rule by Kapos, cruel mistreatment by the SS, and a high mortality rate. The differences in treatment were obvious to all inmates. 'The prisoners [housed in this camp] gave us each three blankets, marvelling at the special treatment these Jews were getting,' recalled one new arrival in the Neutrals' compound, 'I had to pull our blankets out of a prisoner's hand. He clung to the bundle, embracing it, refusing to part from the rough warmth. When I took the blankets, he gazed at me, then down at his meagre, empty hands.'[59] From the Prisoners' camp, in a daring and highly dramatic break-out, 40 Russians fled in early 1944, digging an underground passage with their spoons and dishes under the camp's fence through which they escaped.

Bergen-Belsen as a whole was thus a conglomerate of different camps, with internal divisions and different treatment according to the citizenship of the inmates and the reason for their imprisonment.

Transformation into a Concentration Camp, 1944

While the conditions in the camp in early 1944 were bad enough, worse was in store. In the course of 1944, the 'detention camp' with relative 'privileges' took on an entirely different character. A new purpose for the camp was devised by the SS Economic Office, whose main concern during this period was to force prisoners to work for the German armaments industry. As this was impossible in Bergen-Belsen, the camp was earmarked in March 1944 to receive sick and exhausted prisoners from other concentration camps – the SS chose to call this a 'Recuperation camp' (*Erholungslager*). It was this gradual integration into the camp system throughout 1944, when exhausted prisoners, forced labourers and evacuees from other camps flooded into Belsen, which initiated the final catastrophe of disease, overcrowding, and starvation.

The first transport of invalids arrived in the Prisoners' camp in Belsen in March 1944, consisting of 1,000 mostly tubercular prisoners from the underground factory making V-weapons in Dora-Mittelbau. Not one doctor accompanied them, indicating the type of 'recuperation' intended – death by deliberate neglect. The invalids were terrorised by sadistic Kapos, housed in empty barracks without blankets or hot food. As a result, mortality rates were horrific: only 57 of these 1,000 lived to see the end of the war. With the arrival of more transports, about 4,000 people were delivered to the Prisoners' camp by 1 January 1945, although until then its average population never reached 2,000 because of the high death rate. Until July 1944, in fact, nearly 90 per cent of the deaths in the entire Belsen camp occurred in this section, indicating its abysmal conditions. Moreover, during the summer of 1944, a prisoner 'head nurse', Karl Rothe, killed some 200 people through cardiac injections – he was finally lynched by the prisoners in early September.[60] A German Social Democrat, arrested in 1933, described his arrival from Sachsenhausen in this 'recuperation camp' in February 1945 as follows:

Through deep puddles, with feet and trousers wet, we entered the camp. We saw for the first time that compound in which we would have to stand day after day for so many hours … Gradually the sky became overcast, and snow and rain began to fall – but we stood as before. I looked around for the special accommodations for sick people. But I saw only dirt, water, rubbish and dark, wretched, partially ruined huts.

At last we were allowed to enter the wooden huts … There were no beds, no chairs, no benches, and no light. The windows were broken, and there were neither palliasses nor straw to lie upon, only the floor, which was muddy, as the rain came through the roof. We learned that we would get nothing to eat for the next two to three days ... .

We slept on the floor, packed tight like herrings. There was no room to move or to turn over ... It must be remembered that all these people were either ill or convalescent.[61]

After the establishment of this 'Recuperation camp', it was the creation of the 'Women's camp' which initiated the new phase and final catastrophe in Bergen-Belsen.[62] From August 1944, thousands of Polish and Hungarian women arrived in the camp in transition from ghettos and labour camps in the East, where the Red Army was advancing, to work in the munitions factories of the Buchenwald and Flossenbürg concentration camps. Several further large transports of women followed in the autumn from Auschwitz-Birkenau; but these women, who were mostly sick and weak, remained in the extremely overcrowded and filthy Belsen camp, where, by 2 December 1944, the almost 8,000 women had become the single largest group of inmates. Even those coming from Auschwitz, for example a group of 3,000 women who arrived in early November, found conditions in Belsen shocking.[63]

The women had to live in large tents where they slept on straw on the ground, until a November storm tore away several tents leaving the women standing in the pouring rain without shelter of any kind. To make room for the women in the huts, the inmates of the Star camp were further squashed together in cruelly hasty moves, but the arrivals from Auschwitz also provided them with first-hand information about the atrocities in the extermination camps. Herzberg, for instance, found the reports on gassing 'impossible to believe'.[64] Conditions in the Women's camp deteriorated rapidly as many new transports arrived. Among the thousands who perished there in the following months was Anne Frank, only 15 years old.[65]

These arrivals initiated the last phase of the camp's history. Belsen held some 15,000 inmates by December 1944, when it became the destination for innumerable further transports from concentration camps near the front lines. Its transformation from a 'detention' camp with 'privileges' to merely one of the camps within the concentration camp system was accompanied by a change in the camp's leadership. On 2 December 1944 the command was handed over to SS Captain (*Hauptsturmführer*) Josef Kramer, who, as camp commandant in Auschwitz-Birkenau, had been responsible for the murder of several hundred thousand Hungarian Jews, and who arrived in Bergen-Belsen with many other SS staff after the evacuation of Auschwitz.[66] The camp was now a 'proper' concentration camp. 'Exchange Jews' lost any remaining special privileges, Kapos from the Prisoners' camp were in charge of all inmates, thrashing and work squads became the general rule, and the remaining modest institutions of Jewish self-administration were abolished. The final catastrophe of Belsen had begun.

The Inferno of the Final Months

As one of his first measures, Kramer ordered that no food at all be given to Jews (men, women and children, sick or well) for an entire day. At this time, about 50 per cent of the internees already had hunger oedemas. From this time on, hunger dominated life and death in the camp. Even in mid-1944 hunger had been rampant, food the main topic of conversation.[67] By November 1944, rations had been reduced to a daily bowl of so-called 'soup', turnips cooked in water without meat or fat, and a daily slice of bread of about one and a half inches thick. In February 1945, this ration was still augmented by a teaspoon of butter and a slice of sausage or cheese twice a week, and occasionally so-called 'coffee'. But rations continued to shrink. From mid-March there were several occasions when there was no bread at all for days.[68] It is difficult to imagine what this meant to the starved victims. Some tore up grass and boiled it.[69] When vats full of rancid soup were carried to the huts, any spillage was lapped up from the filthy ground by frantic people, and five guards had to accompany the vat carriers to prevent sudden attacks by the starving internees.[70] Besides their overwhelming misery, inmates were disgusted at the degradation and humiliation of having to scramble for their food on the filthy ground. One noted in his diary:

> in the hospital I hit the 'jackpot': the bottom fell out of a food bowl, the contents fell on the floor, and from there I spooned

all the 'thick' bits into my tin: pieces of potatoes and turnips. An Albanian boy shovelled straight from the floor into his mouth and stole the best morsels from under my nose. This instance as a reminder should I ever become supercilious.[71]

In the Prisoners' compound there was nothing to eat for six days running; they scrambled for the rotten, discarded bits of carrots which inmates of the Star camp tossed over the fence to them, and here the first cases of cannibalism occurred.[72] (It should be emphasised here that the British liberators found in the camp's storerooms 1,700 cans of Ovaltine, and hundreds of Red Cross food parcels containing canned meat, milk and biscuits, filling a room four by five metres and three metres high.[73] This could have alleviated at least some of the starvation.)

Hunger was accompanied by thirst. In the second Prisoners' camp, there were no water taps; drinking water came only from dirty cisterns. In the last days before the camp was handed over to the British, there was no water at all in the entire camp, because a bomb had destroyed the pumping station. No alternative supplies were provided for the prisoners, either through water trucks or through tapping a nearby brook. That this could easily have been accomplished was proven shortly afterwards by the British, who four days after the takeover had all the kitchens connected to water pipes.[74] It is evident that the neglect of inmates was not an inevitable consequence of the chaos in a collapsing country but instead, a policy of deliberate and premeditated murder was implemented.

Housing conditions corresponded to this general picture of purposeful neglect. Entirely unworthy of human beings by the autumn of 1944, intolerable barracks became catastrophic in the winter months. As more and more transports arrived, the number of camp inmates expanded quickly. The second half of the former POW camp was incorporated into the concentration camp and the Women's camp relocated there, but the shortage of space was not alleviated. From 18,000 on 1 January 1945, the number of prisoners rose to nearly 42,000 on 1 March (most from Auschwitz, Buchenwald and Sachsenhausen). After a new wave of transports arrived from the concentration camps in northern Germany (Neuengamme and Dora), some 60,000 prisoners were eventually liberated in Belsen. Yet these figures understate the number of prisoners sent to the camp because they ignore the enormous mortality rates – 18,000 died in March 1945 alone.[75] All these people were cramped, during the winter months, into shoddy barracks with leaking roofs, often no beds, no blankets, no benches, no lighting and no sanitation. A British Lieutenant Colonel summed up the overcrowding in one women's hut: 'It would have held 83 soldiers by British Army standards, we removed from it 1,426 women and that does not count the dead.'[76]

Sanitation was appalling. In November 1944, the Star camp with 4,000 people had one washroom with 12 taps. Throughout the spring of 1945 the entire second Prisoners' camp with some 8-10,000 inmates did not have a single toilet or a single water faucet. (Again, the material for these installations existed close by, but was deliberately withheld.)[77] The compound soon resembled one single latrine, especially since many of the weakened and dying prisoners suffered from diarrhoea. People could not drag themselves to the latrines but relieved themselves wherever they were; sometimes dirty laundry from diarrhoea patients was kept on the beds for weeks.[78] 'We are engulfed in our own stinking sea of germs, lice and fleas, and everything around us is putrid and slimy', one inmate wrote in December.[79] Hygienic conditions reached their horrifying low when the corpses of thousands of victims were simply left lying in the compound:

> During the last week all hygiene was given up and no attempt was made to succour the dying thousands enclosed within the wire. There was no fresh water, no food. The only water tank of any size had at least one corpse floating around in it. Beside the pump, the people died in hundreds – crawling towards it, raving and shrieking, while the brutal guard there beat the queue; and all the time the other guards went on firing, till in the end this half square mile of soil held more suffering than had ever any spot upon earth.[80]

One young girl remembered having been left for dead on one of these piles of bodies:

> I am convinced that many of the bodies heaped on to the piles

to await cremation still had life, though only just. Maybe they had collapsed from starvation and had been collected from the ground as though they were dead. This is how I was found when the allies marched into Belsen. On top of a heap of corpses, awaiting my final resting place – the funeral pyre.[81]

In such circumstances, disease naturally abounded. Many people arrived sick. Those evacuated from labour camps were exhausted, and all had suffered during the horrific transports. In one case, 20 per cent of a transport were dead on arrival, the rest mortally ill.[82] The sick-bays lacked the most elementary preconditions for the care of the sick. In one compound with some 15,000 sick women, the doctors received the grotesque amount of 300 aspirin for a whole week. Once again, stocks of medicine and instruments existed.[83] Thus, only token attempts were made to deal with illness. Epidemics, which were bound to break out under the circumstances, could only lead to massive mortality. An epidemic of abdominal typhus (a bacterial infection spread through food) had raged through the Prisoners' camp in the summer of 1944 and was repeated throughout the entire camp in the winter. Thousands were suffering from dysentry and stomach diseases, tuberculosis was common, and from early 1945 typhus (spotted fever, carried by lice) spread rapidly. Some prisoner doctors – without help from the camp administration – made huge efforts to clean the sick-bays systematically, isolate patients, and to struggle against demoralisation. But they were plainly fighting a losing battle.[84]

Degradation, privation and suffering thus accompanied the agonising deaths of thousands. The SS guards, together with prisoner Kapos, continued to harass people, to impose 'punishments', and to torture their victims by endless roll-calls, which only ceased in the last few weeks when the SS men, afraid of infections, virtually withdrew from the camp, abandoning the inmates to their fate. The guards and staff rarely killed people by actual mistreatment and direct shooting, however; the method of execution in Belsen was through deliberate starvation and neglect. One inmate, Hanna Lévy-Hass, who heard in January 1945 about the gassing in Auschwitz, thus decided that 'The end is the same – only the means are different. In Auschwitz it is a quick, ruthless procedure, mass murder in the gas chambers; in Belsen it is a sadistic, long-drawn-out process of starvation, of violence, of terror, of the deliberate spreading of infection and disease.'[85]

Hunger, thirst, hard work, mistreatment, disgusting housing, filth, lice, diarrhoea, typhus, virtually no medical care – it seems a miracle that anyone survived these months. One inmate described watching everyone, including herself, die:

> Death has become an everyday event and leaves us completely indifferent. We have given up thinking about being rescued and have stopped counting the days as we used to. There is no point in knowing when the Allies will arrive ... For the present our closest and most loyal ally is death. And if we do begin to count the days again, then it is not with an eye to the moment of our liberation but in order to see how long the one or the other of us can still survive. There is a kind of medical curiosity in us, a strange obsession ... I give myself only ten or fifteen days at the most.
>
> This brief semi-existence that is left to me I spend in the company of other corpses, some living, some dead. The corpses are still here, lying in our beds. There is no one to take them away and nowhere to put them in the crowded hut. In the yard outside they lie piled on top of each other in great heaps that grow higher every day. The crematorium is not capable of burning them all ... .
>
> Death is everywhere, hovering above us, threatening to pounce at any moment.[86]

Mortality rates confirm that extermination awaited everyone. In February about 7,000 people died, in March another 18,000. In the first half of April approximately 9,000 more; after the liberation, about 9,000 more succumbed to exhaustion and disease within two weeks, and another 4,000 died before the end of June 1945. A total of 50,000 people were murdered in the concentration camp at Bergen-Belsen.

The End: Evacuation and Liberation

With the advancing frontline, the SS realised by early April that the camp was soon to be taken by the British Army. They took their final measures: to evacuate the original 'exchange Jews', to hide as much as possible of the atrocities in the camp, and to negotiate a hand-over.

The horrors of the evacuation transports in the collapsing Third Reich defy description, and the surviving inmates of the Star camp, the Neutrals', Hungarians', and Special camps were not spared this last misery. Three trains left between 6 and 11 April, apparently destined for Theresienstadt, with approximately 7,000 prisoners in total. Their journeys mirrored the evacuation transports and death marches from all the other camps which had flowed into Bergen-Belsen. Overfilled carriages with dead and dying among the passengers were forced to stop-and-go through destroyed towns with days of unexplained stand-still, in freezing weather. The trains carried no provisions and were bombed almost daily. Abel Herzberg recalled the exhausting walk to the station, when luggage felt so heavy that some even threw away the swede which was their only ration:

> When we arrive, [the train] is already packed. It was to hold a total of two thousand four hundred people. Of these two thousand four hundred people, two thousand four hundred have dysentery. Besides, seven hundred of them are also sick: typhus, paratyphoid, spotted fever, camp typhus, neck cramp and similar diseases. Not counting oedema. It is crawling with lice. And all that is setting out on a journey together, around the world.[87]

The evacuees' good spirits and hope for an end to their misery soon turned to despair under the miserable conditions of the transport. Only after two weeks did Allied troops finally reach all three trains, and the nightmare ended for the evacuees. Hilde Huppert, who had been in Bergen-Belsen since 1943 with her eight-year old son, described her liberation near Magdeburg:

> The first U.S. army jeep passed by at about ten o'clock. ... Four dusty soldiers wearing helmets sat inside. They stopped the jeep and came up to us hesitantly, looking at the motley group. Women and children dressed in rags; a few men. Pitiful scarecrows. They asked, 'Who are you?', and we shrieked, in English, 'Hello! Friends! We love America!'
>
> Then, in chorus, 'We're Jews, Jews!' The Americans took off

their helmets and wiped their faces. One of them indicated a Star of David which hung on a chain around his neck, 'I'm a Jew, too' ... .

Boxes of bread and canned goods were unloaded. A field kitchen was got up at the roadside, and a cheerful cook began to prepare a hot meal.

The American soldiers were kind and friendly. They were ready to listen, although they found our stories hard to believe. They wanted to help. As for us, we hugged and kissed every soldier in sight, out of sheer joy and thankfulness.[88]

But the vast majority of Belsen inmates had not been evacuated and remained in a state of suspense in the last few days:

We just knew that one way or the other ... the end was at hand. It was painfully clear that without food or water we could not live too much longer – and with the knowledge that the Germans might not want to leave traces of their misdeeds behind, – it was really like a race. Who would get to us first. – We were very aware that unusual things were happening. – We saw less and less SS Personnel. In fact we hardly saw anybody at all. – We were just there – abandoned, and although we should really have been elated by the thought that the end was near, – we were not. – I remember that I was angry most of the time. – We had been holding out for so long, and suffered so much, and all this only to be blown up at the end of it all. It must have been the absence of the SS which made us so suspicious and convinced that this was precisely what was going to happen.[89]

Moreover, many inmates were forced to participate in the camp's final monstrous scene. For four days, all prisoners still able to walk had to carry the partly decomposing corpses lying around the camp in huge piles into mass graves. Two thousand emaciated figures – the dying scarcely distinguishable from the dead – in a long procession from six o'clock in the morning until dark, dragged their fellow-victims to unmarked graves; as a final insult 'distracted' by two prisoners' bands playing on Kramer's orders.

Most of the bodies did not weigh more than eighty or ninety pounds. But to carry one would have been too much even for

two or three of us, in our state of weakness. There were not
hundreds but thousands of corpses, and everyone in the camp
who could walk was ordered out to help. Leather straps, belts
or strips of blankets were fastened round each ankle and each
wrist of a dead body, and four men dragged it along the
highway to the far end of the camp. Nearly every dead body was
naked, the clothes having been stolen if they had been good, or
burnt if they had been in bad condition. There was practically
no flesh to be seen, only skin and bones. Many of the bodies had
lain there for many days and were already rotting. The route
over which they were dragged was partly sandy, partly swampy.
Through mud, through puddles and wheeltracks, over stones,
through piles of rubble – this was the last journey of these men.
Their skin, dry, yellow, sometimes green, was rubbed off the
bones, their backs were ripped, their faces were plastered with
mud and sand ... .

One of the strangest features of those days was the fact that the
utmost terror and suffering was mixed up with a kind of wild
gaiety. Coexisting with the deepest misery was a new hopefulness.
Two bands played dance music all day long while two thousand
men were dragging corpses to the burial-pits. There had always
been violins and guitars in the camp and the gipsies [sic] had often
practised fragments of music in the evenings, but in the last few
days there was a complete band. The SS encouraged them, giving
them cigarettes, and so they played, in the open air, from dawn
to dusk and the corpses jolted over the stones and the SS men and
Capos clubbed and lashed the stumbling prisoners, to the
melodies of Léhar and Johann Strauss.[90]

This truly nightmarish *danse macabre* was the last act ordered by the
SS. On 15 April, as part of a local cease-fire, the camp was handed
over to the British.[91]

The shock and disbelief with which the liberators reacted to the
horrors they found in Bergen-Belsen have been described above. It
seems fitting to close our overview of the history of the camp with an
account of the liberation from the other side, by a survivor. Rudolf
Küstermeier wrote:

On the night of April 14th I lay awake, and fell asleep only in the early morning. I was awakened suddenly by one of the Russian workers in our block. 'Come on! Come on! Quickly! Quickly! There are tanks in the road!' I heard the unmistakable clanking, clattering sound ... .

Slowly I got out of bed. A dozen men were already crowding to the doorway. No one dared to go far, for fear of the Hungarians in the watchtowers ... No shot was to be heard, only the grinding and rattling and roaring of the tanks ... .

Unable to stand up any longer I went back to bed. In the distance I heard the tanks pass the camp gate and a voice calling from a loudspeaker van. I knew that we were free. I lay and pondered. Incessantly I had to fight against the bugs and fleas which never ceased to torment me; I had fever and my head was heavy and dull, but I understood that we were free. More than eleven years of imprisonment had come to an end. I was alive. I would have a chance of recovering. I would be able to help in the work of reconstruction. I had no thoughts of revenge, but I knew that the most devilish tyranny the modern world had seen was losing its last strongholds, and that there would be a chance for new men and a new way of life. I felt deeply thankful.[92]

Conclusion

While the British Army obviously could not stop the dying and suffering of thousands immediately, their arrival ended the deliberate starvation and neglect which had caused the catastrophe in Belsen.[93] If the 'detention camp' had not formally been a part of the planned 'Final Solution', its horrendous consequences none the less entirely accorded with the ultimate intentions of the Nazis' extermination policy. Victims of Bergen-Belsen certainly experienced it as a 'death camp',[94] and just before her liberation the Star camp detainee Hanna Lévy-Hass reached 'the inescapable conclusion that Belsen was ... deliberately established and equipped in order to exterminate thousands of human beings methodically and with scientific thoroughness'.[95] Against this, it has been argued that Bergen-Belsen should not be regarded as part of the 'Final Solution', narrowly defined as including only the systematic killing in the extermination camps in Poland.[96] However, it seems pointless sophistry, and an insult to the victims, to draw such fine academic lines of terminological distinction here. The effect was the same. The overall intention was the same. Only the methods differed. Even the most ruthless extermination ideologue must have – however grudgingly – conceded some adjustments on timing, methods, and tactics in the overall killing programme. But stalling or allowing tiny exemptions to the general principle did not mean abandoning the ultimate aim. Once the reasons for the exemptions from the 'Final Solution' were no longer valid, the previously exempted Jews simply reverted to their original status of victims intended for extermination. After the evacuation of the original death camps in the East all subsequent murders were carried out less systematically, by starvation and brutalities on the marches and transports, but this unintentional change of method was merely a continuation of the previous programme by other means, which in the case of Bergen-Belsen meant overcrowding, starvation and epidemics. As Eberhard Kolb concludes:

> Although it was not simply the 'typical' concentration camp which it is often regarded as these days, its development towards the 'horror camp' of the spring of 1945 was anything but 'accidental'. It was rather in keeping with the internal logic of the concentration camp system and with the mentality of those functionaries who controlled the system or contributed towards its operation. In that sense Bergen-Belsen stands as a symbol for the entire barbarity and crimes of the NS regime.[97]

NOTES

1. Dr Fritz Leo, in Raymond Phillips (ed.), *Trial of Josef Kramer and Forty-Four Others (The Belsen Trial)* (London: William Hodge, 1949, War Crimes Trials Series, Vol. II), p.122.
2. Brigadier Glyn Hughes, *The Belsen Trial*, pp.31–2.
3. Himmler complained that 'he had been very poorly repaid' for the handover of Belsen with the world-wide publicity of conditions in the camp; possibly this convinced him to continue evacuating camps before the Allied advances: Felix Kersten, *The Kersten Memoirs 1940–1945*, with an introduction by H.R. Trevor-Roper (London: Hutchinson, 1956), p.288. Initial reaction to the liberation in the West is discussed in Tony Kushner, *The Holocaust and the Liberal Imagination: A Social and Cultural History* (Oxford: Blackwell, 1994), pp.209–25, who, however, warns against imposing later interpretations on contemporary perceptions of the discoveries.

4. Simon Heinrich Herrmann, who left in June 1944, published *Austauschlager Bergen-Belsen: Die Geschichte eines Austauschtransportes* (Tel-Aviv: Irgun Olej Merkas Europa, 1944). Loden Vogel's diary, written in the camp, and Rudolf Küstermeier's account, written down in August 1945, appeared in 1946.
5. Kushner, *Holocaust*, p.206. This is despite the fact that in Belsen more Jewish survivors were liberated than in any other camp. Even a permanent exhibition in the Imperial War Museum set up in 1991 on 'Belsen 1945' focuses more on the British relief efforts than on the liberated Jews: Kushner, *Holocaust*, p.264.
6. Introduction, in *The Belsen Trial*, pp.xxiii–xxiv.
7. M. Broszat, 'Nationalsozialistische Konzentrationslager 1933–1945', in Hans Buchheim *et al.*, *Anatomie des SS-Staates* (Munich: DTV, 1967), Vol.2, p.20. See Eugen Kogon, *The Theory and Practice of Hell: The German Concentration Camps and the System Behind Them* (London: Secker & Warburg, 1950).
8. Falk Pingel, 'The Concentration Camps as Part of the National-Socialist System of Domination', in *The Nazi Concentration Camps: Structure and Aims – The Image of the Prisoner – The Jews in the Camps. Proceedings of the Fourth Yad Vashem International Historical Conference (1980)* (Jerusalem: Yad Vashem, 1984), p.4. A somewhat different classification of stages in the development of the entire German camp system, including the death camps, is put forward in the same volume by Aharon Weiss, 'Categories of Camps – Their Character and Role in the Execution of the "Final Solution of the Jewish Question"', pp.115–32.
9. Broszat, 'Nationalsozialistische Konzentrationslager', p.97. Prisoners' testimonies give sickening details about Buchenwald in David A. Hackett, *The Buchenwald Report* (Boulder, CO: Westview, 1995).
10. For long-term plans linking economic plans to the camp system see, for example, Götz Aly and Susanne Heim, *Vordenker der Vernichtung: Auschwitz und die deutschen Pläne für eine neue europäische Ordnung* (Hamburg: Hoffmann & Campe, 1991). At this point, however, the policy of annihilating Jews had priority over the supply of manpower, even for munitions production: 'Munitions were a means to carry on the war, but the extermination of Jews was one of the goals of the war', Pingel, 'The Concentration Camps', p.15.
11. Broszat, 'Nationalsozialistische Konzentrationslager', p. 104.
12. Hermann Kaienburg, '*Vernichtung durch Arbeit*': *Der Fall Neuengamme. Die Wirtschaftsbestrebungen der SS und ihre Auswirkungen auf die Existenzbedingungen der KZ-Gefangenen* (Bonn: Dietz, 1990), combines the case study of Neuengamme with an analysis of the use of inmates for war production within the entire camp system.
13. On the debate about the decision for the 'Final Solution', see David Cesarani (ed.), *The Final Solution: Origins and Implementations* (London: Routledge, 1994), E. Jäckel, 'Die Entschlußbildung als historisches Problem', in Eberhard Jäckel and Jürgen Rohwer (eds.), *Der Mord an den Juden im Zweiten Weltkrieg: Entschlußbildung und Verwirklichung* (Stuttgart: DVA, 1985), pp.9–17, and H. Mommsen, 'The Realization of the Unthinkable: The 'Final Solution of the Jewish Question' in the Third Reich', in Gerhard Hirschfeld (ed.), *The Policies of Genocide: Jews and Soviet Prisoners of War in Nazi Germany* (London: Allen & Unwin, 1986), pp.97–144.
14. Ronald Headland, *Messages of Murder: A Study of the Reports of the Einsatzgruppen of the Security Police and the Security Service, 1941–1943* (London: Associated University Presses, 1992), p.105, arrives at a total of at least 1,152,731 persons killed by them up to Dec. 1942; but see generally the older study of Helmut Krausnick and Hans-Heinrich Wilhelm, *Die Truppe des Weltanschauungskrieges: Die Einsatzgruppen der Sicherheitspolizei und des SD 1938–1942* (Stuttgart: DVA, 1981).
15. H.A. Strauss, 'Der Holocaust: Reflexionen über die Möglichkeiten einer wissenschaftlichen und menschlichen Annäherung', in Strauss and Kampe (eds.),

Antisemitismus, p. 220. I. Arndt and W. Scheffler, 'Organisierter Massenmord an Juden in nationalsozialistischen Vernichtungslagern', in Karl Dietrich Bracher, Manfred Funke, Hans-Adolf Jacobsen (eds.), *Nationalsozialistische Diktatur 1933-1945: Eine Bilanz* (Bonn: Schriftenreihe der Bundeszentrale für politische Bildung, vol. 192, 1983), pp.539–71, summarise the murder in the camps.

16. Walter Laqueur, *The Terrible Secret: An Investigation into the Suppression of Information about Hitler's 'Final Solution'* (London: Weidenfeld & Nicolson, 1980); Ian Kershaw, *Popular Opinion and Political Dissent in the Third Reich: Bavaria 1933–1945* (Oxford: Oxford University Press, 1983), pp.358-72; David Bankier, 'German Public Awareness of the "Final Solution"', in Cesarani (ed.), *The Final Solution*, pp.215–27.

17. See especially *Auschwitz: Geschichte und Wirklichkeit des Vernichtungslagers* (Reinbek: Rowohlt, 1980), and H.G. Adler, Hermann Langbein, Ella Lingens-Reiner (eds.), *Auschwitz: Zeugnisse und Berichte* (Frankfurt a.M.: Europäische Verlagsanstalt, 1984).

18. On the death marches see L. Rothkirchen, '"The Final Solution" in its Last Stages', in Yisrael Gutman and Livia Rothkirchen (eds.), *The Catastrophe of European Jewry* (Jerusalem: Yad Vashem, 1976), pp.319–45. At least a third of the prisoners in concentration camps died during the final evacuation marches in the last months of the 'Third Reich': Broszat, 'Nationalsozialistische Konzentrationslager', pp.132–3.

19. Wolfgang Benz (ed.), *Dimension des Völkermords: Die Zahl der jüdischen Opfer des Nationalsozialismus* (Munich: Oldenbourg, 1991), p. 17, gives figures ranging from 5.29 million to over six million Jewish victims.

20. My account in the following is largely based on Eberhard Kolb's authoritative history of the camp, *Bergen-Belsen: Geschichte des 'Aufenthaltslagers' 1943-1945* (Hanover: Verlag für Literatur und Zeitgeschehen, 1962), of which there is a short and updated English version, *Bergen-Belsen: From 'Detention Camp' to Concentration Camp, 1943–1945* (Göttingen: Vandenhoeck & Ruprecht, 1985), hereafter Kolb, *Bergen-Belsen*, 1962 and 1985 respectively. For additional documents see the recent collection by Rolf Keller *et al.* (eds.), *Konzentrationslager Bergen-Belsen: Berichte und Dokumente* (Göttingen: Vandenhoeck & Ruprecht, 1995).

21. Foreign Office to RSHA, 2 March 1943, quoted in Kolb, *Bergen-Belsen* (1985), p. 21.

22. Decree by Himmler to SS Lieutenant General Müller (RSHA), December 1942, quoted in Kolb, *Bergen-Belsen* (1985), p.21.

23. Abel J. Herzberg, *Between Two Streams: Bergen-Belsen Diary* (ms. translated by Jack Santcross, London, 1994; shortly to be published by I.B. Tauris, London), p.6. – Special thanks to Jack Santcross for letting me see this manuscript as well as his translation of Herzberg's 'Amor fati!' On the negotiations see Kolb, *Bergen-Belsen* (1962), pp.26–32 and 203–7.

24. For details see Kolb, *Bergen-Belsen* (1962), pp.36–7. Amazingly, there were some cases of organised resistance among the Soviet medical staff; Niedersächsische Landeszentrale für politische Bildung (ed.), *Sowjetische Kriegsgefangene 1941-1945: Leiden und Sterben in den Lagern Bergen-Belsen, Fallingbostel, Oerbke, Wietzendorf* (Lohheide: Gedenkstätte Bergen-Belsen, 1991), is a small brochure giving details and photographs. This is just one extreme example of the treatment of the 5.7 million Soviet prisoners of war, of whom about 3.3 million died in German camps and labour squads. Starvation of Soviet POWs in 1941–42 is discussed in Christian Streit, *Keine Kameraden: Die Wehrmacht und die sowjetischen Kriegsgefangenen* (Bonn: Dietz, 1990), pp.128–90.

25. Kolb, *Bergen-Belsen* (1962), pp.37–8, 209.

26. Kolb, *Bergen-Belsen* (1962), pp.44–52. When this group, who had been expecting to go abroad shortly, realised that in fact they had arrived in an extermination camp, they rioted, one woman shot an SS man, others attacked the SS with their bare hands. Every member of this transport of 1,700 people was killed: Kolb, *Bergen-Belsen* (1985), p.25.

27. Figures in H. van der Dunk, 'Jews and the Rescue of Jews in the Netherlands in Historical Writing', in Yisrael Gutman and Gideon Greif (eds.), *The Historiography of the Holocaust: Proceedings of the Fifth Yad Vashem International Historical Conference* (Jerusalem: Yad Vashem, 1988), p.491. Jacob Presser, *Ashes in the Wind: The Destruction of Dutch Jewry* (London: Souvenir Press, 1968) discusses official German exemptions (pp.164-9) and specifically Bergen-Belsen (pp.512-24); see the more recent papers in G. Jan Colijn and Marcia S. Littell (eds.), *The Netherlands and Nazi Genocide: Papers of the 21st Annual Scholars' Conference* (Lewiston: Mellen, 1992).

28. On the exchanges see Kolb, *Bergen-Belsen* (1962), pp.87–103, who also gives details of how the sad physical state of those arriving abroad shocked Swiss public opinion. The reason that such a small fraction of 'exchange Jews' from Belsen ever actually obtained their freedom lay mostly in the attitude of the German Foreign Office. Negotiators dragged their feet, demanded impossible concessions, and were essentially unwilling to concede even small exceptions to their general policy of extermination. It remains open to discussion whether this was a point at which a few otherwise condemned Jews might have been saved, with goodwill and effort on both sides, especially on the part of dissenters within the German bureaucracies and institutions. For negotiations between Himmler and Allied and Jewish organisations at the end of the war to release some Jews, see Kersten, *Memoirs*, pp.275-90, and R. Breitman and Sh. Aronson, 'The End of the 'Final Solution'? Nazi Plans to Ransom Jews in 1944', *Central European History* 25 (1992), pp.177–203; on Himmler's plans see Yehuda Bauer, *Jews for Sale? Nazi-Jewish Negotiations, 1933–1945* (New Haven, CT: Yale University Press, 1994), pp.103–4, and R. Breitman in this volume.

29. Herrmann, *Austauschlager Bergen-Belsen*, pp.54–7 and 62-79, describes the tension of waiting for the exchange to Palestine to become realised. See also *From Bergen-Belsen to Freedom: The Story of the Exchange of Jewish Inmates of Bergen-Belsen with German Templars from Palestine. A Symposium in Memory of Dr. Haim Pazner* (Jerusalem: Yad Vashem, 1986).

30. Renata Laqueur, *Bergen-Belsen Tagebuch 1944/45* (Hanover: Fackelträger-Verlag, 1989), p.58 (diary notes, 28 May 1944).

31. Herzberg, *Between Two Streams*, pp.28–9, 101.

32. Laqueur, *Tagebuch*, p.74 (diary notes, 22 July 1944), where she gives a detailed description of one typical day in the kitchen.

33. Herbert N. Kruskal, 'Two Years Behind Barbed Wire: Factual Report of a Dutchman Describing his Experiences under the German Oppression', typescript, 1981, Wiener Library, p.23. Herrmann, who was on the same exchange (*Austauschlager*, p.46), adds the occasional beetroot salad and fruit-juice to this list.

34. Laqueur, *Tagebuch*, p.76 (diary notes, 22 July 1944). Other inmates also vividly portrayed the effects starvation had on their lives and the panic at mealtimes, see Hanna Lévy-Hass, *Inside Belsen* (Brighton: Harvester Press, 1982), 4 Sept. 1944, p.16.

35. Herzberg, *Between Two Streams*, p.106 (Star camp); Agnes Sassoon, *Agnes: How My Spirit Survived* (Edgware: Todays Woman Publications, 1985), p.48; Rudolf Küstermeier, 'How we Lived in Belsen: A Retrospect', in Derrick Sington, *Belsen Uncovered* (London: Duckworth, 1946), p.112 (Prisoners' camp); statement by Dr Ada Bimko, who worked in the Women's camp hospital, *The Belsen Trial*, p.69.

36. Hilde Huppert, 'Hand-in-hand with Tommy', typed MS., Tel-Aviv, 1978 (first version written down in Palestine in 1945), Wiener Library, pp.82–3.

37. Herzberg, *Between Two Streams*, p.103. Twenty per cent were sick in Oct. 1944, but Arbeitsdienstführer Rau insisted that they all attend roll-call, and instead of the light work or bed-rest the doctor prescribed, they were forced to unload heavy lumber 11 hours a day, giddy from hunger, exhaustion and wretchedness (Herzberg, *Between Two Streams*, pp.93–4).

38. Herzberg, *Between Two Streams*, p.104 (early Nov. 1944). Another transfer of the old people's home in Feb. 1945 was even worse, with Kapos and prisoners brutalising the elderly, infirm and dying, and stealing their bread (Herzberg, *Between Two Streams*, pp.126–7).

39. Lévy-Hass, *Inside Belsen*, p.39 (diary notes, 6 Nov. 1944).

40. Abel J. Herzberg, 'Amor Fati. Attachment to Fate: Seven Essays on Bergen-Belsen', translated from the Dutch by Jack Santcross, MS. (Dutch edition Amsterdam: Em. Querido's Uitgeverij B.V., 1987), p.6. One of the most notorious of SS staff was Irma Grese, whose cruelties received much attention at the trial. While Derrick Sington pleaded that 'a civilised attitude would have seen Irma Grese as a psychological casualty of war' (Giles Playfair and Derrick Sington, *The Offenders: Society and the Atrocious Crime*, London: Secker & Warburg, 1957, p.184), inmates judged her differently: 'In reality she was as mean and vicious as the rest of them' (Anita Lasker-Wallfisch, MS. notes for her children, 1925–46, Wiener Library, p. 68.) Special thanks to the author for her permission to use the manuscript.

41. Herzberg, 'Amor Fati', p. 12.

42. Herzberg, *Between Two Streams*, p.114.

43. Herzberg, *Between Two Streams*, pp.82, 106.

44. Herzberg, *Between Two Streams*, p.39.

45. Lévy-Hass, *Inside Belsen*, pp.36–7 (diary notes, 23 Oct. 1944). On the difficulties in setting up a school see also ibid., pp.7–8, and Herzberg, *Between Two Streams*, pp.55–6.

46. Herzberg, *Between Two Streams*, p.63.

47. Robert Collis and Han Hogerzeil, *Straight On* (London: Methuen, 1947), pp.46–50, 56.

48. Jewish Committee for Relief Abroad, 'Report on the Concentration Camp for Sick People Bergen-Belsen', by Dr Fritz Leo, MS., Wiener Library, p.4.

49. Herzberg, *Between Two Streams*, pp.106, 111–12. Herzberg also relates some individual children's tragedies: One child, born in Westerbork, died in Bergen-Belsen. A mentally retarded boy of 14, whose parents worked in the shoe squad 14 hours a day, was wandering around the camp alone, bullied by the others, and finally caught stealing, 'because he is retarded, ugly, and rather misshapen'; after his parents and a succession of mentors died, he, too, succumbed (Herzberg, 'Amor Fati', pp.30–31). The 'Jewish Elder' Albala's two year old son was resented as the spoilt 'crown prince' and an 'insufferable worm' because of his parents' 'sumptuous' quarter consisting of a tiny separate room with tablecloth, window curtain and bedspreads, where he played 'Appell, Appell', a game of roll-call (Herzberg, *Between Two Streams*, pp.84–5). As one of the obscene incongruities of camp life, an SS Block Leader known as 'Blonde Irmy' (not Grese), who made the camp inmates' lives miserable and regularly meted out beatings in the Women's camp, occasionally went to the orphanage 'to play and laugh with the children. She would tease them, she would take them for walks. She would bring them a piece of chocolate. She would dry their tears and blow their noses. She would stroke their cheeks.' She especially took to a boy born in the camp, whose mother looked after him so well that he looked healthy and rosy-cheeked, and she promised – intending comfort! – that 'If you're all going to be gassed or shot, I'll save this little one' (Herzberg, 'Amor Fati', p. 20). Children were born in the camp, too, see T. Rahe, '"Ich wußte nicht einmal, daß ich schwanger war": Geburten im KZ Bergen-Belsen', in Claus Füllberg-Stolberg, Martina Jung, Renate Riebe and Martina Scheitenberger (eds.), *Frauen in Konzentrationslagern: Bergen-Belsen, Ravensbrück* (Bremen: Edition Temmen, 1994), pp.147–55.

50. Herzberg, *Between Two Streams*, pp.21–2, 32–4 and 77–9, and Herzberg, 'Amor Fati', pp.24–32.

51. Herzberg, *Between Two Streams*, p.30.
52. On the 'forced community' see also Kolb, *Bergen-Belsen* (1962), pp.69–77; for a valuable general analysis see H.G. Adler, *Theresienstadt 1941–45: Das Antlitz einer Zwangsgemeinschaft* (Tübingen: Mohr, 1955).
53. Herzberg, *Between Two Streams*, p.30.
54. Lévy-Hass, *Inside Belsen*, p.15 (diary notes, 4 Sept. 1944).
55. Küstermeier, 'How We Lived in Belsen', p.129.
56. On religious life in Belsen see Herrmann, *Austauschlager*, pp.57–61, and the article by Thomas Rahe in this volume.
57. Herzberg, *Between Two Streams*, p.13. See also ibid., p.29, on intellectual 'distraction', and pp.67–8, 75–7, 92 on individual acts of defiance. See also T. Rahe, 'Kultur im KZ: Musik, Literatur und Kunst in Bergen-Belsen', in Füllberg-Stolberg *et al.* (eds.), *Frauen in Konzentrationslagern*, pp.193–206, and the collection of very impressive and moving drawings by inmates in his *Häftlingszeichnungen aus dem Konzentrationslager Bergen-Belsen* (Hanover: Niedersächsische Landeszentrale für politische Bildung, 1993).
58. The other compounds are described in Kolb, *Bergen-Belsen* (1985), pp.28–31.
59. Huppert, 'Hand-in-hand with Tommy', p.76.
60. Kolb, *Bergen-Belsen* (1962), pp.104–12, 309 and 312; Keller *et al.* (eds.), *Konzentrationslager Bergen-Belsen*, pp.102–7.
61. Küstermeier, 'How We Lived in Belsen', pp.104–5.
62. On the Women's camp see Kolb, *Bergen-Belsen* (1962), pp.112–7, and Stefanie Plattner, 'Die Frauenlager im Konzentrationslager Bergen-Belsen', in Füllberg-Stolberg *et al.* (eds.), *Frauen in Konzentrationslagern*, pp.27–42.
63. Lasker-Wallfisch, MS. notes, p.63 and her testimony in this volume describing her arrival at the camp.
64. Herzberg, *Between Two Streams*, p.102–3. Laqueur heard about the gassings in November: Laqueur, *Tagebuch*, p.84; diary notes of 13 Nov. 1944.
65. See the introduction to David Barnouw and Gerrold van der Stroom (eds.), *The Diary of Anne Frank: The Critical Edition*, prepared by the Netherlands State Institute for War Documentation (London: Viking, 1989). Ernst Schnabel, *The Footsteps of Anne Frank* (London: Longmans, 1959), pp.140–54, summarises witness reports on the last few months of her life and her death in Belsen.
66. The previous commandant, Haas, 'a grim, taciturn man', was allegedly relieved because he had not improved the buildings or the grim hygienic conditions at Belsen: see *Commandant at Auschwitz: The Autobiography of Rudolf Hoess*, introd. by Lord Russell of Liverpool (London: Weidenfeld & Nicolson, 1959), p.163. On the transfer and Kramer's background see Kolb, *Bergen-Belsen* (1962), pp.121–5.
67. Laqueur, *Tagebuch*, pp.75–6 (diary notes of 22 July 1944).
68. Kolb, *Bergen-Belsen* (1962), p.146, summarises many accounts.
69. Lévy-Hass, *Inside Belsen*, p.67 (March 1945).
70. Küstermeier, 'How We Lived in Belsen', p.111. Starving women, who attacked vats full of swede cuttings, had to be beaten back with broomsticks by guards specially occupied with this task only: Vogel, 7 Feb. 1945, in Kolb, *Bergen-Belsen* (1962), p.247.
71. Vogel, 7 April 1945, in Kolb, *Bergen-Belsen* (1962), p.262.
72. Herzberg, 'Amor Fati', p.41; Jewish Committee for Relief Abroad, 'Report', p.3.
73. Kolb, *Bergen-Belsen* (1962), p.197.
74. Kolb, *Bergen-Belsen* (1962), p.139.
75. Details on the evacuation transports arriving in Belsen in Kolb, *Bergen-Belsen* (1962), pp.126–35. Even Rudolf Höss, notorious commandant at Auschwitz, and the head of the SS Economic Administration, Oswald Pohl, were shocked at the wretchedness of the Bergen-Belsen camp on inspection in March 1945: *The Autobiography of Rudolf Hoess*, p.163.

76. Paul Kemp, 'The Liberation of Bergen-Belsen Concentration Camp in April 1945: The Testimony of Those Involved', *Imperial War Museum Review*, No.5 (1990), p.29.
77. Herzberg, *Between Two Streams*, 30 Nov. 1944, p.109; Kolb, *Bergen-Belsen* (1962), p.139.
78. Herzberg, *Between Two Streams*, 19 and 12 Dec. 1944, pp.118 and 115.
79. Lévy-Hass, *Inside Belsen*, p.49 (Dec. 1944).
80. Robert Collis and Han Hogerzeil, *Straight On* (London: Methuen, 1947), pp.48–9.
81. Sassoon, *Agnes*, p.49.
82. Dr Fritz Leo, who worked as prisoner-doctor in the second Prisoners' compound: *The Belsen Trial*, p.122.
83. Statement by Dr Ada Bimko, who worked in the Women's camp hospital: *The Belsen Trial*, p.70.
84. Küstermeier, 'How We Lived in Belsen', pp.118–24. About the difficulties in combatting the lice which spread the spotted fever epidemic (exanthematicus) see Vogel's account in Kolb, *Bergen-Belsen* (1962), pp.257–61.
85. Lévy-Hass, *Inside Belsen*, p.52 (diary notes, Jan. 1945). Another evacuee from Auschwitz also concluded: 'Belsen was not equipped to deal with anything. – It was not equipped to deal with the sick nor with the dead. – It did not have the "Facilities" of Auschwitz, where bodies were "processed" with comparative ease. Auschwitz was a place where people were MURDERED. In Belsen they PERISHED': Lasker-Wallfisch, MS. notes, p.66. Possibly a gas-chamber was to be built in Belsen; allegedly the workmen had already been commissioned in March 1945: Jewish Committee for Relief Abroad, 'Report', p.3; see also Dr Fritz Leo's statement in *The Belsen Trial*, p.124.
86. Lévy-Hass, *Inside Belsen*, p.67 (diary notes, March 1945).
87. Herzberg, 'Amor Fati', p.43. Herzberg described the mood on the transport: 'yet despite everything, no fear. On the contrary. We are in good spirits. We had been shut up for fifteen months. For the first time in fifteen months we saw trees, grass and a plot of land again ... Now that we see nature again, and are in direct contact with it, we feel free. Although our situation is full of danger, we are hopeful and cheerful': Herzberg, *Between Two Streams*, pp.134–5. As the transport went on, however, the mood plummeted, often there was nothing to forage, the nights were frightening, fetching water became the biggest problem, and deaths increased.
88. Huppert, 'Hand-in-hand with Tommy', pp.99–100. The second transport reached Theresienstadt, while Russian troops finally caught up with the third train near Tröbitz-Niederlausitz, and Abel Herzberg described this scene:

> To our left, a thin line of trees. To our right, a wood... The sleepless hours dragged by. Silence, silence, except for the intermittent popping of anti-aircraft fire and the sound of explosions. Occasionally, the crackle of gun fire. We were waiting to come under attack. Nothing happened.
> Russian armoured vehicles had already been in the village, it was reported. – And early in the morning, very early – guards were standing further along the road. Liberty!
> Tovarisjtsji Svoboda. Comrades, liberty!
> They gave us cigarettes. But up till today, 26 April, they have not bothered about us. They show no concern for us, apart from leaving us to the local inhabitants to plunder. And this plundering was done thoroughly and without mercy.
> We have nothing. We are ill. We were quartered on farms ... Nothing is happening ... How is it in Holland? Outside, the birds are chirping. At night I lie awake and count the strokes of the clock. Is this freedom? (Herzberg, *Between Two Streams*, 26 April 1945, pp.139–40).

For the train evacuation to Tröbitz see also the third part of Renata Laqueur's memoirs: *Tagebuch*, pp.99–130.

89. Lasker-Wallfisch, MS. notes, p.69.
90. Küstermeier, 'How We Lived in Belsen', pp.138–9. Herzberg also witnessed this truly obscene concert: 'Amor Fati', p.41.
91. This truce arrangement was unique until then in the Second World War. For the negotiations see Kolb, *Bergen-Belsen* (1962), pp.157–64.
92. Küstermeier, 'How We Lived in Belsen', pp.140–2.
93. Daily death rates remained terribly high but steadily decreased: on 30 April, 548 people died; 97 died on 17 May. The first 500 relatively fit former inmates started their homeward journey to western Europe on 17 May: Headquarters, Belsen Camp, 'Notes on Belsen Camp', 18 May 1945, MS. (Special thanks to Dr. Arnold Horwell for sending me a copy). Brig. H.L. Glyn Hughes and Lt.-Col. R. Gwyn Evans, 'Belsen Concentration Camp: Medical and General Reports Submitted by HQ Second Army', MS., Wiener Library, with reprints from *The Times* and *Lancet*, gives a description of the compound at liberation, lists of required materials, mortality figures, and suggested first measures. The permanent exhibition on Belsen in the Imperial War Museum, London, also gives many moving details.
94. Huppert, 'Hand-in-hand with Tommy', p.90.
95. Lévy-Hass, *Inside Belsen*, p.69 (diary notes, April 1945).
96. John P. Fox, 'Bergen-Belsen in the Nazi "Final Solution" of the European Jewish Question', paper delivered at the 'Liberation of Belsen' conference, 9 April 1995.
97. Kolb, *Bergen-Belsen* (1985), p.50. Further thoughts on how the study of Bergen-Belsen can help clarify certain aspects of the Holocaust as a whole are in Eberhard Kolb, 'Bergen-Belsen, 1943–1945', in *The Nazi Concentration Camps*, pp.332–3.

Himmler and Bergen-Belsen

RICHARD BREITMAN

Any article about perpetrators of genocide runs the risk of diverting attention from the experiences of the victims and in this case also the liberators. None the less, I have chosen to look at Heinrich Himmler's role in the policies and events that led to the creation and evolution of Bergen-Belsen. The documentary evidence on Himmler is by no means complete or ideal, but there are enough independent sources to show at least the general direction of Himmler's activities and his thinking, if not to resolve all points of controversy.

The author of the first scholarly monograph on the history of Bergen-Belsen, the fine German scholar Eberhard Kolb, found it difficult to account for the origins of this unusual camp. Based on the incomplete documentation that survived, Kolb concluded that Bergen-Belsen was the result of an early 1943 initiative by the German Foreign Office to spare select categories of foreign Jews (Jews of Allied, neutral, or satellite countries living in German-controlled territory) who might be exchanged or repatriated abroad. He doubted that Himmler, responsible for most Nazi racial policies and the network of concentration and extermination camps, had championed the notion of releasing even small groups of Jews, because at the same time Himmler was seeking the 'deportation' of the greatest possible number of Jews to the East, in other words, to their death in the extermination camps. With the creation of Bergen-Belsen, Himmler was supposedly bowing to the Foreign Office's determination of what lay in Germany's foreign policy interests.[1] In his more recent general survey of the liberation of the camps, Jon Bridgman simply endorsed Kolb's findings regarding Bergen-Belsen.[2]

Yehuda Bauer's 1994 work *Jews for Sale?*, however, depicted Himmler as open, beginning in late 1942, to negotiations that might release substantial numbers of Jews in return for money or substantial

The author is grateful to Meredith Hindley for supplying the documents listed below from the Franklin D. Roosevelt Library.

benefits for the Nazi regime. Bauer makes much of the payments (at one point allegedly for a complete cessation of deportations to the extermination camps) to Eichmann's colleague Dieter Wisliceny by a Slovak Jewish group in 1942–43, a potential deal which he believes had Himmler's approval until something caused it to fall through in August 1943. For Bauer, such possibilities completely overshadow the arrangements for sending some thousands of Jews to Bergen-Belsen, so that this camp plays little role in his book.[3]

Bauer's account is dependent on the post-war testimony of several of those, including Wisliceny, who had an interest in making broad negotiations to stop the Holocaust seem like a substantial missed opportunity. There is no independent evidence that payments to Wisliceny saved lives in Slovakia, or for that matter, that Wisliceny's manoeuvres had Himmler's blessing for a time. Further research in this area is needed. It is all the more important, therefore, to look at the history of Bergen-Belsen, for it may tell us more about the Nazi regime's flexibility or inflexibility in carrying out the 'Final Solution' in the last years of the Second World War.

Himmler's conception of a special camp for selected Jews was an alternative or a complement to the idea of releasing some Jews, which Himmler and Hitler discussed a their private meeting on 10 December 1942. Himmler's agenda notes, prepared before the meeting, suggest that he personally opposed the idea of releasing Jews in exchange for ransom: he thought that they were more valuable as hostages to maintain some leverage with the Allies.[4] But Hitler, perhaps responding to an earlier initiative by Hermann Göring to make a small number of exceptions for Jews, responded that Himmler could approve individual cases if they really brought in substantial amounts of foreign exchange (*Devisen*) from the outside. During the same meeting Himmler suggested a special camp for those Jews with connections (*Anhang*) in the United States and Hitler's approval was indicated with Himmler's check marks.[5] Taken together, these two proposals made by Himmler to Hitler in the midst of the most lethal phase of the 'Final Solution' go far toward explaining the later creation of Bergen-Belsen. For some thousands of Jews, the alternatives to the 'Final Solution' were to be ransomed or to be kept as hostages. The future site for hostages was Bergen-Belsen.

Before or after this 10 December 1942 meeting (probably before, or the memo would have had a specific date), Himmler drafted an order for Heinrich Müller, head of the Gestapo, to establish a special camp for Jews from France, Hungary and Romania who had influential relatives in the United States. Describing these Jews, whose number he estimated at 10,000, as valuable hostages, Himmler wanted them to work in the camp, but under conditions that would allow them to remain alive.[6] In the process, Himmler highlighted what would become a significant distinction in the *initial* conditions and treatment of prisoners at Bergen-Belsen compared with other concentration and extermination camps.

Efforts by the German Foreign Office to withhold (at least temporarily) the Jews of neutral countries, Allied countries, or satellite countries from the extermination process began in a serious way in February 1943. The Foreign Office wanted to make sure that the neutral and satellite countries would not object to the elimination of their Jews; otherwise, Germany's foreign policy interests might suffer. Later, there was also consideration of exchanging Jews with Allied citizenship or Jews with some ties to the West for German citizens interned in the West.

These Foreign Office initiatives were grafted onto the earlier SS one. Adolf Eichmann, beginning in January 1943, had tried to find a site to hold specially selected Jews. At a meeting in Berlin on 7 January Eichmann supposedly asked Werner Best to find a site in Denmark for 'superior European Jews', but Best discouraged the idea, because it would have a negative effect on Danish public opinion.[7] Eventually, Himmler asked Oswald Pohl, head of the SS-Economic-Administrative Main Office, to find a proper site in Germany, and Pohl went to the Supreme Command of the Armed Services (OKW), which agreed to turn over a portion of the prisoner of war facilities at Bergen-Belsen,[8] in spite of the fact that Hitler had wanted Germany itself entirely cleared of Jews.

By early May 1943 Himmler had recast his original idea. Now the camp in Germany was to be for about 10,000 French, Belgian, and Dutch Jews with connections abroad. Holding such Jews would give Nazi Germany leverage against the West.[9] In other words, Himmler continued to think of holding some thousands of Jews as hostages, even if he had given out a different version of which nationalities might be best suited for the role.

Also in May the Swiss government conveyed a British government request to Germany to allow 5,000 Jewish children from the General Government of Poland and the Nazi-occupied lands of eastern Europe to proceed to Palestine, a proposal not well covered in the literature on Britain and the Holocaust.[10] In late May 1943 Himmler had laid down the binding principles and the degree of flexibility in the German response to such offers:

> ... we cannot agree to the emigration of Jewish children from the German sphere of power and from friendly states. He [Himmler] considers that he might change his views with respect to emigrating from the German sphere only if, in return for the release of Jewish children for emigration from the German sphere, young interned Germans be permitted to return to Germany, on a scale not yet to be determined. As a scale the Reichsfuehrer SS suggests one Jew for four Germans.[11]

The German Foreign Office added to Himmler's stipulations. If released, the 5,000 Jews could not go to Palestine because the Arabs would object; they could, however, go to Britain if Britain was willing to give Germany something (such as interned Germans) in return, and if the House of Commons was willing to sanction this bargain officially. In late June Himmler and Ribbentrop jointly endorsed these terms, which the German Foreign Office recognised the British could not and would not accept.[12]

The first 'exchange Jews' were taken to Bergen-Belsen in early July 1943.[13] By then Nazi Germany had pressing concerns on the battlefronts that should have drawn its full attention. On 5 July German forces launched a massive tank offensive code named Operation Citadel against the Soviet salient at Kursk. It was designed to stabilise the Eastern front and in Hitler's words 'have the effect of a lesson to the world'.[14] It turned out not to be a lesson that Nazi Germany administered. On 10 July, in the midst of the blood bath at Kursk, the Western Allies launched a surprise invasion of Sicily.

That same day Himmler had a long meeting with Hitler about a variety of topics. Probably referring back to Hitler's December 1942 willingness to release small numbers of Jews in return for substantial amounts of foreign exchange, Himmler suggested 'raising foreign exchange (*Devisenbeschaffung*)', but Hitler responded 'no'.[15] This discussion seems to have been a direct response to the British/Swiss request for the release of 5,000 Jewish children. In other words, Himmler suggested an alternative to the recommended (politically impossible) stipulations: instead of releasing interned Germans, etc., Britain could pay Germany for the release of the Jewish children. One can only conclude that under the pressure of military setbacks, and given a formal request from the British, Himmler sought to obtain funds for his SS empire. Hitler, however, reversed his viewpoint of December 1942 that some Jews might be released for sufficient payment. Hitler hated to make concessions of any kind regarding Jews, and all the more hated concessions from a position of weakness.

In any case, Himmler met immediately thereafter with Foreign Minister Ribbentrop, and the two chiefs accepted the Foreign Office stipulations: no Jews to Palestine, release of interned Germans, and acceptance of the bargain by the House of Commons. Ribbentrop's subordinate Wagner notified Heinrich Müller of the Gestapo that 5,000 Jewish children had to be spared for the time being in the event that the British accepted the arrangement.[16] The formal German response to the Swiss was delayed until January 1944, and the British response was conveyed by the Swiss in March 1944: 'The children are to be taken to England. However, an exchange is out of [the] question, since the British government is of the opinion that Germans can only be exchanged against subjects of the British Empire.'[17]

A second effort in the summer of 1943 to sell a select group of Jews their freedom came from Himmler's subordinate Gottlob Berger. Berger reported that Jewish sources were offering to pay $100 each for 10,000 Jewish children from Hungary, Bulgaria and Romania. These children would be sent to Turkey and Cyprus. If approved, Berger proposed to use the proceeds for the construction of new ships. Himmler's precise response is unknown,[18] but the proposal, which may have been invented or misconstrued by Berger, went nowhere. After Himmler's meeting with Hitler on 10 July, Himmler knew enough not to persue this one.

Also in August–September 1943, Dieter Wisliceny told his Slovak Jewish contacts, who had already given him substantial sums allegedly to halt deportations of Jews from Slovakia, that his idea of halting the deportations from across Europe to Poland in return for further payments had to be shelved.[19] Whether Himmler told Wisliceny this directly is most unlikely (there are no indications of any meetings with Wisliceny in Himmler's appointment books), but Eichmann and Wisliceny certainly must have been told that Jews were not to be released for cash payment. Any entrepreneurial activity here was dangerous once the Führer had made a ruling.

If Jews were not to be released for payment, and if they were to be exchanged only under the most politically onerous of circumstances for the Western Allies, the net effect was for Germany to continue to hold some Jews as hostages. So it was that Bergen-Belsen continued to exist and to expand from the fall of 1943 on – primarily as a camp for hostages and subjects for exchange.

I do not wish to go in detail into the largest proposed bargain for Jewish lives – the infamous 1944 'blood for trucks' offer associated with the names of Adolf Eichmann and his Hungarian-Jewish courier Joel Brand. In this murky affair, which began as a local initiative, Himmler came to test Hitler's willingness to release some Jews (though not on the scale of Brand's message that 1,000,000 Jews might be saved), and what he found was that Hitler was willing to release only small numbers of Jews in order to help speed the destruction of all the rest.[20] By the late summer of 1944 Himmler, however, had an ulterior motive for releasing some Jews – to establish a channel to the Western Allies for possible separate peace negotiations. But it was dangerous for Himmler to arrange for the actual release of Jews without Hitler's approval. So it was perhaps not quite an accident that 1,684 Hungarian Jews supposed to be spent to Portugal and released were sent first to Bergen-Belsen instead, where they were kept in a separate section of the camp in relatively favourable conditions.

They did, however, soon get to Switzerland. Three hundred and eighteen were shipped there in late August 1944, and 1,366 more in December. Here Himmler and his procurement specialist Kurt Becher in effect operated behind Hitler's back at a time when the Führer was no longer capable of keeping close touch on events outside the military situation. Himmler does seem to have been willing to consider freeing additional Jews from Bergen-Belsen by January 1945, but the outbreak of typhus in the camp interrupted arrangements at the local level, and Himmler had to be concerned about Hitler's reaction as well.[21]

When a third shipment of Jews, this time 1,210 Jews from Theresienstadt, had been sent to Switzerland in early January 1945, their arrival inspired newspaper articles in the Swiss press, and according to one report, a number of Nazi officials, including friends of Julius Streicher, wrote a letter of protest to Hitler, complaining that Himmler was easing up on the Jews. The result was that Hitler barred further such releases.[22]

The accounts of Himmler's manoeuvres regarding Bergen-Belsen during the last month of the war are problematic, because the various participants' testimony is skewed by selective recollection, self-interest, and mendacity. Himmler's doctor-masseur Felix Kersten published a diary in 1947, on which Eberhard Kolb partly relied, but Kersten's diary turns out not to have been a contemporary diary and is certainly creative in matters of detail.[23] This is not to say that Kersten entirely invented the story of his efforts to turn Himmler toward humanitarian actions.

The most detailed account and most immediate post-war account of Himmler during the last months came from Walter Schellenberg, who composed a blow-by-blow narrative while in Sweden in June 1945.[24] This manuscript is superior in quality and detail to Schellenberg's published memoirs, which were partly ghost-written. But Schellenberg too was looking out for himself and his future, so it is unwise for the historian to be too trusting.

From various independent contemporary and post-war reports, we can none the less trace some of Himmler's movements and vacillations regarding Bergen-Belsen and the reasons for them. On 3 March 1945 Kersten met with Gillel Storch, a Baltic refugee in Sweden active in the World Jewish Congress there. Storch pressed Kersten to use his influence with Himmler to stop the murder of Jews and to allow humanitarian aid to flow to the camp inmates. After meeting with Himmler in Germany, Kersten returned with a letter in which Himmler promised to consider Storch's requests and also to release some 10,000 Jews to Sweden, provided that Storch would go to Germany for negotiations with Himmler.[25]

On 10 March Himmler directed high concentration camp and RSHA authorities to combat typhus in Bergen-Belsen. Himmler instructed them not to spare medicine and had specified that the inmates were under his special protection, which, however, subsequently benefited the inmates not at all. The next day, at a meeting with Kersten and Himmler's astrologer Wilhelm Wulff (as reconstructed by Wulff), Himmler referred to Kersten's efforts to improve conditions for Jews in the concentration camps, but rejected the proposal to release 10,000 Jews and additional Scandinavian prisoners, because transportation of such a large group of prisoners would be noticed, and Hitler had forbidden the release of Jews.[26] Oswald Pohl, head of the SS Economic-Administrative Main Office, however, visited Bergen-Belsen on 19 March, supposedly to pass on an order not to kill any more Jews.[27]

On 12–13 March 1945 Carl Burckhardt of the International Red Cross met with Ernst Kaltenbrunner, chief of the Reich Security Main Office to press for the release of women, children, and the elderly from concentration camps and for the stationing of Red Cross observers in the camps. Burckhardt had hoped to meet with Himmler personally, but the Reich Führer SS sent word that his military duties prevented him from attending.[28] Perhaps the real explanation was, as a Swedish diplomat reported on 21 March, that Hitler had forbidden Himmler's approval of the establishment of a special camp for Scandinavian prisoners under Red Cross supervision.[29]

On 24 March Felix Kersten wrote to Gillel Storch that Berlin would again investigate the possibility of releasing Jews to Sweden or Switzerland, and that he and Himmler had discussed in some detail placement of Jews in special camps with a Red Cross presence.[30] Kersten also claimed that on 24 March Himmler had personally told camp commanders to treat their Jews better.[31] Kersten typically garbled the dates and the details, but he appears to have some vague sense of Himmler's moves earlier that month.

At a 12 April 1945 meeting with Count Bernadotte Himmler apparently promised not to evacuate the inmates of Bergen-Belsen, Buchenwald, and Theresienstadt away from the path of approaching Allied troops. Himmler's real goal was to use Bernadotte as a conduit for peace feelers to the Western Allies.[32] But Himmler's meeting the next day with Hitler went badly. One report had Hitler rejecting the release of any further Jews; another version was that Himmler had to promise not to release Jews without Hitler's personal approval; a third account had Hitler forbid any German, under threat of death, from helping any Jews or American or British POW cross the frontier.[33]

Still, that left the option of simply surrendering Bergen-Belsen and other camps to the Allies. According to another contemporary report from Himmler's Swiss friend, politician Jean-Marie Musy, Himmler and Foreign Intelligence chief Schellenberg pledged not to evacuate 15 of the larger concentration camps if the British and Americans pledged not to shoot camp administrators and guards. The American Minister in Switzerland, Leland Harrison, assured Musy that it was not Allied custom to shoot those who surrendered in uniform. Felix Kersten wrote to Storch of the World Jewish Congress on 4 April that rumours of the impending Nazi evacuation of Bergen-Belsen were false; Himmler had given an order simply to turn it over to the Allies.[34]

But Himmler was no longer in complete control of events, and Hitler was not the only problem. According to Schellenberg, RSHA chief Kaltenbrunner ordered the evacuation of Bergen-Belsen, Buchenwald and Neuengamme.[35] So Himmler appointed his tried-and-true negotiator from the 1944 negotiations in Hungary, Kurt Becher, as special commissar for concentration camps, apparently on 6 April. Becher and his supposed link to the Allies, Hungarian Jewish official Rudolf Kasztner, went to Bergen-Belsen on 10 April and spoke to Commandant Josef Kramer there. Afterwards, Becher reported back to Himmler and allegedly got Himmler's permission to order Kramer to surrender.[36]

Becher (and to a lesser degree Kasztner) had a post-war interest in claiming credit for bringing about a peaceful surrender, so their account is open to serious doubt. Himmler himself claimed credit of a different sort, in a very peculiar setting and manner. Norbert Masur, an official of the Swedish section of the World Jewish Congress, went to Berlin on 20 April and met at Kersten's estate with Himmler, Schellenberg, and Kersten from 2.30am to 5.00am on 21 April. Himmler gave Masur a whitewashed account of Nazi Jewish policy, calling atrocity stories about crematoria 'vicious propaganda': the crematoria were necessary to dispose of the bodies of those who had died of typhus. Himmler specifically claimed that he had ordered Bergen-Belsen and Buchenwald to be left intact with their inmates for the Allies; in return, he complained, he was getting vilified in the Allied press for atrocities.[37] Again, we have an unreliable source who clearly lied about some matters. So it is hard to simply credit his claim and Becher's claim that Himmler approved the peaceful turnover of Bergen-Belsen.

It is now possible, on the basis of contemporary British records made available by Dick Williams at the 'Liberation of Belsen' conference, to reconstruct the German military activity in the immediate area of Bergen-Belsen and to demonstrate that Himmler and the SS shared responsibility with the German army for the surrender of Bergen-Belsen. On 12 April two German emissaries from Army Group Blumentritt under a flag of truce contacted British 8 Corps regarding Bergen-Belsen. They stated that the German army had taken responsibility for the camp two days earlier, that they had never before been allowed into the camp, and that they were horrified by the conditions there. They were in no position to improve the lot of the inmates. They did not want the camp to become part of the battlefield, and they did not want typhus-laden prisoners to escape and wander around the countryside, so they wished to turn Bergen-Belsen over to the British – although they intended to fight on nearby.

During the negotiations the German military had to contact Himmler's headquarters for permission to turn over the camp itself. The German military willingly agreed to retain

> by force if necessary, the SS Administrative Staff: this was necessary since they alone had any idea of the internal workings of the camp and could be made to produce records, statistics and so on. It was made quite clear that no kind of undertaking was entered into with regard to our [British] treatment of the SS. (The Wehrmacht were only too happy to accede to this demand and clearly quite enjoyed the prospect of carrying it out – an interesting side-light on the relations of Wehrmacht and SS.) [his brackets][38]

As a result of these negotiations, Captain Williams was then able to enter Bergen-Belsen, meet commandant Josef Kramer, and survey the camp in advance of the British take-over on 15 April. His report back to 8 Corps Headquarters set in motion the infusion of food and medicine to the inmates.[39]

In retrospect, it seems clear that all of the Nazi participants, but especially Himmler, inflated claims of what they had done for the inmates of Bergen-Belsen; the actual surrender resulted from a military initiative and military negotiations. At the same time, the German military had to get clearance from Himmler even in mid-April 1945 to surrender Bergen-Belsen. And Himmler could honestly state that he had done something. When Hitler blocked further releases of Jews, Himmler, under pressure from Schellenberg, Kersten, Bernadotte, Burckhardt, and Musy, managed to refrain from ordering the evacuation of Bergen-Belsen and consented to the military turnover of the camp.

Bergen-Belsen remained to the end something of an exception. Although Himmler's moves toward sparing the Belsen inmates were limited and were to some extent disregarded by the camp authorities on the scene, the situation for the inmates of Bergen-Belsen compared favourably with that of Dachau. On 14 April, the day before the Allied take-over of Bergen-Belsen, Himmler instructed the commandant of Dachau to evacuate the camp and not allow any inmates to fall into the hands of the oncoming American troops. Evacuations of prisoners occurred as late as 23–27 April. When an American captain arrived in Dachau on 29 April, in advance of American troops, he found a written order signed by Himmler to leave no inmates alive for the Americans to find.[40] This order was only partially implemented; about 30,000 inmates remained.

The history of Bergen-Belsen reveals in part a flaw in the popular understanding of the 'Final Solution' as the Nazi attempt to murder every single Jew. The Nazi leaders certainly wished to eliminate the Jewish 'race', but that objective did not rule out making limited exceptions to the general policy if there were sufficiently strong reasons to do so. Persisting in the belief that the lives of Jews mattered to the Western Allies, Himmler hoped to be able to use some thousands of Jewish hostages to extract money or goods from the West, and in the process, especially towards the end of the war, gain some goodwill for himself. It is striking that as Germany's war situation deteriorated, Heinrich Himmler found more reason for exceptions to the 'Final Solution' than Adolf Hitler.

NOTES

1. Eberhard Kolb, *Bergen-Belsen: Geschichte des 'Aufenthaltslagers' 1943–1945* (Hanover: Verlag für Literatur und Zeitgeschehen, 1962), pp.26–31.
2. Jon Bridgman, *The End of the Holocaust: The Liberation of the Camps* (Portland, OR: Areopagica Press, 1990), pp.35–6.
3. Yehuda Bauer, *Jews for Sale?: Nazi–Jewish Negotiations, 1933–1945* (New Haven, CT: Yale University Press, 1994).
4. Copy in the United States National Archives (hereafter NA), Record Group 242 (RG 242), Microfilm Series T-175/Roll 94/Frame 2615330.
5. On Göring's initiative, see Richard Breitman and Shlomo Aronson, 'The End of the Final Solution? Nazi Plans to Ransom Jews in 1944', *Central European History*, Vol.25, No.2 (1992), p.181.
6. Himmler to Müller, Dec.1942, NA RG 242, T-175/R 103/2625557.
7. Werner Best, diary entry of 1 Jan. 1943, and interrogation of Best, 31 Aug. 1945, NA RG 319, Investigative Records Repository (IRR) Files, Werner Best, Box 410, XE 020967.
8. Kolb, *Bergen-Belsen*, pp.39–41.
9. Kolb, *Bergen-Belsen*, p.33.
10. Bernard Wasserstein, *Britain and the Jews of Europe 1939–1945* (New York and London: Oxford University Press, 1979), does not cover this particular proposal, but does comment (p.243) that Britain tended to favour schemes designed to assist victims of persecution in their countries of residence, rather than projects which involved emigration to unspecified destinations. It also opposed ransom deals.
11. Many of the basic German Foreign Office documents about this proposal were published in translation by John Mendelsohn, *The Holocaust: Selected Documents in Eighteen Volumes: Vol. 7, Jewish Emigration, the S.S. St. Louis Affair and Other Cases* (New York: Garland Press, 1982), pp.170–213. The quote is from p.173.
12. NA RG 242, T-120/R 4202/E 422450-51.
13. Kolb, *Bergen-Belsen*, p.44.
14. Gerhard L. Weinberg, *A World at Arms: A Global History of World War II* (New York: Cambridge University Press, 1994), p.602.
15. NA RG 242/T-175/R 94/2615094.
16. NA RG 242, T/120/R 4202/E 422447–48. Also, Bauer, *Jews for Sale?*, p.113.
17. Mendelsohn, *The Holocaust Vol. 7*, p.206.
18. Himmler's Correspondence Log (Geheim 1943) in NA RG 242, T-581/R 46A.
19. Bauer, *Jews for Sale?*, pp.86–9.
20. Breitman and Aronson, 'The End of the Final Solution', pp.177–203.
21. Kolb, *Bergen-Belsen*, p.150.
22. Gerald M. Mayer to George Backer, Office of War Information, 26 Feb., 1945, NA RG 84, American Legation Bern, 1945 Confidential correspondence, Box 84, Folder 840.1 Jews.
23. See Richard Breitman, 'A Deal with the Nazi Dictatorship: Himmler's Alleged Peace Emissaries in the Fall of 1943', *Journal of Contemporary History*, Vol.30, No.3 (July 1995), pp.412, 426–7.
24. Schellenberg's account may be found in NA RG 226, Entry 125A, Box 2, Folder 21.
25. Storch to Rabbi Weiss, 27 March 1945, reprinted by Steven Koblik, *The Stones Cry Out: Sweden's Response to the Persecution of the Jews, 1933–1945* (New York: Holocaust Library, 1988), pp.283–4.
26. Himmler to Pohl, Glücks, Grawitz, and Kaltenbrunner, 10 March 1945, reprinted by Kolb, *Bergen-Belsen*, pp.222–3. Kolb's interpretation (pp.191–3) is that this instruction was sincere, but was ignored by camp functionaries more accustomed to killing than

to saving lives. Wilhelm Wulff, *Zodiac and Swastika: How Astrology Guided Hitler's Germany* (New York: Coward, McCann & Geoghegan Publishers, 1973), pp.153–4.

27. Kolb, *Bergen-Belsen*, p193.

28. Roswell McClellend to William O'Dwyer, 22 March 1945, War Refugee Board (WRB) Records, Box 70, German Proposals Through Sweden, Franklin D. Roosevelt Library, Hyde Park, NY (FDRL).

29. Koblik, *Stones Cry Out*, p.132. John Winant to Secretary of State, 28 March 1945, WRB Records, Box 70, German Proposals Through Sweden, FDRL.

30. Kersten to Storch, 24 March 1945, WRB Records, Box 70, German Proposals Through Sweden, FDRL. Also reprinted in Koblik, *Stones Cry Out*, pp.281–3.

31. Herschel Johnson to Secretary of State, 28 March 1945, WRB Records, Box 70, German Proposals Through Sweden, FDRL.

32. Schellenberg's June 1945 account, NA RG 226, E 125A, Box 2, Folder 21. Bernadotte's notes of discussions with Himmler analysed by Koblik, *Stones Cry Out*, p.134.

33. Leland Harrison to Secretary of State (with information from Jean-Marie Musy), 9 April 1945, NA RG 319, Box 628; Schellenberg's June 1945 account, NA RG 226, E 125A, Box 2, Folder 21, p.11; Johnson to Secretary of State (with information from Kleist), 11 April 1945, NA RG 319, Box 40, Folder 1 (Sweden).

34. Harrison to Secretary of State, 9 and 11 April 1945, NA RG 319, Box 628; Kersten to Storch, 4 April 1945, in Kolb, Bergen-Belsen, p.224.

35. Interrogation of Schellenberg, 16 July 1945, NA RG 319, IRR Files, Walter Schellenberg, XE 001752, Box 195, Folder 4. Wulff, *Zodiac and Swastika*, p.154, supports Schellenberg's version that Kaltenbrunner and Bormann lobbied Hitler against Himmler. Bernadotte, influenced in part by Schellenberg, acquired a negative impression of Kaltenbrunner and a positive impression of Himmler. See Koblik, *Stones Cry Out*, pp.285–8.

36. Kolb, *Bergen-Belsen*, pp.159–60.

37. Masur's report, 23 April 1945, reprinted in Koblik, *Stones Cry Out*, pp.289–92. Masur's report summarised by Herschel Johnson to Secretary of State , 25 April 1945, WRB Records, Box 70, German Proposals Through Sweden, FDRL.

38. 8 British Corps, 'The Rhine River to the Baltic Sea: A Narrative Account of the Pursuit and Final Defeat of the German Armed Forces, March–May 1945', copy in the Imperial War Museum, London; photocopy provided to me by Major W.R. (Dick) Williams.

39. Major W.R. Williams, 'Belsen: The 50th Anniversary of the Entry of British Troops to the Camp April 1945', paper presented to the Wiener/Parkes 'Liberation of Belsen' conference, 1995.

40. Bridgman, *The End of the Holocaust*, pp.64–6. Report by J. Donahue of interview with Captain Marc J. Robinson, 22 Oct. 1945, NA RG 319, Box 1398, MIS 212785. For additional evidence of a Himmler order not to leave prisoners to be captured, see Henry Friedlander, 'Darkness and Dawn in 1945: The Nazis, the Allies and the Survivors', in *1945: The Year of Liberation* (Washington, DC, United States Holocaust Memorial Council, 1995), pp.18, 21.

Jewish Religious Life in the Concentration Camp Bergen-Belsen

THOMAS RAHE

A number of images that show the bond between Jew and Torah in the concentration camp stand out vividly in my mind: five or six *chalutzim* (Palestine-pioneers) crouching in the little space left between their topmost bunks and the ceiling, dead-tired, practising conversational Hebrew; worship services held at night in the barracks, with people chanting the Sabbath or holiday liturgy while standing in the high and narrow canyons between the bunk beds; a hastily gathered *minyan* (Prayer quorum) near one of the bunks, saying *kaddish* before a corpse was removed from the barracks; a small transport of Tunisian Jews being herded into our compound, and leading them, an old man carrying a Torah scroll; a group of small boys, sitting in a circle on the ground surrounding a teacher who drills into them the conjugation of Hebrew verbs.

That is how Werner Weinberg, who had been deported to the concentration camp Bergen-Belsen in February 1944, remembers the religious activities of Jewish prisoners in this camp, and he adds: 'These are images that simultaneously grip the heart and make one shake one's head in disbelief.'[1]

This ambivalence in the perception and evaluation of religious activities in the concentration camp is not only to be found in the memories of the survivors but is also mirrored in the historical science of the Holocaust, albeit with a different emphasis. On the one hand, the great majority of both publications about the Holocaust and monographs about single concentration camps do not

Translated by K.-M. Meyke

acknowledge the phenomenon of Jewish religious practices in the
Nazi concentration camps at all. On the other hand, in a major part
of the studies about the Holocaust referring to this topic the Jewish
religious life in the concentration camps appears as a sub category of
resistance, as 'spiritual heroism'. But this approach is also highly
debatable, for to regard the religious activities in the concentration
camps primarily as acts of resistance, denies both the importance of
the religiousness in its own right and the religiously motivated
behaviour of the Jewish prisoners; and it tends to forget the fact that
for the prisoners there was no moral (or even religious) duty for
resistance. Above all a presentation which – for good reasons – marks
out the religious activities in the concentration camps primarily as a
continuity of Jewish religious tradition deprives the Holocaust and
the concentration camps of their historical context. If the sheer
enumeration of religious activities of Jewish prisoners in the Nazi
concentration camps serves to prove the inviolability of religious
values and norms, this equals (from the principally terminological
point of view), the glorification of the Communist resistance in
concentration camps by Communist historical science and really
ignores the world of death, fear, despair, starvation and disease,
which was not only the background for religious activity in the
concentration camps but formed and changed it as well.

It is true, Jewish religious life in the concentration camps was also
characterised by an explicit continuity and strict orientation towards
tradition and it was often a kind of resistance too. But justice is not
done to the historical reality if one regards the religious activities of
Jewish prisoners in the camps *primarily* as 'spiritual heroism'; if one
does not consider the relation between religiousness and the everyday
reality of the concentration camp in detail or of one makes religious
activities appear as typical behaviour for Jewish prisoners in Nazi
concentration camps.[2]

The danger of imposing the wrong emphasis here certainly has
also to do with the sources available. As a rule, the official files which
otherwise are the prime source of historical research about the
Holocaust do not contain any information about this topic. Therefore
research about Jewish religious practices in the concentration camps
has to rely almost entirely on the evidence of the prisoners and the
survivors: on diaries, other documentary notes, poems and drawings

which were made inside the camps or on survivors' reports and interviews. Finally, also serving as sources, there are the responses (decisions or answers of an acknowledged Jewish scholar or rabbi to questions regarding the Jewish religious law and ethics) which were made inside the camps, but mostly written down after the liberation.

It does not automatically follow that there is a deficit of sources compared with other aspects of the history of the concentration camps. The difference primarily lies in the nature of the available sources, not in their authenticity. Indeed it is the specific nature of the available sources which enables an adequate reconstruction of religious life among the Jewish prisoners of the concentration camps, which had to be concealed from the SS as much as possible. Even if the Nazi files did contain information regarding religious life they would necessarily provide us with a very incomplete and unobjective picture because of the anti-Semitic perception of the SS.

It is not the seemingly unreliable nature of survivor testimony that is problematic – these sources have to be analysed just as critically as any other kind of source – but it is their selective nature. They only document to a small extent the religious attitudes of the Jewish prisoners and their changes, and further, mostly report on public religious practices, also visible to the other prisoners. Therefore the clearly visible forms of religious practices of the orthodox Jews in the camp are described unproportionally frequently compared to those of the no longer orthodox Jews. It is true, a critical review of the still available sources – despite considerable losses – suggests that a Jewish religiousness manifesting itself actively in the concentration camps was more widespread than is directly indicated in written accounts. This is shown among other things by a comparison of information gained in interviews with survivors with existing pieces of written testimony. Nevertheless, we must not ignore the fact that those Jewish prisoners whose faith was destroyed by their experience of a killing perpetrated with unbelievable cruelty and with the deliberate intention to exterminate each of them, that those prisoners as a rule did not leave any testimony. Their behaviour, if at all, only appears in other prisoners' witness.

From the historiographic point of view there are three consequences arising from the type of source material available. Firstly, because of the sources available and for reasons of content, this topic, to a great extent, escapes any quantifying analysis. How many Jewish prisoners celebrated which Jewish holidays in which year – this is impossible to find out and every attempt at an answer would only lead to a (only seemingly precise) pseudo-objectivity and would fail to point out the essential aspects of the study. Instead, an approach is necessary which emphasises the quality of Jewish religious practices in the camp and focuses on their social and psychological importance for the prisoners. Secondly, therefore, the narrative aspects are important and the description should be individualising (that is, concrete) rather than generalising (that is, abstract). Thirdly, from the formal point of view, this means that the sources will have to be quoted more frequently than is common.

As much as Bergen-Belsen has become a symbol for the Nazi concentration camps – not least because of the photos which British soldiers took during the first days and weeks after the liberation – one must see that Bergen-Belsen initially had a very specific function in the system of concentration camps and the National Socialist persecutions, which consequently had an effect on the living conditions of the prisoners and their social structure.[3]

Bergen-Belsen concentration camp was installed in the spring of 1943 as a 'detention camp' for specific groups of Jewish prisoners who were meant to be exchanged for German internees in western foreign countries. This intention decided the choice of Jewish prisoners (whole families, as a rule) who at first were exempt from extermination and sent to Bergen-Belsen: those holding an enemy or neutral state nationality, a Palestine certificate, or those who were representatives of important Jewish institutions. But only for few a prisoners did hope of an exchange and release actually materialise. Different from nearly all other concentration camps, the Jewish prisoners in Bergen-Belsen did not live together as equals. They were distributed among strictly separated sub-camps with different living conditions according to their different judicial status and nationality. The largest sub-camp was the so-called 'Star Camp' (because there the prisoners had to wear the star of David) in which Jews of Dutch nationality were the largest number. Next to it among other sub-camps there was a 'Neutrals' Camp' for Jewish nationals of neutral states (for example, Turkey, Spain, Portugal), a 'Special Camp' for Polish Jews and a 'Hungarian Camp' from which in the second half of 1944 1,683 Hungarian Jews were released (the so-called Kasztner-group) into Switzerland.

Apart from the initially strictly separated 'Prison Camp' there were originally only Jewish prisoners in Belsen. A change in this social structure but above all a catastrophic deterioration of the living conditions set in towards the end of 1944 when more and more prisoners from concentration camps near the front lines were brought to Bergen-Belsen as 'evacuation transports'. New camp complexes were installed. The number of prisoners increased drastically (at the beginning of December 1944: about 15,000; 1 January 1945: 22,000; 1 March 1945: 41,520) and the living conditions became even worse. If at first they had been better than in other concentration camps – prisoners for the exchange programme were not allowed to report abroad about the real living conditions in the concentration camps – they reached a record low level from the beginning of 1945: in March alone more than 18,000 prisoners died in Bergen-Belsen from starvation, thirst and diseases which the SS did not take any serious measures to prevent. The total number of victims of the concentration camp Bergen-Belsen is estimated at 50,000.

For the existence of religious activities in Bergen-Belsen these conditions were important in three ways. Owing to their special status as 'exchange prisoners' the Jews deported to Bergen-Belsen at first had more opportunities for religious activity than was the case in other concentration camps. This was so also because they had been allowed to take their luggage with them to Bergen-Belsen (which on later evacuation transports, as a rule, was not possible). With this luggage both religious texts and ritual objects came into the camp, important material prerequisites for any religious activity. Secondly, until autumn 1944 the social structure of Bergen-Belsen was relatively homogeneous: the majority of prisoners had come to Bergen-Belsen with their families, in each sub-camp there were mainly prisoners with the same mother tongue and who shared a common cultural background. Many prisoners, above all of the Star Camp, knew each other from before their deportation to Bergen-Belsen. Moreover, because of the SS 'criteria of selection' a relatively high number of prisoners had a cultural or academic profession. They included a large number of rabbis, who were regarded as particularly influential by the SS and were therefore thought of as valuable hostages. Thirdly, until the end of 1944, 80 to 90 per cent of the prisoners of Bergen-Belsen were Jews and even in the following months when the number of non-Jewish prisoners was rising, most Jewish prisoners were held in separate parts of the camp. Until 1944, when the new commandant Josef Kramer introduced the Kapo system, the prisoners with official functions in those parts of the camp occupied by Jews had been Jews, which meant a higher amount of religious freedom was afforded.

Practising the Jewish religion as well as owning ritual objects and texts was not allowed in Bergen-Belsen. At best a blind eye was turned by the SS to religious activities (more in some sub-camps than in others) – a toleration which could, however, be altered at will. Practising the Jewish religion, therefore, was not easy for the prisoners. It was also highly dangerous to cling to their Jewish identity, which in the face of such a situation was particularly important for their self-assertion.

From the diaries written in Bergen-Belsen and the accounts of former prisoners it becomes clear that in all sub-camps of the 'detention camp' in which Jews were interned waiting for an exchange, there existed Torah scrolls and in some cases printed Bibles as well.[4] Also Talmud studies and Talmud copies are mentioned several times in the sources.[5] Tallit, Tefillin and Shofar existed in the various parts of the Bergen-Belsen concentration camp.[6] Even if their number is uncertain a great number must have existed for as late as autumn 1945 parts of Tefillin and prayer-books were found near the crematorium in Bergen-Belsen.[7]

Some examples may demonstrate the importance of these articles to their owners. Eli Dasberg remembers that for Rabbi Selmann, who belonged to a group which was able to leave Bergen-Belsen with an exchange transport in January 1945, his Torah scroll was so important that he put it into his small rucksack to take it with him to freedom, disregarding possible reactions by the SS.[8] Abel Herzberg owned an old, already damaged Shofar – the only piece of heritage from his grandfather: 'For my unusable and useless Shofar I felt such a strange and – even for me – incomprehensible tie that I could not part from it when we went on a transport into German camps. Of course, I only took the necessities and left behind the forbidden articles. But the Shofar, which I did not need at all, I put into my rucksack.'[9] Finally regarded as 'essential' by Herzberg it came to Bergen-Belsen where it was used for Rosh Hashana in 1944. Arieh Koretz deported from Saloniki to Bergen-Belsen as a 16-year-old boy started a diary there. 'The diary copy books', he explains looking back, 'together with my Tallit, Tefillin and prayer-book which I had been given for my Bar-Mitzwa I kept in my bag through all the time in the camp. I looked after them like a treasure through all those difficult unstable months.'[10] Although Koretz does not mention using his Tefillin and his prayer-books anywhere in his diary, in his memory they almost appear as a pledge of his personality, his identity. In Louis Asscher's luggage was a list in which he had inserted a calendar and the dates of death of the members of his family before he was deported from Westerbork to Bergen-Belsen so that precisely on the according day of death he could say Kaddish for his deceased relatives.[11]

Unsurpassable in its symbolic significance was an event which happened at the fence between the Special Camp and the Hungarian Camp from which a group was released to Switzerland in July 1944. Simcha Korngold, who was imprisoned in the Special Camp, reports as follows:

> At that time the Germans brought a group of Hungarian Jews, the so-called Kastner group. A number of them were sent to Switzerland. We gave them a Pentateuch in which we inscribed our real names, and asked them to give it to Jewish organisations so that they would shake the world. The Pentateuch arrived in Palestine and reached the hands of my uncle, my father's brother. From this he learned that I, my three children and my sister were alive.[12]

It might have seemed to each of the people involved as a symbolic act of exodus.

Owning religious literature, however, was also dangerous to the prisoners. Shlomo Samson reports a delicate situation with an SS-man who was nicknamed 'Todtmann' (death man):

> One day when 'Todtmann' was standing very close to me during work he discovered a rectangular thing in my shirt pocket. At that time neither transistor radios nor walkman existed. He

approached me, reached into my pocket and produced a pocket prayer-book demanding an explanation. I told him that it was a very ancient prayer-book which I had been given by my grandfather and that that book was very important to me as a piece of family memories. That was also the reason why I took it to work with me so that it was not stolen in the block during my absence. He scrutinised the Hebrew book with the yellowed pages (it was without any German translation) and asked: 'Where in this book does it say that you Jews are expected to kill all Christians?' When 'Todtmann' asked no dodging was possible – I had to find an answer. So I said that he had probably mixed up the simple everyday prayer-book with the 'Choshen-Hamishpat', a book I had never seen before and I did not know what it contained, either.[13]

Obviously it was more dangerous for those prisoners who had been taken to Bergen-Belsen after late autumn 1944 as evacuees, and who did not have the status of 'privileged exchange prisoners', to possess religious texts. One of the former Hungarian Jewish prisoners remembers two incidents in which prisoners were seriously maltreated by the SS because they owned religious texts (among others a Torah scroll); in one incident a prisoner died.[14]

Although for the exchange prisoners in Bergen-Belsen it was possible more than in many other camps to bring with them ritual objects and religious texts, in principle they still faced the same problems as Jewish prisoners in other concentration camps which often made it difficult if not impossible to keep up some sort of religious life.

The moment Orthodox Jews set foot in the camp they automatically had to relinquish most religious laws and observances. They were forced to work on the Sabbath and holidays, could not maintain the dietary laws, could not adhere to the fixed times for prayer, and were unable to obey most of the other *mitzvot* [religious duties] whose fulfilment had meant a way of life to them. Here the question of quantity enters. If the circumstances made it impossible for the pious person to keep ninety percent of a given *mitzvah*, did it make sense to cling to the ten percent that remained? For instance, should one keep the minutiae of the Sabbath laws after the hours of forced labour, and was there merit in removing the most obviously non-kosher ingredients from the daily soup? Should one perhaps fast on the Day of Atonement, and eat no bread during Passover? [...] Finally, there were *mitzvot* which a religious Jew *was* able to perform even in the concentration camp. Thus a man could keep his head covered except when he had to take off his cap before an SS-man [...] The daily morning prayer contains a listing of important *mitzvot* with which every observant Jew is familiar. Of these, couldn't a camp inmate, for instance, 'perform deeds of loving kindness', 'visit the sick', 'pray with sincerity', and 'make peace between one man and his fellow'? Ethical *mitzvot* of this kind a camp inmate *could* perform, albeit to a limited degree.[15]

That is how Werner Weinberg described the spectrum of obstacles and changes of religious practice encountered by Jewish concentration camp prisoners. To form the Minyan for the service (as opposed to a private prayer) was one of the obstacles which was hard to overcome.

In the Star Camp we still tried to have a service every day ... in complete secrecy, all in hiding and always someone had to stand on guard so that the SS did not notice anything. And it was difficult, very difficult to get together the Minyan – to get together 10 men for the prayer. Mostly it could not be young men, they would otherwise have been missed at roll-call.[16]

In the Neutrals' Camp the observance of the religious rules was concentrated 'on the Minyan, which was held every morning and which rarely comprised more than the number required'.[17] In the men's huts of the Kasztner-group in the Hungarians' Camp a service was also held daily.[18] But with the deterioration of living conditions it became more and more difficult to get together a Minyan. Fritz Vandor remembers that at the beginning of 1945 in the Hungarians' Camp during the week no Minyan was possible and on Sabbath it was only possible because the few pious Jews asked other prisoners to stand together with them so that the Minyan was complete – this in a hut of several hundred prisoners.[19] The prisoners tried to escape discovery, the danger of which was of course greater for a Minyan than for a single person, by gathering at times during which a patrol by the SS was unlikely.[20]

As strictly as the participants in a Minyan may have tried to orientate towards traditions, the service, at least psychologically and in its atmosphere, could not have remained uninfluenced by the camp context. Helmuth Mainz described with lucidity the beginning of a day in one of the huts in the Star Camp:

> Common commotion in the dormitory, unimaginable jostle of half-naked, steaming and shouting men in the washroom. In the common room the handing out of soup, slurping and noisily eating men, babble of voices and shouting. In a corner of the dormitory men in their Tallits and with their Tefillin praying and following the recital from the Torah scroll. The voice of the prayer leader (chazan) almost gets lost in the common restlessness. The 'owner' of the respective places at the table are waiting impatiently for the pious praying men to clear the places for them. At last the morning prayer is over; a last hurried Kaddish, Torah scroll, Talessim and Tefillin disappear and the synagogue changes into a refectory where I sit down to spoon my soup and to eat my carefully measured ration of bread.[21]

The observance of the Sabbath and, in particular, the ban on working was only partly possible. The records in which celebrations of the Sabbath are reported mostly relate to the different parts of the 'detention camp' (that is, the 'exchange prisoners') – and even here mostly refer to 1944 – whereas accounts about celebrations of the Sabbath held by later evacuees to Bergen-Belsen are very few.

> On Friday evenings the scenery in the huts changes. Industrious women's hands had already cleaned tables and benches in the afternoon, freshly washed table-mats and jam jars as well as tins with green twigs served as decoration for the tables. The children were then allowed to put on their best things, normally carefully hidden, the girls were wearing white bows and both men and women changed their torn and dirty working clothes for their only untorn suits and intact dresses from old times.

And so in the huts a joyful, peaceful and festive mood was created which put everybody under a spell. Very many among us felt they had had no contact with their Jewishness until then. Here, in the huts when the hymn for the reception of the Sabbath sounded all without any difference were one reverent congregation. The shine of the many candles increased the solemn mood. Though it was strictly forbidden to burn candles in the huts, yet they did.[22]

What Simon Heinrich Herrmann describes for the Star Camp in the first half of 1944 had become unthinkable towards the end of 1944 and in the sub-camps outside the 'detention camp' such forms of celebrating the Sabbath never existed. Here a symbolic celebration of the Sabbath was confined to the burning of a piece of paper, for example, because no candles existed; 'substitute candles' would only have been possible to produce if they had used the small ration of margarine fat which was essential for survival – practically the only kind of fat which the prisoners received.[23]

But also inside the 'detention camp' there were considerable differences in the way the Sabbath could be observed. The relatively greatest freedom was given to the prisoners of the Kasztner-group in the Hungarians' Camp, where it was even possible not to work on the Sabbath.[24] Even within the Star Camp Sabbath celebrations differed from hut to hut. In the minutes of an interview with Bernhardt van Leeuwen we read:

Every Friday evening van Leeuwen was invited by a Jewish woman – Flora Pfeiffer. She worked in the kitchen and was then able to serve him with a double ration of food. There was no light, and they could not see each other; some other prisoners were present during those Friday night meetings. Mr. van Leeuwen cannot forget the deep impression it made on him when on demand of the prisoners he said the prayer (before the meal) and suddenly in the darkness all participants started to sing.[25]

The role which the initiative of single persons played in the observance and creation of Sabbath is mirrored by this report of the author of juvenile literature Clara Asscher-Pinkhof:

With an enormous persistence which in the free world I had never assumed every Friday I read passages from the Torah which in the respective week was read all over the world. In a very strange way it connected me with the free world. So in the previous camp [Westerbork] I had read each morning one of the 150 psalms in Hebrew together with the young teacher. A hundred and fifty mornings which in one way or another protected me against everything that the day would bring and what it had brought the day before. In the weekly section you could always find one sentence which created a story for the women beside me. On the first Friday evening when I sat down at the table in the common room of the hut and told the women surrounding me that I intended to tell a story because it was Sabbath it took a long time until the noise had changed into an expectant quiet. The second time I only had to sit down at the table and it was quiet immediately [and I was] supported by a few screaming voices demanding quiet. The third time they behaved like begging children who demand what they are entitled to: a story.[26]

Similarly, a report about Hans Goslar (the former Prussian government spokesman) notes:

I remember, how on Friday nights we would assemble in a barracks that was filled with 'beds' three tiers high. In the beds lay people with typhus and other diseases; all were hungry, suffering, and fearing for their lives daily. In conditions that defy all description, Goslar would sit on one of the upper bunks and speak to us about Sabbath rest, about the joy of Sabbath, about the holiness of Sabbath. True, we were far removed from any Sabbath rest; we were all forced to toil on the Sabbath as on any other day of the week. But as we were listening to the words of Goslar who spoke to us with a face shining with the light from another world, his voice ringing with the trust of a steadfast faith, entirely transfigured by a great joy, we forgot our gruesome state and on the wings of his inspiring words we were transposed to the tables in our fathers' houses on the Sabbaths and Holy Days of times gone by ... Often we would burst out into the traditional Sabbath *Zemirot* (table songs). Though our voices were subdued because of the guards, yet we sang with trembling, and how happy we were![27]

Also for the orphans in Bergen-Belsen, who were housed in a hut of their own, a Sabbath ceremony was held regularly.[28]

Despite everything, not least the exceptional emotional importance of the Sabbath celebrations, they should not be idealised by historians. 'We also "celebrated" Friday evenings, Pessach, etc. Life was hard, very hard, but our faith in the forthcoming exchange gave us great strength to persevere. To be sure, not all were strong enough. Many succumbed to utter despair, many too got tired and lost all interest in their fate; a certain amount of mental decay became ever more noticeable', so Israel Taubes described the context of these Sabbath celebrations, opposing any idealisation.[29]

Psychologically the Sabbath celebrations – and the religious chant in particular – were parallel to the cultural activities in the camp. It is not surprising, therefore, that there existed, as it were, secularised forms of Sabbath celebrations. In Hanna Lévy-Hass's diary, she was a Communist Jew who had been deported from Yugoslavia into the Star Camp, and who in Bergen-Belsen intensively looked after the children, we read under the date of 11 November 1944:

> It has been decided in the whole camp to use the Saturdays for children's festivals which mostly are supposed to have a religious character. In our hut we use the Saturdays likewise, to provide the children with a programme which cheers them up, but we mostly adapt it to our people's mentality. Recitations, singing soloists, and choirs, little theatre performances.[30]

An analogy to the cultural activities can also be found in the sources where the presentation of Bible and Talmud studies are often mentioned together with lectures about cultural or political topics.[31] But the transition between religious and cultural practices was indistinct in other fields too, for example, when children were taught Hebrew,[32] when poems were written which had a prayer as their topic or were prayers themselves,[33] or when for the traditional prayer which is celebrated during the opening of the Torah shrine and the lifting of the Torah scroll a melody was composed.[34]

There are also examples that the Bible and the Talmud were not only important for the strictly orthodox Jews in Bergen-Belsen. The then 18-year-old Gabor Czitrom was one of those prisoners of the Hungarians' Camp who were released to Switzerland in December

1944. In Bergen-Belsen, he recalls, 'I had a glimpse of how highly interesting biblical exegesis could be. There was a fascinating series of lectures by these young rabbis on various chapters of the Bible, putting it into historical context. I do not recall facts, but I do exactly recall the huge interest of it, and that I discovered quite a new perspective.'[35] A further example is mentioned by Abel Herzberg who remembered

> a woman who had been sentenced to eight days of bunker with water and bread by the Nazis for various insignificant matters which on top of it all were untrue and who went into the cell with the Tenach (Bible) under her arm. [...] She was far from religious. But persecuted as a Jew she wanted to draw strength from the old tales, the words of the Prophets and the lyrical songs of the Psalmists which could keep up a person under any circumstances.[36]

Here, too, however, one must warn against idealisation and overestimation from the statistical point of view. After mentioning talks and lectures about the Torah and its significance S.H. Hermann notes: 'I am sorry to say that the meetings were infrequent and after a promising start soon a certain fatigue set in. One has to take this literally. 11 hours work per day and a rumbling stomach by and by stifled the interest in mental exercise.'[37] And in the same context referring to the Hungarians' Camp and the Kasztner-group, respectively, M. Weiss comments: 'The Bible and Jewish history were studied. There were also some who learned Talmud. The majority passed their time playing cards.'[38]

About individual prayer in Bergen-Belsen there are very few reports, probably not least because it belonged to a kind of religious practice which was barely noticeable to fellow prisoners. As a rule individual prayers and their significance are only described when personal behaviour is concerned, as in the case of Ada Levy: 'Extreme willpower was necessary to survive, every day brought with it new terrors, how was it possible for me to overcome this inferno?! It must have been my daily prayer, pleading for the survival of my beloved mother and my Willy that kept me alive.'[39]

The more Bergen-Belsen became a death camp, the more its reality surpassed the worst nightmares the stronger hope mixed with desperation in prayer. In Abel Herzberg's diary, reflective, philosophical passages recur; everyday camp life is often described with an ironical distance and with the help of a play on words. But when in March 1945 more than 18,000 prisoners die, when starvation drives the first prisoners into cannibalism and madness, the prayer also comes into Herzberg's diary, beside the matter-of-fact resignation: 'God Almighty, put an end to our suffering. I beg you.'[40] The inferno which Bergen-Belsen became in the last months and weeks before the liberation did not bring with it a loss of importance for the prayer, it rather brought about a shift of meaning; even more so the less it was possible to keep up other forms of religious life. In this situation 'perhaps the only religious manifestation was an occasional desperate prayer offered in a moment of dire need. Fear of God was replaced by fear of man. The verse from the *Hallel*, "God is with me, I shall not fear, what can man do unto me?" (Ps. 118:60), seemed to have lost all meaning. Why, man could and did do everything to me, everything thinkable and unthinkable.'[41]

In the concentration camp religious belief and religious practice were not necessarily at one. The Jewish tradition explicitly allows one to disregard the rules of the Torah if, through their observation, life and health are placed in danger. Therefore many prisoners did not regard it as a contradiction when they stuck to their religious belief in Bergen-Belsen but, at least in everyday camp life, did not practise their religion. Ruchama Pinkhof, who had been deported to Bergen-Belsen as a youth, remembers a situation during the roll-call: 'Then a woman behind me said if that exists, no God exists. And very quickly I realised, this woman had never had a God, she had never believed in God when she said, as I am in a difficult situation, as we are in danger, there is no God. That is too simple, I very clearly remember this moment, the woman's words and my reaction inside.'[42] Atheism as a reaction to what she had to experience in Bergen-Belsen was out of the question for Pinkhof, but her attitude did not result in any religious or religiously motivated activities, either.

Even if it did not become apparent, one should not underestimate the significance of religious attitude, the significance of conversations about religious topics among the prisoners or individual reflections about religious questions. To survive the concentration camp a high degree of willpower and psychological energy was necessary. When, according to the memories of the Dutch psychiatrist and Bergen-Belsen prisoner Louis Tas, there was only a very small number of suicides, that was the case because for anyone who did not want to live on, no active form of suicide was necessary.[43] To give oneself up, to have no will or courage of survival, not to stem oneself against the process of dehumanisation, deindividualisation and depersonalisation – this within a very short time almost automatically was followed by one's own death. In this context it was of great importance to keep up a religious, a Jewish identity. Probably in no other testimony does this become more apparent than in Abel Herzberg's diary. In view of a weary, meaningless kind of work, a barely tolerable permanent hunger, spiritual efforts had to be made even in the work commandos: 'You must try to form your own circle, therefore, to have at least some kind of distraction, some standard. Sometimes it succeeds. There is much philosophising, politicising, debating the jewels of Hebrew literature, translating the psalms from memory, or verses by Judah Halevi. At such times we know only too well what the difference is between the Scharführer and us.'[44] In September 1944 shortly before the Jewish holidays there are pages full of reflections in his diary about the specific character and the theological superiority of Jewish monotheism. In the everyday degradation and the threats of life by the SS he also sees a religious dimension:

> Roll-call is like a religious rite, or at least a sacred act for that bunch of inferior anthropoids who, unfulfilled by the human ideals that their teachers and priests had taught them, and partly out of genuine indignation at all manner of fine cant, have invoked with pounding hearts a stark and lewd heathendom, which taught them that the absolute binding power of ethics and morals was nonsense, and that as a matter of principle, everything that was advantageous would always be permissible.[45]

For Herzberg, the convinced Zionist, the common religion in Bergen-Belsen becomes the expression and guarantee of Jewish unity and therefore also of collective self-assertion:

> Indeed, the religion, that is the Jewish unity. [...] I say it, even

though I do not practice the ancient religion myself, but still lay claim to my share of Jewish unity. To this day the Jewish religion is followed by every group of Jews according to exactly the same model. Behold! Two thousand years ago two brothers said good-bye to each other. One went this way and the other that way, the one died and then the other died, and also their children died and their children's children. And after endless wanderings the descendants of the one arrived in a town on the North Sea, along the Mediterranean Sea, somewhere in the east, in Greece, in Tripoli, in Italy and Yugoslavia – it does not matter where. And Adolf, the world's madman, brought them together in camps, and what transpired? They speak different languages, they dress differently and want something different, but when they turn to their God, they are so alike within and without that you could exchange the one for the other and you would not notice it.[46]

The food rules belonged to those rules whose observation was particularly difficult. The Kasztner-group in the Hungarians' Camp was an exception, which with the permission of the SS could obtain kosher food, a possibility which, following M. Weiss's memory, approximately one quarter of the prisoners made use of.[47] But in the other parts of the camp the total observation of the food rules was impossible unless one accepted one's own death. From the Neutrals' Camp Rudolf Levy mentions the fate of the Yeshiva-teacher Burak from Antwerp: 'weakened by hunger and carried off by the cold he died, as he refused for ritual reasons to accept the hot lunch during his entire stay in the camp – with the exception of the last days before his death.'[48]

From other parts of the Bergen-Belsen camp there are similar sceptical observations from fellow prisoners. 'A religious group of prisoners – 34 people – tries to organise kosher food in a separate corner of the washroom. A hardly manageable undertaking', Jozef Gitler-Barski writes in his diary in the Special Camp for the Polish Jews.[49]

Whether and to what extent prisoners in Bergen-Belsen were able to eat kosher food depended on their living conditions as a whole: 'The exemption of the Hungarians from forced labour was practically much more important than the question of kosher food. The difficulties and tortures in the various labour parties and the whole complex belonging to labour, finally resulted in malnutrition and starvation.'[50] At best compromises were possible: 'I always took all pieces of meat out of my soup and gave them to people, mostly children who were already in a very bad state, because in danger of life these rules have to be transgressed. But I had no possibility to do without the broth in which this meat had been cooked.'[51] Apart from that one could only hope to make the food 'more kosher' by bartering:

> Very quickly together with ten table companions the food is gulped down. You are offered to barter, vegetables for potatoes, potatoes for evening soup, orthodox Jews try to exchange their ration of mussels which is supposed to be handed out in the evening against white cheese or potatoes; they are met with little sympathy and find themselves in severe conflicts of religious and practical nature, because nobody here can afford to do without that little food handed out without anything in return.[52]

It is not surprising that the attempt to eat kosher in a concentration camp, although the Jewish tradition does not only allow, but even demands the transgression of the food rules in such a situation, was met with lack of understanding by many fellow prisoners. 'Were these people fanatics or martyrs? No, I think that they just *could* not eat the horse meat in the soup, that they *could* not bring a bite over their lips on the Day of Atonement', that is how Weinberg, looking back on this almost suicidal religious consistency, tries to understand it.[53]

Showing last respects towards the deceased belonged to the ethical *Mitzvot* and, to some extent, could be observed by the 'exchange prisoners'.

> Our compound in Bergen-Belsen was a Vorzugslager, and one of the privileges that we enjoyed, was that the dead, unlike in the compound next to ours, were not tossed naked onto a cart, but were taken to the crematorium in a coffin, which would then always be returned empty. The ceremony of washing and

dressing the corpses was not prohibited, and was therefore carried out with the utmost dedication and devotion, until our strength gave way even for that.[54]

The dependants were then allowed to accompany the deceased as far as the fence around their part of the camp.

But to fulfil this *Mitzvah* was not always as easy, as Herzberg describes it here. In a recorded statement by the 'Jewish eldest' Josef Weiss, it says: 'The deceased of the camp were transported on a horse-drawn cart to the crematorium – always in the same coffins. As far as the barbed wire a Minyan always went along, although initially the Germans forbade it. But when they saw that not even beatings could stop the people from paying their last respects to their friends they allowed it.' In this connection Weiss remembers the Albanian women, mostly illiterates. 'These [women] worked in the SS kitchen. Even when they saw a funeral procession from the distance they rose from their work until the procession was over, even beatings could not make them continue working. During this funeral there was always a rabbi saying Kaddish, also for the christened Jews.'[55]

How much the prisoners were exposed to the mood of the SS-men, even in this situation, is shown by two entries in diaries from August 1944. 'August 30th, 1944: There was another big scandal this morning. Rabbi Dasberg and a few other people paid their last respects to a deceased as far as the fence of the crematorium. The SS announced that this was forbidden, and the sad consequence was that Rabbi Dasberg had to go to work, and what kind of work!'[56] A few days later Abel Herzberg wrote about the transport of the deceased from the Star Camp:

> The coachman, a giant of an SS man, smokes his cigarette. He remains so completely indifferent, so completely unmoved by the event that he must be an outstanding pupil of his master. Behind the motionless mask of his face he thinks – assuming that he is still capable of thinking – of what importance is a human being? At least another Jew less. And when he thinks that the coffin is not being loaded on to the cart quickly enough, he shouts: 'Los, los, Sauvolk, rasch, sonst hau' ich euch einen in den Arsch. Ihr glaubt wohl wir hätten Zeit für eure Juden-Kadaver. So was gibt es nicht. Es ist kein General gestorben!'

[Hurry up, hurry up, you swine, quickly, or I'll kick you in the arse. You must think we have all day for your Jewish carcasses. Don't deceive yourselves. It is not a General who's died.][57]

However, the greater the number of deceased after the beginning of 1945, the more impossible it became to keep up paying one's respects to the deceased.

The large number of children and youths in Bergen-Belsen also led to Bar-Mitzvah ceremonies.[58] In one case in Bergen-Belsen even the circumcision of a Libyan-Jewish baby by a Dutch Jew is verified.[59]

The situation of the rabbis in Bergen-Belsen is a chapter on its own. Compared to other concentration camps their number in Bergen-Belsen was relatively high, because the SS regarded them as 'leaders' of Judaism, so to speak, and therefore regarded them as particularly valuable exchange hostages. The rabbis deported to Bergen-Belsen ranged from militant anti-Zionists like the leader of the Szatmar Chassidim, Joel Teitelbaum, to explicitly Zionist rabbis like Simon Dasberg from the Netherlands.[60]

Their importance as 'exchange prisoners' whose maltreatment was forbidden to the SS in Bergen-Belsen made the situation of the rabbis in Bergen-Belsen more tolerable than in other concentration camps. They could, for example, like several other orthodox Jews in Bergen-Belsen, wear their beards and so fulfil the Biblical rule not to shave – which was unthinkable in almost all other concentration camps. Sara Berkowitz, who had been taken from Auschwitz to Bergen-Belsen late in summer 1944, remembers how astonished she was: 'At one camp we could not believe our eyes. The inmates were orthodox Jews; the men wore beards and the women wigs, and they had their children with them. It was the first time I had seen children since I had left the ghetto. We learned that they were Jews from Holland. It was very rare to see Jews whose beards had not been cut off or women who were allowed to cover their hair.'[61]

The beard was symbolic both for the orthodox Jews and for the SS. Abel Herzberg describes the case of an Orthodox prisoner:

One of them was a man with a beard. Not a particularly beautiful beard, but an ordinary man with a filthy, kosher and brown beard. Nothing, however, raised more anger in the eye of the Nazis than a Jew with a beard. In their opinion every Jew with a beard was a rabbi or equalled them and a rabbi was an upper-Jew and therefore tortured especially, was continuously punished, had to stand by the fence without any food when the others were having lunch, but he did not cut off his beard. Everyone advised him to do so, but he only laughed about it.[62]

And about Rabbi Selmann it is written in Herzberg's diary:

Rabbi S. is not cutting off his beard. The Third Reich hates Jews and among the Jews, the Rabbis in particular. Rabbis have to do extra work here. And everyone who wears a beard is called 'Rabbi.' Beards must be shaven off, therefore, but R. S. refuses. Surprisingly, the SS relent. However, R. S., complete *with* beard, is assigned to a hard labour party. Rabbi S. laughs and triumphs. But the outdoor party is stronger than R. S., and one evening when he has to stand at the gate for punishment, he collapses. He is carried to his bed and everyone advises him to cut off his beard. The next morning R. S. rises at five o'clock, goes to his work, combs his beard and grins.[63]

On the whole it was only a small minority of the Jewish prisoners who in everyday camp life in Bergen-Belsen stuck to their orthodox way of life and practised their religion. A wide spectrum of forms and intensities of religious practices were in evidence. Observing the religious rules under concentration camp conditions was mostly done episodically; as a rule religion was practised individually or in small groups, often in a hurry, in fear of being detected. It was important to use the few opportunities that arose as it was uncertain when, and if, they could be repeated. The single religious activities were therefore mostly marked by a lack of continuity. Unlike the ghettos, there was no permanently accessible 'haven', where the prisoners could take spiritual refuge. Secondly, religious activities oriented around the Jewish religious law had to remain fragmentary – as described by Weinberg. Finally, the social and psychological context of religious practice changed radically, losing to a large extent losing its traditional dramaturgy and aesthetic aura in the camps.

These deficits in Jewish religious activities due to the conditions in the concentration camp were contrasted by positive social functions. Even if the group of Jewish prisoners in Bergen-Belsen, compared to other concentration camps, was relatively homogeneous, on the whole, Bergen-Belsen also represented a heterogeneous forced community with all its resulting social and psychological conflicts.

Prussian civil servants and Greek fishermen, Polish rabbis and Hungarian students, Yugoslavian communists and Dutch Zionists – apart from their Jewish origin, which had been the reason for their deportation into the concentration camp – mostly they had hardly anything in common. Furthermore, the whole organisation of the concentration camps was geared in such a way that the Jewish prisoners in particular should not only have their identity, self-esteem and courage to face life taken away, but should also be exposed to a process of social atomisation which was meant to effect a fight for survival among the prisoners, thus suffocating social community and solidarity. In view of this situation the practising of the Jewish religion had an important social function. In order to fulfil certain religious rules social communities were formed, centred around just these religious practices. If a prisoner had no Tefillin which he could use for prayer, he associated himself with fellow prisoners who had Tefillin and who, just like him, had risen from bed earlier to say their morning prayers. For a service according to Jewish law, a Minyan was required, that is, a minimum number of ten praying males of at least 13 years. Also, for the production of certain utensils, above all, for the Sabbath and Jewish holidays, co-operation between the prisoners was necessary.

While the practising of religion in everyday camp life was only an affair of single persons or small groups, the celebration of Jewish holidays was also a social event in which a far greater number of prisoners took part. What Mina Tomkiewicz states for the Special Camp might also refer to the other parts of the 'detention camp' in Bergen-Belsen:

> Just as festively the holidays were celebrated in which irreligious people took part as well, fasted on Yom Kippur, prayed and so on. Those traditions were held up predominantly by whole families. The single prisoners envied them and felt their loneliness even harder. Sometimes, however, the single prisoners were also 'adopted' or associated with each other. These family or festive traditions taught us never to lose

courage, not even under the most extremely bad conditions and taught us that such ceremonies of communal life are part of life and of God, whatever people thought about life and God otherwise.[64]

The stronger the parallels between the respective festival and the situation of the Jewish prisoners in the concentration camp, the greater was its importance. It is not surprising, therefore, that Passover, the festival in memory of the liberation of Israel from slavery in Egypt, is the festival mentioned most frequently in the records. On the eve of Passover, on Seder evening, according to tradition the youngest present asks: 'Why is this night so different from all other nights?', which is answered by the narration of the Passover-Hagada. In the camp this question contained a richness and intensity of meaning that it had never assumed before. The Seder evening was different from all other evenings in the concentration camp, during which the liberation from Egypt was not just remembered as past, but as present, full of hope, quite in accordance with the exhortation of the Jewish tradition, that in every generation every person ought to regard himself as if he had walked out of Egypt: 'This is the bread of misery which our forefathers ate in Egypt. Everyone who is hungry may come and eat! Everyone who is distressed, may come and celebrate Passover with us. This year – still here; in the following year – in Israel! This year – still slaves; in the following year free men!'[65] Was there a greater affinity imaginable between remembered past, suffered present and a hoped for future than becomes apparent in this passage of the Passover-Hagada?

Both in 1944 and in 1945 the celebration of Passover is mentioned in the records. There is, however, no uniform picture in the records about how far the festival (and other holidays) were tolerated by the SS. S.H. Herrmann reports on the Star Camp in 1944: 'the Passover festival was celebrated in the dignified way without the Germans interfering.'[66] But for the same time and same part of the camp it states in a different report about the celebration of the Seder evening: 'But very soon we were interrupted, a German came into the hut, forbade the "celebration" and so our evening of celebration ended.'[67] Apparently there was no common and co-ordinated behaviour by the SS in this respect, but it depended on the mood of the individual SS-man if religious activities were tolerated when noticed. It was wise to be cautious. Thus the physician Philip Arons celebrated a Seder evening in one of the hospital huts, 'because there were relatively few controls in the hospital' as 'the Germans were very frightened of catching a disease'.[68]

A further difficulty was to obtain the unleavened bread (matzah) for Passover. J. Gitler-Barski noted in his diary in the Special camp on 1 April 1944: 'It is planned to organise Seder on April 8th. A list of people has been set up who should try and get flour (for the matzah) and fresh vegetables instead of soup.'[69] But when four days later it was discovered that postcards had been smuggled out of the Special Camp, the SS punished the prisoners collectively: 'First Grossfeld is no longer senior spokesman of the camp, it is forbidden to bake the matzah, we are driven to work.'[70]

Although some prisoners in the Star Camp from Westerbork had been able to bring matzah to Bergen-Belsen[71] and others were able to bake matzah with the help of an improvised electric cooker and 'organised' flour[72] it was impossible for all those prisoners who wanted to celebrate Passover to obtain matzah. Therefore, three Dutch chief rabbis from the Star Camp explicitly allowed and recommended that under these circumstances leavened bread (hametz) could be eaten as a substitute. For the occasion they wrote a prayer which was said before the eating of the leavened bread on the Passover days:

> Before eating leaven, one should say with deep devotion: 'Our Father in Heaven. It is evident and known before You that it is our desire to do Your will and to celebrate the festival of Passover by eating matzah and by observing the prohibition of hametz. With aching heart we must realise that the enslavement prevents us and we are in danger of our lives. Behold, we are prepared and ready to fulfil Your commandment: 'And you shall live by them [the commandments of the Torah] and not die by them'. And we are warned by Your warning: 'Be careful and guard your life very carefully'. Therefore we pray to You that You maintain us in life and preserve us and redeem us speedily so that we may observe Your statutes and do Your will and serve You with a perfect heart. Amen'.[73]

As printed or written Hagada copies were lacking, its most important passages or those parts which individual prisoners could remember were recited from memory.[74] Those prisoners who celebrated Passover in Bergen-Belsen surely felt the parallels between Jewish past and present just as intensively as described by Clara Asscher-Pinkhof:

> When Passover came nearer, the festival of liberation from Egypt, the children and I lived between narration and reality, between history and present. It really was the same. When our men were put in front of a manure cart instead of horses and when they were driven on with shouting when the SS guard yelled: 'You are lay-abouts' [...] it was as if they were speaking the language of the Bible. I did not have to say much about the slavery in Egypt; that was too well known. But about the liberation; that was still unknown. We once talked about it when an SS-man came into the hut. We stood to attention until he left the hut but when he had gone into the dormitory of our hut and we were beyond his reach, I said still standing to attention: 'Don't forget that while we were talking about the Egyptians he came in.' We really did not need any textbooks.[75]

A then nine-year-old girl remembers going to another hut to celebrate Passover there: 'And I remember a man walking by and looking and making [faces], you know, saying what nonsense that was, [...] and I remember sitting there and looking from that man to my father and looking back and really knowing those were the two choices.'[76]

By March 1945 the living conditions had reached such a low level that many prisoners were driven into madness by hunger; numerous cases of cannibalism are reported in the records. The fact that even under such conditions Passover was still celebrated in numerous huts in Bergen-Belsen – if only by a small minority – underlines the exceptional, psychological importance of this festival for Jewish prisoners in the camp. In Simon Gutmann's diary these weeks and days are summarised thus:

> 40 degrees temperature, 40.5 to 41° [...] Eight days without consciousness – typhoid fever – thanks to my brother Jacob's care and attention I regain consciousness. The daily food

consists of three quarters of a litre of Kohlrabi [a kind of turnip] soup and three cms of bread. After a few weeks there is no bread any more. Right and left of me people die of starvation. [...] Passover comes. The first Seder evening we spend by my bed, Jacob and Zwi Neuberger are there, too. Some have baked small Mazzoths and so we can perform Kiddusch.[77]

And in Abel Herzberg's diary in which earlier one can find pages of reflections about religious and philosophical questions it states succinctly and laconically: 'Despite everything, we celebrated Seder last night. Oh, oh ... ! A historical Seder. There was no need for bitter herbs. And still it was more than last year. Matzos were baked with flour that had been given us. And they tasted good.'[78]

On that Seder evening Joseph Weiss visited several huts of the Star camp to deliver a short speech for Passover:

In the evening I visited all huts of our group [...] and in short said something like the following: 'It may be paradoxical to quote the sentence from the Hagadah: 'Everyone may come and eat with us.' For today the opposite is true, we are all starving, we in charge cannot provide you with anything any more, our food supply looks very depressing. I cannot give you any bread, I can only encourage you with words, endure the last five minutes. They are the last five minutes, even though we don't read any newspaper and don't listen to the radio, we feel it. We belong to the few European Jews who survive this genocide, we must persevere because we will have to take part in bringing about the renaissance of our Jewish people.[79]

The impact on his fellow prisoners can best be described in the words of a then juvenile prisoner who did not pursue any religious activities in the camp:

Last wartime Seder evening, in Bergen-Belsen. It was in the evening, pitch-black night. We were lying on our beds, there were almost continuous air-raid warnings. A faint, flickering light and Joseph Weiss enters the hut holding a candle and speaks calmly, seriously and full of emotion. It was a feeling that even touched me. He talked about the approaching end, the coming liberation. Everybody listened holding their breaths.[80]

The context in which Jewish prisoners celebrated Passover in the concentration camp had changed so radically, past and present had intertwined so much in the light of hope for liberation, that both the course of events and the .procedure of the Passover festival had changed, and not only because Hagada copies and other material prerequisites were lacking.

The records also report on the celebration of other Jewish holidays. For Simchat Torah prisoners of the Kasztner-group placed a Torah scroll in the window of a hut and children with self-made little flags paraded past.[81] There are similar reports about the Special Camp.[82] The leader of the Szatmar Chassidim (and militant anti-Zionist) Joel Teitelbaum together with his followers celebrated the Jewish holidays in Bergen-Belsen in a particularly emotional way. On Simchat Torah, Hermann Adler remembers, 'the Szatmar rabbi holding a Torah scroll danced in the whole camp in such an ecstatic way as I had never experienced it before.'[83] Also referring to Simchat Torah a fairly unusual document from 1944 states: 'We, the undersigned, hereby testify that on the last Simchat Torah Reb. Elieser, son of Reb. Uri de Pauw was elected bride-groom of the Torah in hut 17 in Bergen-Belsen camp, while we were locked in imprisoned. The bridegroom of the Bereshith was Reb. Uri, son of the honoured Reb. Ahron de Pauw.'[84]

Where other Jewish festivals are mentioned in the records the close connection between religious activity on these holidays and cultural activity is apparent, for example, when for Shavuot a poem (of non-religious content) was written and recited, 'not as a religious expression, but rather as a conscious effort to observe it on some level',[85] when for Channukka lectures of cultural historical content were held,[86] or when, also for Channukka, Margot and Anne Frank together with other girls sang 'Dutch and Yiddish songs, also cheerful ones like "Constant hat een hoppelpaard"'.[87] And something else is striking in the records about the Jewish holidays in Bergen-Belsen: the relatively frequent mention of the involvement of children, particularly in connection with festivals like Channuka, Purim, Simchat Torah or Sukkot, which in themselves, through their symbolic character, had a special emotional quality.[88] To some of the Jewish prisoners the celebration of the festivals in Bergen-Belsen provided a demonstration of the religious-cultural diversity of

Judaism: 'I shall never forget', Abel Herzberg wrote in his diary on 10 October 1944, Simchat Torah,

> how they danced in the much too small space of hut 15. Among the North Africans everyone is devout, hence everyone joins in. The religion they practice is very primitive. They are really still believers in every letter, every little point of the law. The Balkan Jews are quite different. In part already as much assimilated as we are, naturally to *their* environment. A substantial number of them are baptised, Greek Catholic, to be exact. A Dutch Jew who had lived in Yugoslavia for decades was also baptised a Greek Catholic and stole just as much as many of the others. In a Jewish sense, not much happens there. There is a group of very devout individuals among them. Some remind one of Arabs. Above all the Albanians. Others, with their majestic bearing, seem to be absorbed in cabbala.[89]

As at Passover, the behaviour of the SS, as it is described to us in the diaries and testimonies of prisoners, was in no way uniform on the other holidays either. Meir Weiss remembers that an SS-man, on the request of Jewish prisoners, brought a prayer-book from the Hungarians' Camp to the Special Camp at Rosh Ha-Shana.[90] However, there are more frequent reports about the aggressive behaviour of individual SS-men in which their rudimentary knowledge of Jewish traditions, among other things the dates of the Jewish holidays, is mirrored. As central as the racist ideology was to Nazism, it cannot be ignored that its anti-Semitism also had religious overtones. Oskar David Berg remembers meeting the SS-Scharführer Chris on the highest Jewish holiday, Yom Kippur, a strict day for fasting:

> Strictly speaking he was a really sadistic person. In the morning he shouted: it is Yom Kippur, a day of fasting. Which of you is fasting? I then said I had tried until that day. And we raised our hands, five or ten. He said: those who are not fasting need not go to work, the others will come along. So we did that hard work. We worked in the kitchen from three in the morning until ten in the evening, with one break. And at midday he came with a piece of pork. I said: I am not eating that, I stuck to it.[91]

In spiteful contrast, on the Christian festival of Christmas in 1944 the Jewish prisoners received better food than usual.[92] Also at Yom Kippur the SS ordered that all inmates of the Star Camp had to have a shower on just that day.[93] Yehudith Ilan-Onderwyzer remembers that she (then 11 years old) and her mother regarded it as so humiliating that they hid in their hut so that they did not have to shower, risking maltreatment by the SS had they been detected.[94]

> All religious observance is forbidden in an SS camp for Jews, including above all the celebration of Yom Kippur. The result of this prohibition is that religious observances take place in *every* hut, despite the work that still has to be done that day, despite roll-call being repeated three times, despite the air-raid warnings, despite the pouring rain. We are able to meet before work, before six o'clock in the morning. Those who remain inside the camp also meet between roll-calls, and after half past six in the evening, when the parties have returned, there is an opportunity for the final prayer, that poetic mystical web of verses and avowals which, in the evening twilight, creates a mood all of its own. With their tallith over their wet working clothes, the men stand in the closing darkness full of nostalgia for their God.

So Herzberg describes Yom Kippur 1944 in Bergen-Belsen.[95] But this contrasting description also belongs to the image of Yom Kippur in Bergen-Belsen:

> The service was over, the soup was distributed to the hungry, what was left was to be distributed to those who had been fasting all day. Then real life started again: Yom Kippur over; sins forgiven; at once the fight for survival which here is particularly hard brings new ones. Again and again I heard: 'But you have eaten at lunch-time', or 'you have already had second mug full', or 'You have received a mug unjustified' and so on. I noticed how life very quickly pushed aside religion and that life itself then is stronger than all ethical principles![96]

In the concentration camp tight limits were set on religious thinking and theological reflections. Nevertheless, even if theological disputes were rather a rare exception, and sheer survival absorbed nearly all mental energies, the question of the why of the Jewish suffering in the concentration camps was inescapable to most prisoners. This question was particularly urgent for two reasons. As opposed to politically motivated persecution, the Nazi persecution of the Jews could not be attributed to individual actions or attitudes. One could not recognise a comprehensible motive for the persecution, as was possible, for example, for the Communist prisoners who clearly knew for which ideals and actions they had been deported to the concentration camp. Secondly, according to Jewish understanding eschatological salvation also has a concrete historical dimension; but was this promise not historically negated through the events in the concentration camps?

In view of the long history of the Jewish people's suffering and its continuous theological reflection there were many links for a specifically Jewish answer to this question. Identifications with figures in biblical history such as Abel, Isaac or Hiob presented themselves, but they could hardly offer more than a partial answer – and also only for a minority of Jewish prisoners. The same is true for interpretations which, referring to traditional patterns of explanation of guilt and punishment, integrated political phenomena into the explanation. Joel Teitelbaum, the leader of the Szatmar Chassidim, explained the Nazi persecution of the Jews as punishment from God for Zionism through which man had interfered in eschatological actions reserved for God (Teitelbaum was released from Bergen-Belsen in 1944 with the Kasztner-group as a result of Zionist negotiations!).[97] But such patterns of explanation through guilt and punishment oriented at orthodox standards were unacceptable for the great majority of the Jewish prisoners.

There were mainly two religious basic ideas which were meaningful to the Jewish prisoners in the concentration camps. Kiddush Hashem ('sanctification of God's name'), that is, the century-old formula for Jewish martyrdom, a religious interpretation of violent death for the sake of Jewish belief, was used by Jews in the concentration camps to give their forced fate a minimum of dignity and meaning. The transfer of this concept to the situation of the concentration camp emphasised the continuity and parallelism to the Jewish history of suffering that had gone before. But some questioned whether this comparison was possible. Was it not true, unlike earlier times, that by turning away from Jewish belief through Chillul Hashem ('desecration of God's name') it was impossible for the victims of this persecution to flee from violent death? And so another concept gained in importance, Kiddush Hachayim, the 'sanctification of life'. With this concept a religious motive was created for the numerous very different forms of Jewish self-assertion and resistance. 'For all the other resistance fighters inside and outside Nazi-occupied Europe resistance was a doing. For Jews [...] caught by the full force of the Nazi logic of destruction, resistance was a way of being.'[98] In comparison with Kiddush Hashem it was also a religious concept which was clearly more strongly oriented at behaviour (and towards active doing), which for the Jewish prisoners in the concentration camp was motive and guideline alike without standing in contradiction to Jewish tradition. Only superficially do Kiddush Hashem and Kiddush Hachayim appear as opposite theological concepts. Kiddush Hachayim did not just refer to physical survival, but also to the Jewish shaping of it (and in doing so giving sense to it), indeed both were regarded as linked inseparably. The two religious concepts are rather to be seen as different religious answers to different situations during the persecution: 'Kiddush Hachayim often stood at the end of a desperate and futile fight for survival, for the "sanctification of life".'[99]

For the majority of the Jewish prisoners in Bergen-Belsen it seems Emil Fackenheim's dictum is true: in the Holocaust one will never be able to find a religious meaning, only a religious answer (an answer, Y. Amir has added, which cannot be thought but can only be done).[100] This idea corresponds to the sources available about religiousness in Bergen-Belsen: while there is an impressive quantity of records about religious activities in Bergen-Belsen there are hardly any texts which contain religious interpretations. Also in Bergen-Belsen the answer to the urgent question about the meaning of one's own, of the Jewish suffering in Bergen-Belsen and in other camps, was that of religious acting (or not acting), not that of articulate theology.

For those who stuck to their orthodox way of life and convictions even in the concentration camp the persecution they suffered was nothing substantially new in Jewish history but parallel to the many persecutions which Jewish tradition reports. For these people this new persecution first and foremost made topical a basic pattern of

Jewish history, whose religious significance had been reflected time and again, whose questioning of the religious law connected with it had repeatedly been answered in a pragmatic way. Therefore they did not question the validity of the traditional religious laws and the decisions accompanying them (with this, by the way, in most cases a motive was missing theologically to interpret one's own fate in the form of text).

Evelien van Leeuwen, who had been baptised, noticed this

> Single orthodox families manage to stick to their Sabbath celebration until the very last moment [...] here it becomes obvious that tradition is neither an empty formula nor simply a habit. The old familiar words and the strict discipline give meaning and strength to the unwavering belief. No orthodox Jew's lips will pass the question about God ('Where is God, since our suffering is so great?'). With them the knowledge that being chosen and suffering go hand in hand is very strong.[101]

Further, this self-interpretation serves as such an act of self-assurance by putting one's own fate on a parallel with earlier periods of Jewish suffering. When the Dutch chief rabbis in the prayer quoted above allowed the consumption of Hametz this was not just an instruction of behaviour for their fellow prisoners which was in accord with tradition and which could take up the examples of the religious tradition as far as even the terminology, this was also a direct interpretation of 'Kiddush Hachayim'.[102] This concept which made the preservation of life its centre at the same time had both an individual and a collective dimension and it is not surprising therefore that in the camp an almost osmotic correlation of religious and national, Zionist self-assertion and self-interpretation developed. 'When the situation in Bergen-Belsen sank below the bearable, a shift from the religious to the secular must have occurred within me. Emotions and actions which I would formerly have called religious or religiously motivated now ranked in my mind as "Jewish-cultural", "Jewish-national", or "spiritual-ethical".'[103] What Weinberg, looking back, observed about himself, Abel Herzberg registered even more clearly in his diary following a visit to the hut of the Chalutzim (Palestine pioneers) at Simchat Torah:

The same prayers, the same songs, but the religion practised entirely in a nationalist light and aimed at the reality of Palestine. With an indomitable rhythm, they tunefully and passionately sang prayers for the reconstruction of Jerusalem. Once again, as happens constantly in Jewish history, religion and nationalism are being inseparably interwoven. The idea bound to politics, the principle of eternity to the opportunity of the moment.[104]

NOTES

1. Werner Weinberg, *Self-Portrait of a Holocaust Survivor* (Jefferson, NC and London: Mc Farland & Co., 1985), p.164.
2. For the following see also Thomas Rahe, 'Jüdische Religiosität in den nationalsozialistischen Konzentrationslagern', *Geschichte in Wissenschaft und Unterricht*, Vol. 44, No.2 (Feb. 1993), pp.87–101.
3. For the following see Eberhard Kolb, *Geschichte des 'Aufenthaltslagers' Bergen-Belsen 1943–1945* (Hanover: Verlag für Literatur und Zeitgeschichte, 1962); idem., *Bergen-Belsen. Vom 'Aufenthaltslager' zum Konzentrationslager 1943–1945*, (Göttingen: Vandenhoeck & Ruprecht, 1991).
4. See, among others, Jozef Gitler-Barski, '"Aufenthaltslager" Bergen-Belsen. Dziennik Wieznia', *Biuletyn Zydowskiego Instytutu Historycznego*,Vol.95, No.3, (1975), p.81, (entry of 28 May 1944); Abel Herzberg, *Tweestromenland. Dagboek uit Bergen-Belsen* (Amsterdam: Querido, 1980), pp.94 ff., 152 (entry of 9 Sept. 1944 and 10 Oct. 1944); Clara Asscher-Pinkhof, *De danseres zonder benen* (Gravenhage: H.P. Leopolds Uitgeversmij N.V., 1967), p.220; Rudolf Levy, 'Das Neutralen-Lager Bergen-Belsen' (Wiener Library eyewitness testimony (WL) P. III. h. (Bergen-Belsen), No. 294a), p.5; Simon Heinrich Herrmann, *Austauschlager Bergen-Belsen. Geschichte eines Austauschtransportes* (Tel Aviv: Irgun Olej Merkas Europa, 1944), p.58; Joseph Weiss, 'Eiduth' (Yad Vashem 03/947), p.7; statement by Hermann Adler (Basel, 9 June 1992) and statement by Prof. Meir Weiss (Jerusalem, 30 Aug. 1992); author interview with Fritz Vandor (Budapest, 8 July 1992).
5. Herbert Kruskal, 'Two Years Behind Barbed Wire' (Wiener Library P. III. h. (Westerbork), No. 137), p. 54; Helmuth Mainz, 'Erlebnisse 1940–1944', (WL P. III. h. (Holland), No. 722), p. 74; statement by Weiss; '"Je moet het je kinderen vertellen". Verhalen uit de geschiedenis van de Familie Dasberg' (Tel Aviv, 1966, unprinted private manuscript), p.149.
6. See, among others, Weiss, '"Je moet het je kinderen vertellen"', p.149; R. Levy, 'Das Neutralen-Lager', p.10; statement by Weiss; interview with Vandor; H. Mainz, 'Erlebnisse', p.65.
7. Lecture, Eliahu Ben-Yehuda at the Bergen-Belsen Memorial (video recording from 5 June 1994).
8. See Eli Dasberg, 'Dagboekfragmenten, notities en gedichten uit het kamp Würzach, van 20 Januar 1945 tot aankommst Amsterdam, 30 Juni 1945', 1965 (unpublished manuscript, 1965), p.14.
9. Abel Herzberg, *De man in de spiegel* (Amsterdam: Querido, 1980), p.249.
10. Arieh (Leo) Koretz, 'Bergen-Belsen Tagebuch eines Jugendlichen 11.7.1994–30.3.1945' (quoted from the authorised, unpublished German translation), p.6.

11. The original is still in possession of the Asscher family (copy at the Bergen-Belsen Memorial).
12. Abraham Shulman, *The Case of Hotel Polski. An Account of One of the Most Enigmatic Episodes of World War II* (New York: Holocaust Library, 1982), p.173.
13. Shlomo Samson, *Zwischen Finsternis und Licht. 50 Jahre nach Bergen-Belsen. Erinnerungen eines Leipziger Juden* (Jerusalem: Rubin Mass, 1995), p.255.
14. Interview HB-MK (Summer, 1984) (Jerome Riker International Study of Organized Persecution of Children, Sands Point, NY).
15. Weinberg, *Self-Portrait*, pp.162 ff.
16. H. Wielek, *De Oorlog, die Hitler won* (Amsterdam 1947), p.414.
17. Levy, 'Das Neutralen-Lager', pp.9 ff.
18. Statement by Weiss.
19. Interview with Vandor (Budapest, 8 July 1992).
20. See Herrmann, *Austauschlager Bergen-Belsen*, p.58.
21. Mainz, 'Erlebnisse', p.65
22. Herrmann, *Austauschlager Bergen-Belsen*, pp.58 ff.
23. Interview RH-M/JK (14.4.1983) (Jerome Riker International Study of Organized Persecution of Children, Sands Point, NY).
24. Statement by Weiss.
25. Bernhardt van Leeuwen, 'Vom Konzentrationslager zurück in die Schweiz & Freiheit' (WL P. III. h. (Bergen-Belsen), No. 845), p.6.
26. Asscher-Pinkhof, *De danseres*, p.220.
27. Quoted from Eliezer Berkovits, *With God in Hell. Judaism in the Ghettos and Death Camps* (New York and London: Sanhedrin Press, 1979), p.15f.
28. Statement by Michael Gelber (Rotterdam, 20 June 1993).
29. Israel Taubes, 'The Persecution of Jews in Holland 1940–1944. Westerbork and Bergen-Belsen' (Yad Vashem 01/117), p.33.
30. Hanna Lévy-Hass, *Vielleicht ist das alles erst der Anfang. Tagebuch aus dem KZ Bergen-Belsen 1944–1945* (Berlin: Rotbuch, 1982), p.38.
31. See, among others, Abel Herzberg, *Tweestromenland*, p.272 (entry of 29 Aug. 1944); Mina Tomkiewicz, *Tam sie tez zylo* (Hove: Polska Fundacja Kulturalna, 1984), p.10.
32. Asscher-Pinkhof, *De danseres*, p.224.
33. See, for example, the poem 'Brot' by Ninka Gitlerowna, contained in the diary of Jozef Gitler-Barski (entry of 29 Dec. 1944) or the poem 'Gebet' by Hans Presseisen, *Gedichten. Hans Presseisen 1921–1944* (Rotterdam: Rotterdamse Kunststichting, 1977), p.34.
34. The composition is by Josef Pinkhof, of which another musical version exists. Both original versions composed in Bergen-Belsen in February 1944 are still in the possession of the Pinkhof family.
35. Quoted from Deborah Dwork, *Children With a Star: Jewish Youth in Nazi Europe* (New Haven, NC and London: Yale University Press, 1991), p.132.
36. Herzberg, *De man in de spiegel*, p.422.
37. Herrmann, *Aufenhaltslager Bergen-Belsen*, p.61.
38. Statement by Weiss.
39. Ada Levy, 'Theresienstadt and other Concentration Camps' (WL P. III. h. Auschwitz, No. 16), p.8.
40. Herzberg, *Tweestromenland* (entry from 17 March 1945), p.213 (here and further on quoted from the forthcoming English translation by Jack Santcross).
41. Weinberg, *Self-Portrait*, pp.164 ff.; see also Herzberg, *Tweestromenland* (entry of 24 Sept. 1944), p.121.
42. Author interview with Ruchama Pinkhof (Bergen-Belsen, 15 June 1993).
43. See Louis Tas, 'Psychical Disorders among Inmates of Concentration Camps and

Repatriates', *Psychiatric Quarterly* No. 20 (Oct. 1951), pp.679 ff.
44. Herzberg, *Tweestromenland* (entry of 29 Aug. 1944), p.45.
45. Ibid. (entry of 14 Aug.1944), pp.15 ff.
46. Ibid. (entry of 4 Sept.), pp.70 ff.
47. Statement by Weiss; See also Avraham Krauss, 'Bericht über die Deportation ungarischer Juden nach Bergen-Belsen und ihre Freilassung in die Schweiz 1944' (Yad Vashem), p.4.
48. Levy, 'Das Neutralen-Lager', p.10.
49. Gitler-Barski, "Aufenthaltslager" (entry of 30 Dec. 1943), p.73.
50. Samson, p.314.
51. Ibid., p.313 ff.
52. Mainz, 'Erlebnisse', p.70.
53. Weinberg, *Self-Portrait*, p.163.
54. Herzberg, *Amor fati. De aanhakelijkheid aan het levenslot. Zeven opstellen over Bergen-Belsen* (Amsterdam: Querido, 1987), pp.66 ff.
55. Weiss, *Eiduth*, p.6.
56. Diary A. Koretz, p.34.
57. Herzberg, *Tweestromenland* (entry of 31 Aug. 1944), p.55.
58. See J. Weiss, 'Eiduth', p.7.
59. See Dan Michman, 'Jewish Religious Life Under Nazi Domination: Nazi Attitudes and Jewish Problems', *Studies in Religion* 22, Vol.19, No.2 (1993), p.164.
60. The fate of the rabbis will be described more extensively in a separate article about 'Rabbis in the concentration camp Bergen-Belsen', which the author is preparing.
61. Sara (Bick) Berkowitz, *Where are My Brothers?* (New York: Helios Books, 1965), p.85.
62. Herzberg, *De man*, p.420.
63. Herzberg, *Tweestromenland* (entry of 18 Sept. 1944), pp.110 ff.
64. Tomkiewicz, *Tam sie*, p.24.
65. *The Passover Haggadah*, translation by Philip Schlesinger and Josef Güns (Tel Aviv, 1976), p.3.
66. Herrmann, *Austauschlager*, p.60.
67. Jehudit Ilan-Onderwyzer, 'Spannungen der Kindheit' (authorised and unpublished German version of the original Hebrew edition from 1981), p.26.
68. Report from memory by Philip Arons (WL: P.III. h. (Bergen-Belsen) No. 839), p.146.
69. Gitler-Barski, Dziennik, p.77. About the same complex another report exists which is arranged in legendary style and which apparently also refers to the Special Camp: Yaffa Eliach, *Träume vom Überleben. Chassidische Geschichten aus dem 20. Jahrhundert* (Freiburg: Herder, 1987), pp.35–9.
70. Gitler-Barski, "Aufenthaltslager" (entry of 5 April 1944), p.78.
71. See H. Kruskal, 'Two Years Behind Barbed Wire' (WL : P. III.h. (Westerbork), No. 137), pp.47 ff.
72. See interviews by the author with Chanoch Mandelbaum (Hanover, 28 Aug. 1989 and 14 July 1988); S. Samson, pp.383 ff.
73. As the Hebrew original text of the prayer does not contain any information about the author one cannot definitely identify him. Apart from the Chief Rabbi of Rotterdam, Aaron Davids the Chief Rabbis Simon Dasberg (Groningen) and Abraham Levinson (Leeuwarden) are most likely the co-authors. The text was written down by Jacques Asscher. For this information and a copy I thank Mrs. Tsofia Langer-Asscher. About the text of the prayer, see also Deborah Schechterman, 'Concepts of Suffering', *Remembering for the Future. Working Papers and Addenda*, Vol.1 edited by Yehuda Bauer (Oxford/New York: Pergamon Press, 1989), pp.975–86.
74. Ilan-Onderwyzer, *Spannungen*, p.39.

75. Asscher-Pinkhof, *Danseres*, p.224.
76. Interview Judith Kerstenberg with S.W. (Jerome Riker International Study of Organized Persecution of Children, Sands Point, NY, 5 Aug. 1987).
77. 'The Last Weeks in Bergen-Belsen' by Simon Gutmann and his brother Jakob (Yad Vashem 033/29), p.1.
78. Herzberg, *Tweestromenland* (entry of 30 March 1945), p.216.
79. Report from memory of Joseph Weiss, written down on 7 June 1945 in Tröbitz (Rijksinstituut voor Oorlogsdocumentatie: Amsterdam [II] 09 Weiss), p.10.
80. Shmu'el Hacohen, *Zwijgende stenen. Herinnering aan een vermoorde jeugd* (The Hague: Uitgeverij BZZTôH, 1990), p.333.
81. See Statement by Weiss.
82. See minutes of an interview with Josef Galler (Jewish Historical Institute, Warsaw: 1137).
83. Statement by Adler.
84. The Hebrew original text from which has been quoted is printed in *Keshev. Studies and Sources*, Vol.1, No.1 (Dec. 1985), p.36. Chatan Torah is he who may read the last passage from the Torah on Simhat Torah, Chatan Bereschit is he who is asked to read from the first chapter of the story of the Creation.
85. Statement Erica Herz Van Adelsberg (26 July 1994). Her poem which she wrote together with Marietta Moskin, was entitled 'Kakaogedicht für Schawuoth 5704 in Bergen-Belsen' and pulled prisoners' legs. I thank E. Herz Van Adelsberg for surrender of the unpublished poem.
86. Gitler-Barski, "Aufenthaltslager" (entry of 29 Dec. 1943), p.72.
87. Lin Jaldati/Eberhard Rebling, *Sag nie, du gehst den letzten Weg. Erinnerungen* (Berlin: Der Morgen, 1986), p.422.
88. See, among others, Gitler-Barski, "Aufenthaltslager" (entry of 9 March 1944), p.76; Asscher-Pinkhof, *Sternkinder* (Hamburg: Friedrich Oetinger,1986), pp.189–91; Yaffa Eliach, 'Jewish Tradition in the Life of the Concentration-Camp Inmate', *The Nazi Concentration Camps. Proceedings of the Fourth Yad Vashem International Historical Conference*, (Jerusalem: Yad Vashem, 1984), p.201; Diary Zielenziger (entry of 12 Oct. 1944), p. 4.
89. Herzberg, *Tweestromenland*, pp.152 ff.; also see Levy, 'Das Neutralenlager', p.10.
90. Statement by Weiss.
91. Author interview with Oskar David Berg (Iserlohn, 14 July 1988). Also see Gitler-Barski, "Aufenthaltslager" (entry of 27 Sept. 1944), p.85.
92. Herzberg, *Tweestromenland* (entry of Christmas 1944), p.196.
93. See diary A. Koretz (entry of 26 Sept. 1944), p.51.
94. See Ilan-Onderwyzer, 'Spannungen', pp.30 ff.; also see Marietta D. Moskin, *I am Rosemarie* (New York: Dell Publishing, 1972), pp.174 ff.
95. Herzberg, *Tweestromenland* (entry of 28 Sept. 1944), pp.123 ff.
96. Selma van Leeuwen-Gerzon, 'Bergen-Belsen, Jom Kippur 1944/45' (Joods Historisch Museum, Amsterdam: 922/735H).
97. See Joel Teitelbaum, *Sefer Va' Joel Moshe* (New York, 1982). See for the following more detailed Rahe, 'Jüdische Religiosität'.
98. Emil Fackenheim, 'The Spectrum of Resistance During the Holocaust', *Modern Judaism 2* (1982), pp.127 ff.
99. Leni Yahil, 'Jewish Resistance: An Examination of Active and Passive Forms of Jewish Survival in the Holocaust Period', in *Jewish Resistance During the Holocaust: Proceedings of the Conference on Manifestations of Jewish Resistance* (Jerusalem: Yad Vashem, 1972), pp.40 ff.
100. See Yehoshua Amir, 'Jüdisch-theologische Positionen nach Auschwitz', in Günter B. Ginzel (ed.), *Auschwitz als Herausforderung für Juden und Christen* (Heidelberg:

Lambert Schneider, 1980), pp.453 ff.
101. Evelien van Leeuwen, *Späte Erinnerungen an ein jüdisches Mädchen. Autobiographische Erzählung* (Trier: éditions trèves, 1984), p.32.
102. The three rabbis probably had in mind a prayer said to have been written by Rabbi Alexandri (third century B.C.) (bab. Berakhoth 17a) reading: 'Master of the worlds/it is revealed and known before Thee/that it is our will to do Thy will./But what prevents?/ The leaven in the dough and the oppression by the Kingdoms./May it be Thy will/O Lord, our God/ to subdue these, fore and aft/that we may again abide by the laws of Thy will, with all our heart.' Meyer Perath, *Rabbinical Devotion. Prayers of the Jewish Sages* (Assen: van Gorcum & Co, 1964), p.12. I am grateful for this hint by Tsofia Langer-Asscher.
103. Weinberg, *Self-Portrait*, p.164.
104. Herzberg, *Tweestromenland* (entry of 10 Oct. 1944), p.153.

THIS IS THE SITE OF
THE INFAMOUS BELSEN CONCENTRATION
Liberated by the British on 15 April 1945

10,000 UNBURIED DEAD WERE FOUND HERE
ANOTHER 13,000 HAVE SINCE DIED
ALL OF THEM VICTIMS OF THE
GERMAN NEW ORDER IN EUROPE.
AND AN EXAMPLE OF NAZI KULTUR

1 The notice erected by the British at the entrance to Camp I (Jo Reilly)

2 Female internees preparing food in Camp I after liberation. In the background is a huge pile of boots and shoes (Wiener Library)

3 One of the mass graves marked by the British (Jo Reilly)

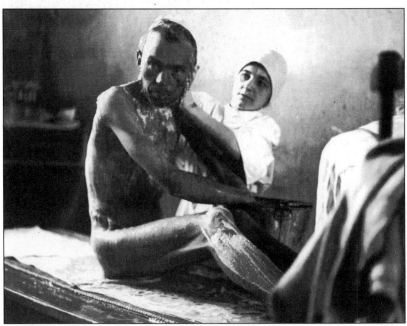

4 Inside the 'Human Laundry': an internee is washed before being transferred to Camp II (Wiener Library)

5 The Panzer Training School, one-and-a-half miles from Camp I, established by the British as a hospital centre and known as Camp II (Jo Reilly)

6 An ambulance of the Jewish Relief Team from Britain (Wiener Library)

7 Young mother in Belsen Displaced Persons' Camp (Jewish Relief Unit Archive, Wiener Library)

8 The unveiling of the Jewish memorial stone on the site of Camp I, April 1946
(Wiener Library)

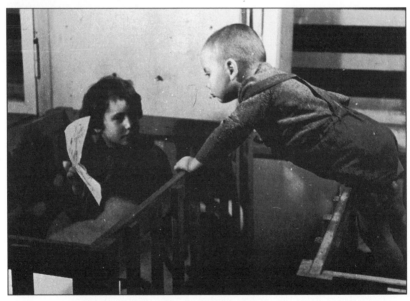

9 Children recovering in Belsen Displaced Persons' Camp (Jewish Relief Unit Archive,
Wiener Library)

PART III: THE LIBERATION OF BERGEN-BELSEN

French Internees and British Liberators

ANNETTE WIEVIORKA

In contrast to the British who consider Bergen-Belsen as the perfect example of a concentration camp, largely because *they* liberated it, the French have no collective memory of the camp and its image remains unclear to them. Several memorials were built in memory of the various Nazi concentration camps inside the Père Lachaise cemetery, near Le Mur des Fédérés where the last rebels of the Paris Commune were shot. The Bergen-Belsen memorial is the ninth and last. It was inaugurated only recently, on the 23 March 1994, thanks to the Bergen-Belsen Memorial committee whose president, Albert Biegelman, was deported to Belsen as a child, with his mother. Simone Veil was also present, both as ministre d'Etat and ministre des Affaires sociales (one of the highest-ranking ministers in the French government in charge of welfare and city affairs) and as a former internee of a camp to which she was transferred from Auschwitz, along with her mother and her sister, in January 1945. In their choice, the designers of the memorial settled on a replica of the existing memorial at the camp. On its base, one can read a double dedication: 'They suffered and hoped. You fight for freedom' and 'Their bodies were broken, but not their spirit'. Further inscriptions serve as a reminder of the various transfers from other camps: Neuengamme, Auschwitz, Buchenwald ... According to its designers,

> The lower part of the monument is closed by a tapering wall whose meaning is either to welcome or hold back; down its middle, a breach opens into nothingness. This breach is partly filled by a jutting obelisk rising towards hope. The rails and the footprints are symbolic of the arrivals. The names of the camps from which the deported came are engraved on the plaques affixed to the lower part of the wall supporting the rails.

A twig of briar, brought from the camp, was planted at the memorial on the day of the inauguration. Eventually, briar from the camp site will cover the ground on either side.[1]

The fact that Bergen-Belsen was only a transit camp, a place where many died at the end of a long journey through several camps, probably explains why, contrary to what happened in the case of other camps, no active friendship society of former Bergen-Belsen inmates developed. This also explains why the memorial was only recently erected. In fact, we can establish three categories among the internees from France: a small number who were sent there from other camps to 'recover', or so it was said; a larger number who were deported during the last months of the war; and a few hundred women and children sent there as hostages in May and July 1944.

Indeed, only a small number were sent to Bergen-Belsen, to 'recover'. 'One day, they give us striped clothing and we leave the Schonung*' recalls Michel Fliecx, of his time as a prisoner in the Dora concentration camp which supplied slave labour for an underground rocket factory. 'There are about a thousand of us in there. A thousand of us competing in this new trial, and I am one of the most handicapped. They have brought the sick from the Schonung, on stretchers, the ones who come from the Revier** are laid on stretchers, and others come from the tunnel.' The next afternoon, after they had spent the night in that shelter, Fliecx recalls that,

> they give us some bread, margarine and some meat … as in a blurry dream, I follow the alley that runs through the camp. What a weird parade! The head of the camp and all the B.V.s around him are bent with laughter: 'Nach Sanatorium … ' (to the sanatorium) they shout laughing at us as we go by. Coming from them, a very sinister joke. The worst is to be expected.[2]

The first group of 'recovering sick' that appears in the accounts made by internees, arrived on 27 March 1944 from Dora. These men, labelled 'Political prisoners', were put in two shacks left vacant by those who had built the camp. They did not work. Aimé Blanc

---

* Schonung means 'convalescence'. Here it is the place where the inmates stayed when they were convalesing.
** Camp 'hospital'.

indicates that all the work was done by the Jews. Dr Fréjafon remembered that almost all the men had tuberculosis and described this so-called rest camp thus:

> Bergen Belsen was the rest camp to which the other camps sent those they had no use for any longer: the old, the sick, the physically disabled, all of them worn out and hoping to find the peace, the quiet, the medical care and the most basic humane treatment they had been dreaming of for so long. They only found a slow and inescapable death, the 'night and the fog of Nacht und Nebel' … One after the other, the Reviers of Auschwitz, Buckenwald [sic], Mauthausen and all the other major labor camps would transfer their miserable patients to the recovery camp.[3]

In May and July 1944, two small convoys of French Jewish prisoners arrived from Drancy bringing to Bergen-Belsen the wives and the children of prisoners-of-war as well as a handful of VIPs. Unlike the first arrivals, these were hostages to be used in the Nazis' bargaining plans.[4]

In the summer of 1944, because of its location in the heart of the Reich, Bergen-Belsen became one of the places into which were emptied the inmate population of the Eastern camps, threatened by the advance of Soviet troops. In October and November 1944, the evacuation of Auschwitz began and the first convoys of women arrived in Belsen. Some remained there only a few months before they were sent to other camps attached to factories engaged in the German war effort.

With the exception of the wives and the children of the Jewish prisoners-of-war, we have no precise statistics as to the number of French men and women who went through Bergen-Belsen. The only reliable figures concern the later period. At the end of April 1945, there remained 1,241 French men and women in the camp.

What were the feelings of the survivors when they saw the British liberators? How did they live their first moments without the Nazis? Nothing is harder to grasp for the historian whose only sources here are violently conflicting testimonies. Fliecx recalls:

> On the morning of Sunday, April 15th, as I come out of the barracks, all is unusually quiet. Not one SS in sight: there is almost nobody outside, except for the dead whose bodies are

everywhere … Along with a few comrades, I look at this horrible but familiar scene. The sun shines, it will be a beautiful day. Oh yes, a beautiful day, the most beautiful day ever!

In the distance, serious gunfire can be heard coming from the direction of Winsen, on the road to Celle; it is punctuated by canon shots; it's Them! they have come and they are fighting for us. Who are they? What are they? American or English? Doesn't matter, bless them. Doesn't matter if the fighting comes all the way here. We said it often enough: Let the sh**hit if this is the way it has to be, but let's get it over with!

The SS and the Hungarian camp guards were by now wearing white armbands: the camp was to be surrendered without fighting. The internees began to loot the clothing stores. A few internees were already beginning to talk about 'settling accounts'. 'The women's camp is opened', continues Fliecx.

Several inmates are already making new acquaintances. With a few others, we try to see the few French women who are still in more or less good health. This meeting with the women, that too smells of the end, and of freedom.

Around noon the gunfire ceases. Nothing. Again, we begin to worry. Will they come? Aren't they going to make a detour and leave us like this for several days?

There is almost no water left in the camp. The water for the soup is drawn from disgusting tanks.

And when at three thirty in the afternoon, while the soup is being distributed, we see an impeccable line of tanks at the edge of the woods along the road to Celle, a long, orderly, awesome line of tanks, we begin to shout, we are overcome with joy and emotion. In a minute we identify them: English!

Shouts of joy, tears, excitement. For a few minutes we are drunk with happiness and gratitude.

We finally leave the wire fence and go back to the centre of the camp, as we pass others with a question on their faces, we yell the news at them. Before they ask, we yell the news at all those who cannot walk but drag themselves out of the blocks, at those who lay on the ground dying and look at us with mad hopefulness and for a minute, this mad hope rekindles their eyes, we yell the news at all this humankind which will soon achieve for the second time the miracle of resurrection:

Es sind die Engländer, alles ist fertig!

The English are here, it is all over.

One hour later, as we are discussing this newly discovered happiness, a huge wave of noise brings us out of our barracks: a British army radio car, so beautiful with its Saint George medallion, is coming round, its double loudspeaker repeats in all languages the blessed words: 'You are free!'

As the car arrives near our section, the crowd of the miserable, starved, filthy living dead overflows and smashes the fences, the door flies towards the casks containing the soup which have been arranged across from the entrance to our quarters. Everybody wants to dip their bowls and all is spilled. But in a huge cloud of dust, most of the crowd runs to the kitchens and to the last heaps of rutabaga. 2 or 3 thousand of these ghosts now swarm in the small space between the shacks and the kitchens.

Fliecx goes on to describe the brutal scene, and the powerlessness of the English faced with what looked like an uprising in front of the food stores.

The radio car is sent on another round: 'go back quietly to your blocks. Food is on its way, medicines too. The English troops will not enter the camp for fear of contagious diseases.' It is quite a let down. We won't be able to mix with our brothers, our liberators! However, that evening, tanks drive up and down the alleys of the camp, together with live men. English soldiers look round, they are dumb struck, the next day, the radio will say: 'The Second British Army has reached the camp of Bergen Belsen and so on … , the "desert rats" have never seen anything worse since El Alamein'.

Michel Fliecx chooses to end his account with the vision of two 'tommies' who walk by him smiling 'with so much kindness that my heart is pinched, a forgotten feeling rises in me and tears run down my cheeks'.[5]

This vision of the situation by an 'old' Bergen-Belsen internee seems unique in its unfailing optimism and the exceptional gratitude it shows for the British. But the liberation of the camp was not such a happy time for most of the French prisoners, both male and female: they were in such a bad physiological condition that they could not afford any joy. Also, if there was any joy at all, even a passing sense of joy, it was marred by the endless weeks they still had to spend in the camp and by the excruciatingly slow process of repatriation. Simone Veil says:

> The very conditions and the bare facts of our repatriation show that the authorities didn't understand the situation, or were indifferent to it. Though quite a few women were very sick and though we were all very weak, we were repatriated more than a month after the liberation of Bergen Belsen. They crammed us into trucks and we travelled like this for five days before they put us on a train to Paris whereas the French prisoners of war, who had been liberated at the same time as us, had very quickly been repatriated by plane.
>
> For want of medical care and adequate nourishment, many internees died during that period. The British military authorities who had liberated the camp and the French envoys in charge of our repatriation understood the situation but could do nothing because they had nothing and could not take care of us. Why did we have to wait so long? Probably because they feared a typhus epidemic, or more simply because 'that' was totally unexpected. But we had the feeling that our lives did not mean much, though the number of survivors was already very small.[6]

The liberation of Bergen-Belsen was a great disappointment for the office of the Frenay ministry then in charge of repatriation: 'We had great hopes for the Bergen Belsen repatriation now that we were familiar with the geography of the various criss-crossings of the [German] convoys. And [there were] only 1,200 names.'[7] The descriptions of the camp after the liberation are awful. In Camp III, 8–10,000 women were crammed into 20 blocks and lay on three-tiered bunks or on straw mattresses placed on the ground. With so many people and so little space, epidemics spread faster. Many of the women still wore their striped concentration camp suits. Underwear was scarce.

At first, the food distributed by the British was not sufficient: black bread, a few biscuits and some soup, which was nothing but a dark liquid with a few pieces of meat floating in a bowl. Indeed, supplies were scarce in the area and everything was difficult to find. Yet Dr Fréjafon wondered at the contrast between the fate of Bergen-Belsen inmates and the nearby Stalag XIB prisoner of war camp. On the day following the arrival of the allied troops, the POWs, numbering 25–30,000 including the prisoners of the satellite camp at Lichte, received white bread and choice foods. True, there were 10,000 British soldiers among them, but to Fréjafon it was 'still difficult to understand why the British were not fair when they divided whatever food they had at their disposal. Was the fate of the internees in Camp III, mainly "genuine resistants and racial internees" not as worthy of interest as the fate of their neighbours the prisoners?'[8]

Bergen-Belsen was still a miserable place. It remained as awful as ever even though the SS were no longer there to exert their violence. No help arrived from France. An anonymous report dated 10 May stigmatises the absence of UNRRA representatives on the premises of the camp. Help did not come from the liberators but from their neighbours; the indignant French POWs gathered what they could and stole more from the nearby villages. They brought food, underwear and fresh clothes to the camp. National solidarity played an important role. There were few medical officers among the British and so the internees organised themselves. Dr Fréjafon managed to transform part of Block 19 into an infirmary where internees served as sanitary officers. They got help from POW doctors such as Dr Salomon who had come to Belsen in search of his wife. She was, in fact, no longer there having been deported from the camp before the British troops arrived.

The British were very mean in terms of the assistance that the Germans could give. They only assigned two or three Germans to help in the blocks under Dr Fréjafon's care. He complained about this, arguing that he needed more people to bring sanitary conditions up to a minimal level. An Englishwoman replied that 'it is preferable to put the internees to work, it helps for their re-education'. This answer clearly showed the scorn that some British relief workers displayed towards people who no longer resembled civilised human beings, people who the liberators came to look upon as sub-human.

By early May, typhus had spread considerably. The camp was then put under quarantine, the harshness of which inflicted deep suffering on the internees. As Dr Fréjafon noted, 'This unexpected extension of their stay in this cursed place and the uncertainty felt by many as to ever being able to return to their native country progressively changed the atmosphere of the camp. Hundreds died. Fear was on all the faces.' On 15 May, the typhus epidemic reached its peak. The sick were mixed in with the healthy and the conditions in the makeshift hospitals were inhuman. The French women were scattered throughout various buildings. Even after a new hospital was opened on 10 May and hopes for better conditions were raised, the French women were still not united. Of 59 patients transferred from Dr Fréjafon's infirmary to the hospital, only five had beds. The rest were placed in dirty rooms and slept on straw mattresses thrown on the floor. The hospital was staffed entirely by Germans. The French women were only brought together in the same room after the German orderlies were given cigarettes. Thus, it was necessary to reinstate the system of corruption that characterised concentration camp life.

Even though the SS were gone, the fear of an epidemic led to a draconian enforcement of the quarantine and the drastic curtailment of the freedom of the survivors. In order to seal off the camp, the British used whatever personnel were available, including the Hungarians who had previously been serving under SS command in the German armed forces. 'Every morning', says Dr Fréjafon, 'the noise made by these Prussian-trained soldiers marching through the camp added to the feeling that nothing had changed. The guards were not very strict, but even if the cage was gilded, our countrymen were not free, and their thirst for freedom was exarcerbated.'[9]

It is plain from the above that the picture of the British liberators that emerges from French sources is generally negative. Can this be ascribed to the influence of the old anti-English prejudices in French culture? Or does it accurately reflect the behaviour and attitudes of the British liberators? It is quite impossible to give definitive answers to these questions. It is certain, however, that the liberation of

Bergen-Belsen was a bitter episode for the French internees. There were no luxuries and no plentiful supplies; the most basic needs of the internees went unsatisfied. Liberation did not even bring immediate freedom.

NOTES

1. Concerning all the deportation memorials and the genocide, see Serge Barcellini and Annette Wieviorka, *Passant souviens-toi! Lieux du souvenir de la Seconde Guerre mondiale en France* (Paris: Plon, 1995).
2. Michel Fliecx, *Pour délit d'espérance. Deux ans à Buchenwald, Pennemünde, Dora, Belsen* (Evreux, 1947), pp.118–19. Also see Aimé Blanc's account, *Français, N'oubliez pas!* (Paris: reflets de notre temps, 1947).
3. Dr Fréjafon, *Bergen Belsen, bagne sanatorium. Les Derniers jours de Georges Valois,* Preface by L. Martin Chauffier (Paris: Librairie Valois, 1947), p.53.
4. Concerning the wives and the children of Jewish prisoners of war who were deported to Bergen-Belsen, see the account of Marcelle and Robert Christophe, *Le Miracle de nos prisons,* (Paris: Presses de la Cité, 1974).
5. Michel Fliecx, op. cit., pp.190–94.
6. Simone Veil, 'Une difficile réflexion', an interview with Annette Wieviorka; *Pardès,* Vol.16 (1992), p.274.
7. Olga Wormser Migot, *Le Retour des déportés. Quand les Alliés ouvrirent les portes* (Brussels: Complexe, 1985), p.236.
8. This as well as the quotes come from Dr Fréjafon's long report. A political internee, he was transferred to Bergen-Belsen in 1944, probably from Dora. See also *Bergen Belsen bagne sanatorium*, p.101. Dr Fréjafon remained in the camp to take care of his fellow Frenchmen.
9. The 'liberated' found it hard to bear the presence of the Hungarians enforcing the quarantine. On 18 May 1945 Mr Lorion, Embassy secretary, confirmed these facts in a note concerning the circumstances of the French nationals in Germany.

The British Army and the Liberation of Bergen-Belsen, April 1945

PAUL KEMP

'I knew no more than that they had found a concentration
camp and that there was typhus in it ... '.

On 12 April 1945 following the breakthrough of the British Second
Army after the Rhine crossing, an emissary from the 1st German
Paratroop Army came through British lines to declare the presence of
a concentration camp at Bergen-Belsen at which there were some
'1,500' typhus cases. At this stage there was no indication of the true
nature of what lay behind the wire fences and the British were chiefly
concerned with preventing the spread of disease. Consequently the
Chief of Staff of the British VIII Corps, Brigadier Taylor-Balfour, was
empowered to conclude a truce with the Germans by which a 48-
square kilometre area around the camp would be evacuated. German
troops would remain to guard the camp, together with a Hungarian
unit, but a British unit, the 63rd Anti Tank (AT) Regiment, Royal
Artillery (Lieutenant-Colonel R.I.G. Taylor, DSO, MC) would
supervise the Germans who were to be released within six days and
given free passage back to their own lines. The position of the SS staff
was left vague. If the German Army could prevent them from running
away, then they were to stay at their posts. In fact, the majority of the
SS had fled on 13 April but the Kommandant, SS *Hauptstürmbannfuhrer*
Josef Kramer, together with 80 warders (50 men and 30 women)
remained.

Special thanks are due to Dr Ursula Guly MRCP for her advice on the medical aspects of
this article, and to Dr Thomas Rahe of the Niedersächsishe Landeszentrale für politische
Bildung.

The first British soldiers to arrive at Belsen were members of the 1st Special Air Service (SAS). Although the majority of 1st SAS was engaged in providing a reconnaissance screen for the 6th Airborne Division, a section under the command of Major Harry Poat was in the 11th Armoured Division area to check if any members of the regiment or any other allied POWs were incarcerated there. It is not clear when the SAS reached the camp, but they did so before the arrival of a group of staff officers from HQ VIII Corps who were to make an assessment of conditions at the camp and to decide what needed to be done. In charge of the party from VIII Corps was Brigadier H.L. Glyn-Hughes, Deputy Director of Medical Services (DDMS) Second Army and it included Captain W.R. Williams, Staff Captain in the Supply and Transport Branch.[1]

By the time Glyn-Hughes' party had finished their reconnaissance, the main body of 63 Anti Tank Regiment began arriving at the camp where Kramer and some of his staff were waiting. Kramer delivered a report on the numbers of internees and was then ordered to accompany the British officers on a tour of the camp. Taylor ordered Kramer to accompany him on an inspection tour when there were reports of rioting by the prisoners. As Taylor walked down what he described as the 'main roadway' of the camp he began to realise the full horror of the situation:

> A great number of them were little more than living skeletons with haggard yellowish faces. Most of the men wore a striped pyjama type of clothing – others wore rags while the women wore striped flannel gowns or any garment that they had managed to acquire … There were men and women lying in heaps on both sides of the track. Others were walking slowly and aimlessly about – a vacant expression on their starved faces.[2]

The War Diary for the DDMS VIII Corps, Brigadier J. Melvin, CBE, MC, TD, who had also toured the camp that afternoon, starkly portrayed conditions: ' … Death rate 17000 in March. Thousands of corpses lying unburied. Inmates starving to death every day. Water and food finished. No light or sanitation. Hundreds dying.'[3] It was clear to both Glyn-Hughes and Taylor that the situation was well beyond the resources of 63 AT Regiment to deal with, so an urgent request was dispatched to Second Army and VIII Corps for medical help. Under the overall control of Brigadier Glyn-Hughes the relief operation got under way. On 17 April No. 224 Military Government Detachment assumed responsibility for the control of the camp. 11th Light Field Ambulance (Lieutenant-Colonel M.W. Gonin RAMC), 32nd Casualty Clearing Station (CCS – Lieutenant-Colonel J.A.D. Johnstone RAMC) and 30th Field Hygiene Section (Major P.J. Fox RAMC) were the first medical units to arrive.

Lieutenant-Colonel Gonin of 11 Light Field Ambulance (LFA) left an immensely moving description of his first impressions of Belsen which encapsulates the horrific conditions and the hopeless situation his unit was placed in:

> I can give no adequate description of the horror camp in which my men and myself were to spend the next months of our lives. It was just a barren wilderness, as bare and devoid of vegetation as a chicken run. Corpses lay everywhere, some in huge piles where they had been dumped by the other inmates, sometimes singly or in pairs where they had fallen as they shuffled along the dirt tracks. Those who died of illness usually died in the huts, when starvation was the cause of death they died in the open for it is an odd characteristic of starvation that its victims seem compelled to go on wandering until they fall down and die. Once they have fallen they die almost at once and it took a little time to get used to seeing men, women and children collapse as you walked by them and to restrain oneself from going to their assistance. One had to get used early to the idea that the individual just did not count. One knew that 500 a day were dying and that 500 a day were going to go on dying before anything we could do would have the slightest effect. It was, however, not easy, to watch a child choking to death from diphtheria when you knew a tracheotomy and nursing would save it. One saw women drowning in their own vomit because they were too weak to roll over and men eating worms as they clutched half a loaf of bread purely because they had to eat and could now scarcely tell the difference between worms and bread. Piles of corpses, naked and obscene, with a woman too weak to stand propping herself up against them as she cooked

the food we gave her over an open fire. Men and women crouching down just anywhere in the open relieving themselves of the dysentery which was scouring their bodies, a woman standing stark naked washing herself with issue soap in water from a tank in which the remains of a child floated.[4]

Another arrival at Belsen on 17 April were men of the Army Film and Photographic Unit (AFPU) who were to record conditions in the camp. Sergeant William Lawrie, a film cameraman, recalled being given no instructions on what to film. He recalled that the prisoners were totally apathetic about their liberation: 'They were incapable of coherent thought ... it was a very quiet silent business. They sat about, very little movement. Some of them were too far gone to move. There was absolutely no way we could ask them to rehearse a piece for us.'[5]

On 17 April the medical units held a conference to decide upon a strategy for dealing with the camp. It was decided that 11LFA was to deal with medical work inside the camp. Lieutenant-Colonel Gonin succinctly described the problems facing his unit:

> What we had therefore was buildings, eight nurses, about 300 RAMC chaps and a regiment of LAA and at least 20,000 sick suffering from the most virulent diseases known to man, all of whom required urgent hospital treatment and 30,000 men and women who might die if they were not treated but who certainly would die if they were not fed and removed from the horror camp. What we had not got was nurses, doctors, beds, bedding, clothes, drugs, dressings, thermometers, bedpans or any of the essentials of medical treatment and worst of all no common language.[6]

The conference established the nature of the medical problems requiring attention. The camp was riddled with typhus and tuberculosis. Erysipelas, scurvy and starvation disorders were widely prevalent.[7] The control of typhus within the camp and prevention of the spread of the disease to the troops and civilians in the surrounding area was the main priority, a responsibility which was given to 30th Field Hygiene Section. Major Fox was assisted by Captain W. A. Davies of the US Army Medical Corps, a consultant in typhus control attached to 21 Army Group by the US Army's Typhus Commission. Preventative measures were swiftly introduced. Anyone entering the camp was dusted with DDT powder which killed the lice carrying the disease. Speed restrictions on traffic around the camp were also imposed to keep down the dust which was also a factor in the spread of the disease (see the note on typhus at the end of the article for an explanation of this dreadful illness). Those already suffering from the disease would be evacuated from the camp, which the British now referred to as Camp I, to a proper hospital which was being established in the nearby German Army barracks by 32CCS. While these preparations were being made, the dead in the camp had to be buried. The initial estimate of 2,000 unburied bodies was hurriedly revised to nearer 10,000 with a further 17,000 corpses lying in open or barely covered pits.

The SS guards, except Kramer, who had been removed to a POW cage at Celle on 18 April, were put to work collecting the corpses and taking them to pits dug by a bulldozer provided by the Royal Engineers. The guards were given the same ration as the inmates before release and were worked until they dropped. One of the SS men committed suicide after a day of this work while another two were shot while attempting to escape. But the sheer number of corpses awaiting burial meant that a more expedient method of burial had to be resorted to. Frederick Riches, a driver with 11 LFA, recalled watching the Germans throwing the bodies into the open pits:

> ... the officer was getting them to throw the bodies in because none of them had any identification on them, no bracelets, no nothing, just throw 'em straight in. Then another officer come along and said 'Look you're wasting your time doing that ... put your bulldozer back on it'. So he (the bulldozer driver) was put in and this chap didn't like it at first. Then he started pushing them in and that's how it went on from there.[8]

Despite the rough nature of the burials, funeral services were read over the graves by Army chaplains and also by Rabbis from Belsen and other liberated camps. The sight of the thousands of bodies being bulldozed into the ground had a numbing effect on those watching:

> If it had been several hundred bodies one might have been

desperately upset and affected by it mentally or psychologically, at any rate. But no, it was on such a huge scale it was rather like trying to count the stars. There were thousands and thousands of dead bodies and you couldn't really relate to them as people … there were just too many.[9]

While the sickening task of burying the dead went on, 32CCS were converting the lavishly equipped barracks for use as a hospital. It was estimated that upwards of 15,000 beds would be required which were hurriedly made by 32CCS and the gunners. Some 750 beds a day had to be made, or requisitioned from local towns and villages. The plan of evacuation was simple. The very sick would be taken from Camp I to the newly established hospitals. The fitter inmates (those who could climb into a lorry unaided) were to be transferred to barrack accommodation in the Panzer school nearby where Camp II was established for men and Camp III for women. Once Camp I was emptied it would be burned. .

Medical officers from 11 LFA would enter each hut and, making no attempt at a diagnosis, decide who should be evacuated immediately and who could wait in the camp for a few more days before being moved: 'it was a heartbreaking job.'[10] Frederick Riches recalled that once the medical officers had indicated those who had been chosen for hospitalisation:

> We just went down, pointed out three people, out they came. There was no names, no nothing at all, just – we was sorry we couldn't get 'em all out at once. They were all putting their hands up, 'I'm next, I'm next'. They were shouting out, 'Take me, take me'. You went to the front and said, 'Right, you come out you, come out and you come out'. And that was it.[11]

Those selected for evacuation would be stripped, wrapped in clean blankets and taken by ambulance to what became known as the 'Human Laundry' established in the former barrack stables. Here there were 60 tables each staffed by two German Wehrmacht doctors and two German nurses under the command of the pathologist of 32CCS and the men of 7 Mobile Bacteriological Laboratory RAMC. The German medical staff, especially the nurses, were very truculent to begin with but their humanity and professionalism eventually prevailed: 'Those girls worked like slaves, they went down with typhus and they died but others took their place; they grew thin and they grew pale but they worked and they toiled from eight in the morning until six at night. They earned our respect.'[12]

At the 'Human Laundry' the inmates would be shaved, washed, dusted with DDT powder, wrapped in clean blankets and taken to a ward in the hospital in a 'clean' ambulance. Rigorous precautions were taken to ensure that there was no transmission of disease between the camp and the hospital. Inmates' clothing and the blankets in which they were wrapped for their journey were burned and the 'dirty' ambulances were regularly scrubbed out. Likewise those inmates transferred to Camps II and III were also thoroughly deloused. 63 officers and men from 11LFA were involved in this work and despite wearing protective clothing and being regularly sprayed with DDT, 22 of their number contracted typhus. The authorities hoped to begin the evacuation on 20 April but a day was lost after the Germans evacuating the barracks destroyed the water supply. On 21 April 320 inmates were moved to hospital. Evacuation to Camps II and III began on 24 April but only 23 people were transferred. On 25 April 515 were transferred to Camps II and III while 628 went to the hospital. From then until 9 May the evacuation continued at about the rate of 1,100 a day. Thereafter numbers declined. During this period the death rate steadily fell from 500 per day on liberation to 300 per day by the end of April. On 11 May the death rate fell below 100 for the first time.

While the evacuation was in progress, work continued in Camp I to alleviate conditions. 63 AT Regiment were relieved on 18 April by 113th Light Anti-Aircraft Regiment (Durham Light Infantry) Royal Artillery with 1575th Artillery Platoon RASC. Other medical units sent to the area included 76th Field Hygiene Section (Major F.R. Waldron RAMC), 9th General Hospital (Lieutenant-Colonel A.R. Oram RAMC) which arrived on 27 April, 163rd Field Ambulance (Lieutenant-Colonel M. Herford DSO RAMC) which arrived on 8 May, 35th CCS on 14 May and 29th British General Hospital on 19 May. The military relief effort was supplemented by civilian relief teams. The British Red Cross contributed six teams of helpers, while the Swedish Red Cross greatly relieved pressure in the camp by agreeing to take 6,000 inmates for treatment to Sweden.

As death and evacuation reduced the numbers in Camp I, so the British tried to alleviate the conditions for the thousands forced to remain there. As each hut was cleared of those going to the hospital or to Camps II and III, the huts were either burned, if their condition was too dreadful, or deloused and fitted out by the British troops, using the Hungarian guard battalion for labouring duties, with bunks, lighting and sanitation. These refitted huts would, in turn, also be burned as their occupants were transferred out of the camp.

Feeding the inmates was the chief problem. There were five cookhouses within the area of Camp I, each of which was made the responsibility of an RA officer or Warrant Officer. Messing strengths averaged 10,000 to each cookhouse with one serving 16,000 inmates. A central messing office was established in order to coordinate the food supply. Water and other services were speedily restored or improvised by the RASC Artillery Platoon working with the relevant RAMC units, using equipment requisitioned from the local area if necessary. But merely supplying food for the inmates was not enough since many of them were too sick to eat. In any case the rich food which made up the staple diet of the British soldier in 1945 would have killed many of them (and probably did) in the days immediately following liberation when generosity by British soldiers outweighed caution. To deal with the feeding problem two specialist teams arrived in Belsen, the first from the Medical Research Council under the control of Dr, later Dame, Janet Vaughan and a team from UNRRA led by Dr A.P. Meiklejohn, who later assumed responsibility for administering the special starvation diet. Both these teams had considerable experience in dealing with the starving, particularly as a result of coping with famines in India during the inter-war period, when a mixture consisting of dried milk, flour, sugar and molasses had been developed, known as Bengal Mixture.

Also included in Dr Meiklejohn's team were 96 medical students who were in their final clinical year at the various London medical schools. The students had been asked to volunteer for famine relief in Holland but were asked to go to Belsen at short notice where they arrived on 30 April and set to work in pairs in the huts in Camp I. Their tasks were twofold, first to help the Army in clearing out the accumulated filth from the huts, creosoting the floors, dusting them with DDT powder and generally making them fit for their occupants.

Secondly, and more important, they had to organise the feeding of those too sick to feed themselves and to ensure that the food was distributed equally and not taken by the fittest in each hut.

The students were in for a veritable baptism of fire. Dr I.R. Proctor remembers walking into his allocated hut, 'we walked into the hut, held our noses, walked round, walked out again, looked at each other and said "where do we start?"'[13] Dr Proctor's memories of that hut are typical of the conditions facing the medical students:

> It was full of the most emaciated people I have ever seen in my life. There was supposed to be a loo at the far end but they couldn't get up to go to it. It [the hut] was almost up to the top of one's boots in excreta. One just stumped about in it. People by now were too weak to use it [the lavatory] and were just lying there in their own faeces and urine which dripped down from one bunk to the next – quite appalling.[14]

Michael Coigley, a final year student from St Thomas's Hospital described their routine:

> We go there every day of the week and work from 8am till 6pm with one and a quarter hour break for lunch. I feel dead at the end of it. That is not the end though for we have a conference from 6.15 to 7.15 to check upon the chaos here ... Each one [of us] is in charge of a hut and it is his job to see that the inmates are properly fed.[15]

Feeding the inmates was now the main priority since 'anything else they'd either died from it already or were going to die from it very soon and one really couldn't do anything much about it'.[16] One of the five cookhouses in the camp was directed to produce nothing but the Bengal famine mixture but could not cope with the demand. Michael Hargrave, another of the medical students, was allocated to a hut which had been cleared of the very sick and had been fitted out by the RASC men with two latrines and rudimentary bunks each containing two people. Dr Hargrave's 'ward round' would constitute a nightmare for a modern physician. There were six rooms in the hut each containing 40 people: two rooms were full of active typhus cases, three of post-typhus convalescent cases and one room containing active Tuberculosis cases. During his first evening in the hut Hargrave acquired enough Bengal famine mixture together with some slabs of chocolate, Horlicks, Ovaltine, cocoa and biscuits which he scrounged from the Army. That evening each of the 240 people in the hut was able to receive one cup of a mixture of Horlicks, Ovaltine and cocoa, two cups of Bengal famine mixture, one biscuit and one square of chocolate.[17] The only medication available was opium for diarrhoea and aspirin for post-typhus ailments. Proper medical or surgical practice was impossible: Michael Hargrave remembers using a razor blade heated over a naked flame to open a breast abscess. No anaesthetics were available and the patient must have been in 'gross agony'.[18]

Problems soon arose with the distribution of the Bengal famine mixture. Many of the sick were too weak to swallow it. Intravenous transfusion was tried on a few occasions but the students found it nearly impossible to administer. The SS doctors had used injections of benzol or creosote to murder the inmates and the sight of an intravenous feeding kit sometimes produced hysterical reactions from the sick: 'you came in with a tube and a needle and they all thought they were going to be slaughtered'.[19]

Dr J.R. Dixey, one of the medical students, recalled another difficulty in distributing the Bengal Mixture:

> It was very nutritious, but it was also very sickly and sweet. And I have a tremendous recollection of three Czechoslovakian Jewish doctors who were reasonably well preserved – they were very thin and emaciated but very much 'on the ball'. And they said to us, 'Look, it's all very well giving us this mixture, we are East Europeans and sweet food does not come nicely to us because we eat sour things, and this sweet food is just revolting and what can you do?' ... But sadly, this Bengal mixture made them all sick and they rejected it.[20]

Overall the picture was not as bleak as painted by Dr Dixey. Dr Meiklejohn estimated that the Bengal mixture, though unpopular, was responsible for halving the death rate from starvation. Dr Meiklejohn paid tribute to the work of the medical students in organising their huts and administering the feeding programme: 'It was a joy to see the change which took place in the patients when they found themselves under proper ward conditions with adequate medical attention. There can be no doubt that the large majority of the patients in this Students' hospital owed their lives to this achievement.'[21]

On 19 May the last 421 inmates were evacuated from Camp I and on the same day there was only one recorded death in the camp. Problems abounded, however, including an increasing sick rate in Camps II and III where people originally deemed fit were now falling ill. However, the comprehensive medical services now at Belsen ensured that these new outbreaks were kept under control. On 21 May the last of the huts in Camp I was ceremonially burned down and with its destruction the first phase of the relief of Belsen came to an end.

Attention was now focused on the hospital area and on the inmates in Camps II and III who were categorised under the undignified acronym of DPs – Displaced Persons. The medical students were transferred to the hospital where the remaining 12,000 sick were housed. Most of them were assigned to the former officers' mess, known as the Roundhouse, which was being used for treating those still suffering from malnutrition. As the condition of the majority of the inmates improved new problems were emerging. When some of the fitter inmates recovered their strength, they began to engage in an orgy of destruction of German property: ' … they are making such an infernal mess of this camp, and all their destruction is so wanton as they destroy anything which is of no use to them at the present moment, irrespective of the fact that they might want it later, and they still live by the "law of the clutching hand"'.[22] Assaults on German nursing staff on the wards at night became common and British QAIMNS nursing sisters from the various military units were forbidden to do ward duty at night since their safety could not be guaranteed. Russian and Polish inmates were the chief troublemakers and an early decision to employ groups of Russian inmates as armed guards had to be revoked.

Newly-arrived British medical staff sometimes betrayed a lack of understanding of what had been achieved, an attitude that was highly irritating to those who had worked in the dreadful conditions in Camp I: 'Some Army nursing sisters and a Major from 29 British General Hospital had arrived and there were several blow-ups between the nursing sisters and our chaps – the sisters tried to order them around in their own wards and as we were still in charge they were told, none too politely, where to get off.'[23] The problems of discipline were solved with the gradual return of the inmates to their home countries. But the Jewish inmates, who were by far the largest single group in the camp, had no wish to return to their pre-war European countries. Instead they wished to settle in Palestine. Initially the British were reluctant to recognise the Jews as a separate 'ethnic' group, preferring to categorise them under their country of origin. This attitude was to change after vigorous lobbying by a committee set up on 18 April under the chairmanship of Josef Rosensaft.

The struggle of the Jewish internees in Belsen to reach Palestine lies outside the scope of this article. Suffice it to say that Belsen had to remain their home until it was finally possible for them to leave. Belsen acquired the unique status of a self-governing Jewish community within the British Zone of Germany with schools, hospitals, theatres and a police force set up in the camp. Relations with the British were not always smooth and this was bound to be the case since both sides had different priorities, yet Rosensaft admitted that the British 'did everything in their power, both materially and administratively, to help and to ease the physical suffering and mental anguish'.[24] The last internees did not leave Belsen until 6 September 1950.

The British units involved in the relief would also in time disperse to other duties in Germany or demobilisation in the UK. 11 Light Field Ambulance had to undergo a period of quarantine in Norway, its officers and men having worked in the most disease-ridden areas of the camp, before the unit could be redeployed. The medical students would return to the UK on 28 May, their place being taken by medical students from hospitals in Belgium. None would ever forget what they had seen in Belsen. A common theme running through their letters and diaries is a fear that their terrible experiences would not be believed by those at home. Michael Coigley wrote simply that, 'I would never have believed had I not seen this'.[25] Most moving of all is the concluding paragraph of a letter written on 20 May by Gunner George Walker of 113 LAA Regiment, who had seen conditions in the camp at their worst: 'This letter will read like fiction and will seem to be an exaggeration but I swear that as sure as there is a God in heaven that what I have told you is the Gospel truth'.[26]

The achievement of the British Army in the liberation of Belsen was remarkable. Perhaps the last word should be left to Dr Hadassa Bimko-Rosensaft, an internee doctor at Belsen: 'The work of the doctors and nurses who came to us from the British Army and from voluntary organisations will for ever remain a ray of sunlight in those dark and tragic days. They may have the satisfaction of knowing that those who recovered are everlastingly grateful for the humane service rendered them so generously'.[27]

A Note on Typhus

The greatest problem confronting the British at Belsen was the treatment of typhus which was widespread throughout the camp. Some notes on the disease and its treatment may therefore be useful.

Typhus is caused by an organism of a particular class named the Rickettsiae, smaller than bacteria but larger than viruses. The Rickettsiae are carried in insects, the louse being a particular favourite, until they attack the human victim. Rickettsial infections are acute with a very high degree of mortality.

In Europe typhus manifests itself in two forms: Murine and Epidemic or 'Fleck' Typhus. It was the latter, caused by the Rickettsiae Prowazekkii which was the scourge of Belsen. It is spread in a cycle: an infected louse will settle on a person and bite. The wound is then contaminated with louse faeces which are laden with the Rickettsiae Prowazekkii, leading to infection. The cycle of the disease is completed when the louse picks up the Rickettsiae Prowazekkii from the blood of infected people. Thus a cycle of man-louse-man is established.

The main symptoms in man are skin rashes (hence the name of 'Fleck' Typhus), followed by fever, acute headache and pain in the joints, renal failure, blockage of small blood vessels leading to gangrene and reduced resistance to other illness such as pneumonia. The invasion of the Rickettsiae Prowazekkii into the central nervous system produces a peculiar agitation followed by delirium while a falling blood pressure and increasing pulse indicate that the disease has reached the circulatory system. In this state a terrible death, accompanied by convulsions and agonal screaming, follows within 24 hours. In an uncontrolled state Epidemic Typhus has a mortality rate of at least 60 per cent.

Treatment of the disease in 1945 was by prevention and immunisation. Immunisation (injections of dead Rickettsiae Prowazekkii give immunity against typhus) was out of the question given the scale of the problem at Belsen so the effort was concentrated on prevention. Vector (that is, louse) control was of paramount importance in preventing the disease. High standards of personal hygiene and use of insecticides such as DDT can eradicate body lice. The control of dust carrying the infected louse faeces was also important: hence the traffic restrictions around the camp.

What happened in Belsen, and in all the other liberated concentration camps, was the last major epidemic of typhus in human history. When broad spectrum antibiotic drugs like Chloramphenicol and Tetracycline appeared in the late 1940s typhus suddenly became a minor nuisance rather than a lethal, large-scale scourge.

FURTHER READING

Caiger-Smith, M. (ed.), *The Face of the Enemy: British Photographers in Germany, 1944–45* (London: Dirk Nishen Publishing, 1988).

Crew, F.A.E., 'Medical History of the Second World War', *Army Medical Services, Campaigns Vol IV, North West Europe* (London: HMSO, 1962).

Donnison, F.S.V., *Civil Affairs and Military Government in North West Europe 1944–46* (London: HMSO, 1961).

Feig, Konilyn, *Hitler's Death Camps* (New York: Holmes & Meier Publishers, 1979).

Kolb, Eberhard, *Bergen-Belsen, Geschichte des Aufenthaltslagers 1943–45* (Hanover: Verlag für Literatur und Zeitgeschehen, 1962).

Kolb, Eberhard, *Bergen-Belsen: From Detention Camp to Concentration Camp* (Niedersächsische Landeszentrale für politische Bildung: Sammlung Vandenhoeck, 1985).

Leivick, H. *et al., Belsen* (Tel Aviv: Irgun Sheerit Hapleita Me'haezor Habriti, 1957).

McBride, Brenda, *Quiet Heroines, Nurses of the Second World War* (London: Chatto & Windus, 1985).

McLaughlin, R., *The Royal Army Medical Corps* (London: Leo Cooper, 1972).

Juliet Piggott, *Queen Alexandra's Royal Army Nursing Corps* (London: Leo Cooper, 1975).

NOTES

1. See Major W.R. Williams, RASC, TS account, Imperial War Museum (IWM), Department of Documents. Also see the eye-witness testimony section in this volume for Major Williams' account of his first reconnaissance into Belsen.

2. War Diary of 63 AT Regiment RA, Appendix 1, PRO WO 171/4773.
3. War Diary of DDMS 8 Corps, 15 April 1945. PRO WO171/343.
4. TS Lecture by Lt. Col. M.W. Gonin., RAMC, IWM Dept.of Documents 85/38/1.
5. Sgt. W Lawrie, interview, 1984, IWM Dept. of Sound Records, 7481/3.
6. Gonin, op. cit.
7. W.R.F. Collins, MD, FRCP, FRCPI, DPH, 'Belsen Camp – A Preliminary Report', *British Medical Journal*, 9 June 1945, pp.814–16.
8. Private Frederick Riches interview, 1987, IWM Dept. of Sound Records, 009937/03.
9. Dr J.R. Dixey, MB, Bchir, FRCGP, interview, IWM Dept. of Sound Records, 008936/02.
10. Gonin, op. cit.
11. Riches interview, op. cit.
12. Gonin, op. cit.
13. Dr I.R. Proctor interview, 1986, IWM Dept. of Sound Records, 9309/2.
14. Proctor, op. cit.
15. Dr Michael Coigley, IWM Dept. of Documents, MISC 89 Item 880.
16. Proctor, op. cit.
17. Dr Michael Hargrave, TS account, IWM Dept. of Documents.
18. Hargrave, op. cit.
19. Dixey, op. cit.
20. Dixey op. cit.
21. 'The Medical Students at Belsen', *British Medical Journal,* 23 June 1945, pp.883–4.
22. Hargrave, op. cit.
23. Ibid.
24. H. Leivick *et al.*, *Belsen* (Tel Aviv: Irgun Sheerit Hapleita Me'haezor Habriti, 1957), p.31.
25. Coigley, op. cit.
26. Gunner G. Walker, letter, 20 May 1945, IWM Dept. of Documents, 94/2/1.
27. Leivick, *Belsen*, p108.

Cleaner, Carer and Occasional Dance Partner? Writing Women Back into the Liberation of Bergen-Belsen

JO REILLY

This contribution seeks to redress an imbalance which exists in our common perception of the liberation of Belsen. When we think of the liberation we do not usually associate it with women. Indeed, popular images suggest that women did not play a significant role in the relief effort at all. Amongst the many reels of photographs and film shot by the British Army and newsreel camera crews, only a handful of images inform our collective memory of the months which followed 15 April 1945. Most dwell on the victims of Belsen, and the conditions they were enforced to endure, but many also document the ways in which the British Army attempted to relieve the situation. The cameras followed the men of the Royal Artillery as they forced the SS guards at gun point to bury the thousands of corpses which lay around the camp. They documented the men of the Field Ambulance unit who worked untiringly stretchering people out of the filthy huts of Camp I to the waiting ambulances.

Image after image depicts the soldier in uniform as liberator, against the stark backdrop of Belsen, the shame of the German nation. These images are found repeated again and again in modern representations of the Belsen camp, and they are used frequently in film documentary and television presentations dealing with the Holocaust period. The same images form a large part of the Belsen exhibition on display at the Imperial War Museum and the accompanying publication uses them extensively. In that 32-page booklet, titled *The Relief of Belsen*, only one female relief worker, who may or may not be British, is portrayed.[1] Yet women were involved and indeed played a crucial role in the liberation period. This article seeks to establish the nature of this role, to examine the way in which their role was perceived by their male colleagues and also attempts to explain why they are so overtly missing from, the admittedly limited, historiography on the subject.

As is stated by Paul Kemp in this volume, in the first phase of the liberation period, the military, in addition to adjusting to their new role and circumstances, were concerned primarily with the practical matters of establishing food and water supplies to the camp, and with burying the dead. From the end of April and throughout May, Camp I was slowly evacuated and on 21 May the typhus-ridden huts were burned down. Meanwhile an extensive hospital area had been established in the grounds of the nearby German Panzer Training School and further medical staff and volunteer helpers were continuously drafted in. Gradual but heartening improvements were visible around the new camp, both in terms of the facilities available and the physical condition of the internees. Slowly increasing in strength and morale, they were able to communicate better their needs and also articulate some of what had been their experience under the Nazi regime. The experience of the British personnel working in the hospital camp was thus different to that of the original liberators. The first combatant troops who entered Belsen faced an impossible situation: a mass of emaciated indistinguishable forms who, it seemed, would never physically and mentally recover from the degraded state to which they had been reduced. The medical staff, however, who went on to treat the sick in subsequent months, experienced far more personal contact with the internees and were able to witness the positive results of their actions.[2]

It is difficult for us, from the perspective of the 1990s, to appreciate just how long the first stage of the relief process lasted. With the war still going on, not nearly sufficient units could be deployed to the Belsen camp. Vital medical teams were still advancing as late as six weeks after the British arrived in the camp. Until the arrival of 96 medical students from the London teaching hospitals at the end of April and beginning of May, only a small number of British personnel had been inside the huts in Camp I and the patients had not received any direct medical care.[3]

A decision was taken early by the military authorities that the women amongst the liberating forces should not be admitted to the main camp.[4] Hence in the first weeks the women working in Belsen were employed in preparing those buildings in the Panzer Training School, known as Camp II, which were to make a hospital area. As the relief operation got properly under way, and more units were directed to Belsen, so the number of women amongst the liberators in the camp increased. At an early stage, various teams of voluntary relief workers were on the scene. These included the British Red Cross, a Girl Guide team and a party from the Friends Relief Society. With the Quaker team was Jane Levy, notable for being the first British Jewish relief worker in the camp (by two months), giving a great psychological boost to her co-religionist internees.[5]

By 3 May the first 7,000 beds had been prepared. After the arrival of the British General Hospital units and a second Casualty Clearing Station, the hospital had been expanded to 14,000 beds by 19 May. The first 320 patients from Camp I were evacuated on 21 April. Other nurses and relief workers were directed into this area on their arrival at the camp.[6]

The working conditions in the Belsen hospitals were gruelling from the start, even before the patients arrived. Preparing a former banqueting hall, recreation rooms and even the beer cellars for the arrival of thousands of sick patients was no easy task. The eight QA's of 32 Casualty Clearing Station had to supervise the stripping and cleaning of rooms, which were to act as wards, and to organise a catering system. Their work included the distribution of food and clothing to former internees who were not hospital cases but were also accommodated in the barracks of the Panzer School. Perhaps one of the most difficult tasks was that allocated to the Red Cross sister who had to set up a registry of patients in Camp II – this involved dealing with 22 different nationalities.[7]

When the patients were evacuated from Camp I they were taken first to the 'Human Laundry'. There German nurses, seconded from a German military hospital nearby, waited to wash them down, dust them with DDT powder and wrap them in clean blankets. They were then transferred to the hospital. Needless to say the hospital wards never approached the exacting sterile standards usually demanded by the medical profession. Indeed, newly arrived British nurses, who had not witnessed the chaos of the Belsen camp immediately following the liberation, were often horrified at the conditions in the wards. They found it difficult to believe that what they were now witnessing represented a marked improvement.[8]

One nurse remembers:

> I was detailed to find square 10, block 61, in an enormous compound ... every building was the same, dull looking, of grey stone with small windows ... passing through the door of block 61, I was astonished to hear the sound of hundreds of tongues; and the dreadful smell, only to be associated with Belsen, was indescribable ... There was not an open window, the floor was filthy, straw littered with human excreta. Thousands of flies were recreating the typhus circle, by settling on broken plates which held pieces of black bread, turnip tops and sour milk ... no one had been able to compile a register of patients ... Many [of the patients] had forgotten their identity. However, with Nurse, I visited the human remains lying in the straw palliases, covered with filthy blankets. At first glance we were unable to define their sex. Several were lying on top of their blankets, their heads shorn. The agony of their suffering showing clearly in their expression, with eyes sunken and listless, cheekbones prominent, too weak to close their mouths, with arms extended in an appealing manner ... with the aid of a British medical officer every patient was examined. 90% were found to have TB in addition to other specific fevers and post-typhus conditions ... .[9]

The nursing staff were faced with a range of illness from typhus and tuberculosis to gangrene and various forms of skin disease. The majority of patients – probably 80 per cent – were suffering from diarrhoea and most were confined to their beds. A visitor to the hospital on 24 May, six weeks after the take-over of the camp, was also struck by the nauseous smell of the large wards. The patients, she wrote, 'mostly lie motionless in their beds, gazing into space and occasionally whimpering like an animal. One can hardly believe that human beings reduced to such an emaciated condition can live. There is of course no privacy of any sort and no attempt to screen off those who are dying'.[10] The high death rate in the hospital was difficult to cope with. One of the most dreadful tasks the nurses had to face every morning was to try to identify and remove the night's fatalities.

The routine reminded one nurse of the terrible childhood stories told to her of the Black Death in the Middle Ages and the ringing, daily cries of 'Bring Out Your Dead!'[11]

The acute shortage of staff and even the most basic equipment such as bed-pans, meant that there was only a limited amount the staff could do for the patients. They concentrated on administering a suitable recovery diet and simple treatments and tried as far as possible to make the patients comfortable. A hospital block of 150 beds was supervised by one army sister and perhaps two British, and later Belgian, medical students. There would also be one or two ex-internee nursing staff to do the day duty and some German nurses, drafted from the towns nearby, to cover night duty. There was generally just one doctor to each square of five blocks. Staff from the Red Cross teams who had volunteered as drivers or welfare workers, and had never worked in a hospital before, found themselves running wards of 50 beds containing typhus patients. Often this small staff created as much work again as they were able to complete. It had been hoped originally that the internee nurses would be able to work in the wards unsupervised but this proved impossible. They too had been through the camp system and had many of the same mental scars as their patients. They were prone to apathy and it was not unknown for them to take food from their patients. On the whole the German nurses were seen to be professional and motivated and so gained the respect of their British colleagues. Their presence also helped to break down language barriers and they were of particular value in explaining the use and dosage of the German drugs. The scarcity of British nursing staff meant that the authorities gave little thought to the negative feelings that the patients might have to being treated by German nurses. Some patients did in fact display their resentment and revelled in openly humiliating the women. In one recorded incident, a group of Russian women stole the German nurses' uniforms, attacked them while they were sleeping and succeeded in shaving the hair off a number of them.[12]

In the words of Annig Pfirter, a member of the Red Cross, life in the hospital centre was quite different from anything anyone had ever experienced. 'It seemed to us sometimes that we were living on another planet; we had in fact to forget all our habits, our ideas of tidiness, cleanliness, moral considerations and human dignity in order to try to comprehend our patients psychological and mental state.'[13] In truth, of course, even the most experienced doctors in Belsen had no experience of dealing with concentration camp victims, people whose lives had been torn apart through the implementation of a vicious, all-embracing racial policy; people whose physical and mental health had been most cruelly eroded. There were very few doctors there who had any psychiatric training. The situation demanded hundreds of such trained people, but in reality the nursing staff had to deal with their patients as best they could.[14] Psychological trauma manifested itself in many different ways. The medical staff, for example, learned a painful lesson about the nature of Nazi camps when some patients reacted hysterically to the sight of a syringe or a needle. For many of the internees a preoccupation with food overrode all other interests and hoarding was common. The nurses would find slices of bread and meat under a patient's pillow, sacks of stolen potatoes under their beds, and on one memorable occasion even half of a small calf. Further, as the patients regained their strength they often became restless, impatient and difficult to manage. Many felt indignant at the restrictions the hospital imposed and took to wandering about at night, stealing food and raiding locked stores.[15]

Yet how were the nurses to react when patient after patient attempted to unburden their painful stories? On one occasion documented by Pfirter, a nurse asked a patient to state her name, nationality and place of birth. In reply, the woman managed only to pull up the sleeve of her night-gown, exposing the Auschwitz tattoo on her arm, and stammer, 'me ... no name – only number – no country, just a Jewess, do you understand? I am only a dog. How I wish I were like you – a human being'. Naturally, such pitiful words left the nurse shaken – 'the unfortunate woman's eyes seemed to reflect the multitude of nameless people who could no longer believe they were human beings'. Indeed, the language barrier was a hindrance everywhere in Belsen but particularly when a patient needed to tell her story and explain her traumatic experiences. Somehow the nursing staff managed to interpret the descriptions. To quote Pfirter again: 'the past came back so vividly that we were able, from their gestures and the expressions on their faces, to understand what they were trying to tell us'.[16]

Not all the wards were quite so dispiriting. The children's block, run by Robert Collis, a volunteer with the Red Cross, was said to be the happiest in the camp.[17] Although many were still poorly, the younger children in particular soon laughed and smiled and seemed to show none of the terror symptoms so evident in the adults in Belsen. For similar reasons Eva Kahn-Minden felt lucky to have started her work as a nurse in Belsen in the maternity ward. There at least the internees began to show signs of caring again, investing their energy and placing their hopes for the future in their new born babies. Not that the work here was any easier. Many of the babies, described by one onlooker as the 'most pathetic objects it has ever been my misfortune to see', were born to mothers who had typhus and not surprisingly some were lost. The few babies who had been born before the liberation were in a pitiful state. The sister in charge of the maternity block related that because the babies had not been washed since birth, when she had undressed the poor mites to bathe them, their skin had come away with the clothes.[18]

It is certain that the women in this block particularly appreciated the presence of female nurses in whom they could confide. Eva Kahn-Minden was given a gold locket, probably held to be very precious, by one of the new mothers who told her: 'I want you to have it because you have listened to me when I unburdened myself for the first time about the worst period of my life. Since that talk I feel free and am now happy to be going home with my baby.'[19]

As these few example show, women were certainly present during the liberation of Belsen and clearly fulfilled a crucial role in the relief process. Yet they are largely missing from the historiography relating to the camp. I would like to turn now to the issue of why this might be the case.

There is of course nothing new about he exclusion of women from war narratives. As noted by one First World War historian, the spectacular service of the many women doctors and nurses who did so much to alleviate suffering in the front line hospitals remains little known and barely acknowledged.[20] Women are integrated so rarely in official wartime documentation and, as a consequence, the depiction of women in war is often removed from reality. Marion Korzak, reviewing a 1970s exhibition, 'Women at War – A Celebration' in the Imperial War Museum, directed her criticism at the fact that the

depiction of women in the contemporary propaganda posters –
'Smiling faces, jaunty girls, uniformed, spruce, brave nurses' – was
rarely challenged in the exhibits chosen. Patronising praise was given
in the exhibition and the word 'sacrifice' glibly used but the actual
results of women's war effort did not emerge.[21]

By the end of the Second World War there were nearly half a
million women in the Forces. Many were exposed to considerable
dangers but perhaps none more than the nurses in the combat zones.
In 1943 they were granted wartime commissions and wore the
insignia of a military rank (although they had the rank of an officer,
they did not receive an officer's salary). Yet no matter how their
presence was appreciated by the individuals they nursed or by
colleagues on the ground, their perceived role in the general scheme
of the war was summed up neatly at a briefing conference given by
general Montgomery: 'The most important people in the army are
the Nursing Sisters and the Padres – the sisters because they tell the
men they matter to us – and the Padres because they tell the men they
matter to God – and it is the men who matter.'[22] In Belsen the army
nursing staff mattered to the relief operation; nowhere more than in
the easing of suffering in the concentration camps of Germany did
women establish their ability to equal their male colleagues.

In her *Women Workers in the First World War*, Gail Brayburn
demonstrates skilfully the consistency of male attitudes towards
women's work, even in the exceptional time of war. Her study
concentrates on women on the home front and refutes the commonly
held view that the demand for women's labour during the First World
War led to a fundamental change in opinions on women's position
and role in society. Brayburn argues that, ' ... women's work, and
men's attitudes towards women, should not be seen in isolation. The
four years of war cannot be separated from the rest of history, and
women's work cannot be detached from the broader issues
concerning work roles [and] sexual stereotyping ... .'[23]

Penny Summerfield explores similar issues in relation to the
Second World War and challenges the standard interpretation,
advocated, for example, by Arthur Marwick, of the role of the war in
the social history of women. In the spheres Summerfield examined,
namely domestic work and paid employment on the home front, she
found that in spite of the 'challenge and expectation of change'

during the war, there was in fact a considerable amount of continuity with 'pre-war attitudes and practices' towards women.[24] The same consistency of male attitudes to women's work, it is argued here, can be identified in examining women's work in Belsen. It might be imagined that under the extreme circumstances that post-liberation Belsen presented, traditional gender roles would have broken down, that the tremendous urgency of the situation, the lack of personnel, the shock, the determination to save lives, would in some way have led to a blurring of the customary male/female ascribed functions. In fact, traditional roles were maintained in the relief of Belsen, if not further entrenched. The crisis situation led to a reinforcing of subconscious, gendered behaviour patterns. In such a military environment, where power was resolutely in male hands, the demarcation of established work roles and sexual stereotyping was firm.

It was ruled by Army officials that the conditions in Camp I were so terrible that women should not be permitted entry at all: hence the absence of women from the main liberation photographs. This decision reflects the paternalism of the time and was clearly motivated by a desire to protect the sensibilities of the women who could not, it was assumed, withstand such horror. The imperative towards protection was probably nowhere stronger in British society than amongst the class that produced Army officers. It seems, for example, that a senior nursing sister with vast experience, including battles across Normandy and Holland, was in some way deemed less suitable to work in the camp than a 21-year old man not yet out of University.[25] It was probable that the majority of women working in Belsen were extremely grateful not to have to work inside Camp I. Yet one cannot escape the feeling that the reason for totally excluding them was not only to do with offending sensibilities but also with the expectations of the female capacity to cope professionally with the situation.

In Belsen after the liberation, the women's role, whether internee or personnel, was viewed as cleaner, carer, and occasional dance partner in the officer's mess.[26] When Camp I was evacuated, the first to be moved were women who were fit 'and suitable for employment in the laundry and cookhouses' in Camp II. Internee 'seamstresses' were put to work on producing hundreds of standard Belsen nightgowns for the sick. Similarly, when an officer wanted to use the SS guards to scrub out several huts in Camp I he chose six female guards. These women, however, were taken away after a few days by a superior officer who believed it most undignified for an officer and a gentleman to make women work in such a way.[27]

The nature of women's work in the camp was arduous, emotionally draining and crucial. Yet, because it was confined to the hospital sphere, to the traditional female arena of caring, like so much of women's work it is 'lost', taken for granted and deemed not worthy of special mention or credit. Certainly, the involvement in the Belsen relief operation of so many women received very little acknowledgement from the predominantly male official report and dispatch writers.

In 1945, two officers from the Royal Army Medical Corps felt it necessary to write to the *British Medical Journal* in order to right an imbalance they felt was present in the coverage of the medical aspects of the liberation of Belsen. Major Hilda Roberts and Captain Petronella Potter observed: 'In the recent literature on what had been done in Belsen Camp, reference has been made to the excellent work of medical students, research teams, civilian workers and combatant units, but so far no mention had been made of the work of the Army nursing sisters.' Describing the conditions under which the nurses worked, they reminded their colleagues that the Army sisters 'showed a willingness and initiative that deserves the highest praise' and that they too 'came to Belsen immediately following a hectic and gruelling time dealing with casualties of the Rhine crossing, and at the end of nearly a year's service with the BLA [British Liberation Army]'.[28]

The liberation is not a period which has been studied extensively by scholars. Holocaust historians have tended to view the liberation as a neat ending, a tying up point for the Holocaust. As a consequence, they have chosen not to dwell on the details of the relief operation or the impact on the people involved. Rather, the liberation of the camps has become a part of the military history of the Second World War, a discipline notoriously dominated by male historians and not a context in which one would expect to find discussions of female work roles. In recent years a significant body of academic work has been undertaken to document women's participation in the war effort generally, but crucially, women remain absent from the military history of the Second World War, included, if at all, as a token addendum. The role of women in the war has been marginalised into specialist volumes. Thus, for example, we have Brenda McBride's *Quiet Heroines, Nurses of the Second World War* and Juliet Piggot's work on the Queen Alexandra's Royal Army Nursing Corps.[29] Both of these texts are keen to highlight the liberation of Belsen as an important episode in the work of the British Army nursing sisters and yet neither are able to draw on a great deal of eyewitness testimony; the Piggot book, in particular, relies entirely on official army records.

The fact is that there are very few written accounts from Belsen by women in the public domain. This could be for one of two reasons: either because women did not write about their experiences or because the documentary holding centres have not attempted to correct biases in their collections. Both explanations are probably valid. At the time of writing, in the growing collection of documentary and oral evidence from liberators in the Imperial War Museum, there are only three contributions from women: one letter, one diary and a longer document detailing the experience of an UNRRA worker.

Of the contributions by men, many of the longer testimonies and diaries, which do not fall into the category of official war documents, are those written by some of the 96 medical students for whom Belsen was a singular wartime experience outside London. They were young and held a unique position within the camp and perhaps felt more inclined to record the episode on paper. It could be argued that for the nursing staff, in contrast, the work in Belsen was a continuation of their war service. The location was new and conditions were the worst they had ever seen; nevertheless, there was some sense of continuity in their rountine and perhaps for this reason they did not feel the necessity to write down their thoughts. This may be a partial explanation. It is difficult, however, to believe that it is the sole reason why a dearth of womens' testimony exists in the public domain. One must presume that some diaries and letters were written by women in the camp and that some still exist; the onus must be on curators to track them down. If anything, the differential in the weight of testimony produced by men and women has widened over the past 50 years. The same officers who were in a position to write official reports during the weeks after the liberation, are those who later in life are most likely to produce memoirs of their wartime experiences, reinforcing the accepted history and distorting further the already heavily-gender-biased memory of Belsen's liberation.

NOTES

1. Imperial War Museum (IWM), *The Relief of Belsen, April 1945: Eyewitness Accounts* (London: IWM, 1991).
2. For a general description of the camp and the early relief efforts see, for example: Derrick Sington, *Belsen Uncovered* (London: Duckworth, 1946); Paul Kemp, 'The Liberation of Bergen-Belsen Concentration camp in April 1945: The Testimony of those involved', *Imperial War Museum Review, No. 5*, 1990. Other sources are cited in Joanne Reilly, 'Britain and Belsen', Ph.D thesis, Southampton University, 1994, Ch.1.
3. See E.E. Vella, 'Belsen: Medical Aspects of a World War II Concentration Camp', *Journal of the Royal Army Medical Corps* (1984), No.130, pp.34–59; Reilly, 'Britain and Belsen', Ch.1.
4. R. Wilson, *Quaker Relief. An Account of the Relief Work of the Society of Friends 1940-48* (London, 1952), p.222; J. Greenwood, *Quaker Encounters* (York: Sessions, 1975), p.319; *The Times*, 16 May 1945; See IWM, Department of Sound Records 11540/2: Hughes, reel 1: by the time he had arrived in Belsen in May 1945 'things were more civilised and we were able to have British nurses'.
5. Wilson, *Quaker Relief*, p.227; Brenda McBryde, *Quiet Heroines. Nurses of the Second World War* (London: Chatto & Windus, 1985), p.182; W.R.J. Collis, 'Belsen Camp. A Preliminary Report', *British Medical Journal*, 9 June 1945, p.814.
6. Public Record Office (PRO) War Office (WO) 177/849: War Diary 11th Light Field Ambulance; Kemp, 'The Liberation of Belsen'.
7. McBryde, *Quiet Heroines,* p.182.
8. IWM, Department of Documents 76/74/1: Michael Hargrave, 26 May 1945.
9. Report of a QR Nursing Sister quoted in Ian Hay, *One Hundred Years of Army Nursing* (London: Cassell, 1953), pp.329–30.
10. CMAC RAMC 1218/2/18: Pfirter.
11. McBryde, *Quiet Heroines*, p.184.
12. Ibid.
13. Wellcome Institute Archive, CMAC RAMC 1218/2/18: Annig Pfirter, 'Memories of a Red Cross Mission'; see the comments by a Belsen nurse in *The Times*, 16 May 1945.
14. Initially only one Psychological Warfare team was directed to Belsen but even this was removed before the evacuation of Camp I got under way: PRO WO 171/4604: 10 Garrison HQ War Diary, Report on Belsen 18–30 April; Major R.J. Phillips, Advisor in Psychiatry to Second Army visited the camp: CMAC RAMC 1218/2/14: letter, Phillips to Glyn Hughes, 31 May 1945.
15. McBryde, *Quiet Heroines*, p.184; CMAC RAMC 1218/2/18: Pfirter; Eva Kahn-Minden, *The Road Back. Quare Mead* (Jerusalem: Gefen, 1991), p.8.
16. CMAC RAMC 1218/2/18: Pfirter.
17. See Robert Collis and H. Hogerzeil, *Straight On (Journey to Belsen and The Road Home)* (London: Methuen, 1947) and also Robert Collis, *To Be a Pilgrim* (London, 1975), *passim*.
18. Hay, *One Hundred Years,* 331; Collis and Hogerzeil, *Straight On,* p.61.
19. Kahn-Minden, *The Road Back*, p.11.

20. See Monica Krippner, *The Quality of Mercy: Women at War, Serbia 1915–18* (Newton Abbot: David & Charles, 1980).
21. Marion Kozak, 'Report Back: "Women At War – A Celebration"', *History Workshop*, No.4 (Autumn 1977), pp.239–40.
22. In J. Smyth, *The Will to Live: The Story of Dame Margot Turner* (London: Cassell, 1970), p.xxi.
23. Gail Brayburn, *Women Workers in the First World War* (London: Croom Helm, 1981), pp.31, 232.
24. Penny Summerfield, *Women Workers in the Second World War* (London: Croom Helm, 1984), p.1; see Arthur Marwick, *Britain in the Century of Total War* (London, 1968).
25. See poem by Joy Trindles, 'Until Belsen', in V. Selwyn (ed.), *More Poems of the Second World War* (London, 1989). Also comments by Maureen Gara on her part in the Normandy Landings: 'it was dust, dirt, blood and mud' in 'Angels of D-Day', *Outlook*, April/May 1994, p.25; Eric Taylor, *Women Who Went to War* (London, 1988), pp.206–9.
26. See IWM, Department of Sound Records 8924/1: Trimmer and IWM, Department of Documents 86/7/1: Bradford, 23 May 1945 on 'Coconut Grove', the improvised dance hall set up in the camp by the forces.
27. PRO WO 171/4604: 10 Garrison report, 18–30 April, App.E; J. Hankinson, 'Belsen', *St Mary's Hospital Gazette* (1945), No.51, p.76; Leslie Hardman, *The Survivors* (London: Vallentine, Mitchell, 1958), pp.35–6 and interview with the author.
28. *British Medical Journal* (1945), No.21, p.100.
29. Juliet Piggot, *Queen Alexandra's Royal Army Nursing Corps* (London: Leo Cooper, 1975).

A Community of Survivors: Bergen-Belsen as a Jewish Centre after 1945

HAGIT LAVSKY

Introduction

After liberation, Bergen-Belsen, a symbol of the Nazi regime's satanic evil, was quickly transformed into the central Jewish Displaced Person's (DP) camp in the British Occupation Zone. Its name has become synonymous with the struggle for survival, rehabilitation and national Jewish pride. In the years following the war Bergen-Belsen played a special role for Jews in the British Zone. Life in the camp became a model of sorts for the whole region. Its organisational system formed the nucleus of all political, social and cultural activity and its leaders strove to create a united body to represent all Jews in the British Zone, including the DPs in the camps and assembly centres and the Jewish communities which sprang up after the war. The Bergen-Belsen leadership also shaped the Zionist outlook of this body and lent it a decisive, even militant character.

In the following analysis an attempt is made to explain how Bergen-Belsen became a Jewish centre, and to illustrate some of its special features.

Bergen-Belsen as the Main Concentration of Jews in the British Occupation Zone

Bergen-Belsen was the largest concentration camp liberated in Germany, and it became the largest Jewish DP camp, holding most of

This contribution is part of an ongoing research project conducted by the author as the incumbant of the Samuel L. Haber Lectureship for She'erit Hapleta, at the Avraham Harman Institute of Contemporary Jewry, The Hebrew University of Jerusalem.

the Jewish survivors in the British Occupation Zone in north-west Germany. Bergen-Belsen had received the majority of transfers from the eastern occupied territories and from the forced labour camps in Germany. These were people who had survived the death marches, though only a few of them stayed alive in the horrible conditions prevailing in the camp in the last phase of the war.[1] In addition there were numerous forced labour camps in the area, especially in Hannover and Neuengamme, which had supplied workers for the ammunition industry. There were many Jews in these camps too – although there is no reliable estimate of how many of them survived to be liberated in or near Belsen.[2]

Despite the absence of statistical data, it is estimated that upon liberation more than half of the 60,000 survivors of Bergen-Belsen were Jews. After a few weeks, when the transfer of the survivors to a former German military camp nearby took place, numbers had been cut by approximately half. The massive death toll was the main factor. About 14,000 died during the first few weeks, most of them apparently Jews. Thousands were sent to Sweden to recuperate from their illness, and an estimated 17,000 were repatriated to Holland, France, Belgium, Czechoslovakia, Yugoslavia, Hungary and Romania. Thus, the population of the camp was much smaller, but the proportion of Jews had grown substantially because the repatriations had involved mainly non-Jews. By the beginning of June, some 12,000 Jews remained in Bergen-Belsen, comprising about two-thirds of the camp population.[3] There was also a constant influx of newcomers, as the large concentration of Jews in Bergen-Belsen attracted survivors from small camps in the British Zone. This inward flow exceeded the number of forced and voluntary departures, further strengthening the Jewish component. Indeed, in the following months the number of Jews rose to the point where the camp was almost entirely Jewish, with only a small minority of non-Jews.[4]

This process also affected overall Jewish demographics in the British Occupation Zone. When the situation became more stable and the number of Jews there declined to 20,000, Belsen's 10,000–12,000 DPs comprised more than half the Jewish population of the Zone. As for the others, between 4,000 and 5,000 were German Jews in the newly established communities of Hamburg, Cologne, Duesseldorf and Hannover and the rest were scattered in small camps or assembly centres near or in towns such as Lingen, Lueneburg, Diepholz, Neustadt, Luebeck, Celle, Kaunitz, Hanover, Hamburg and Brunswick.[5]

These figures remained relatively stable throughout Belsen's existence, despite the growing influx of refugees from eastern Europe, mainly Polish Jews repatriated from the Soviet Union. The number of Polish Jews fleeing to Austria, Germany and Italy reached a peak in the summer of 1946 after the infamous pogrom at Kielce (4 July). By the summer of 1947, when the Polish Jews were joined by the Hungarian and Romanian Jewish refugees, there were nearly 185,000 Jewish DPs in Germany alone. However, most of them were absorbed into the American zone,[6] and the British zone was hardly affected. This was due to the British policy which, unlike that of the Americans, restricted and then barred the entry of refugees into the British Zone while encouraging emigration to the United States, and from 1947, to Palestine (via 'Operation Grand National').[7]

The demographic stability in the British Zone with its relatively small and unchanging Jewish population, allowed Belsen to keep its position as the largest concentration of Jews in Germany.

Socio-Demographic Composition

The numerical stability in Bergen-Belsen also affected the socio-demographic character of its Jewish population, which was unique from the outset. Due to the camp's function as the recipient of prisoners from death and forced labour camps until the very last moment before liberation, its composition was not typical of most *She'erit Hapleta* – the surviving remnant. There was an exceptionally high ratio of women; and of youngsters and children – about 500, who apparently were brought there just before liberation, from Buchenwald and Theresienstadt.[8] Most of the Jewish inmates were of Polish origin, who had declined to return to the graveyard of their people and families; those who did so, soon came back. There was also a large group of Hungarian Jews who had survived Auschwitz, about 3,000 souls, who constituted at least one-quarter of the camp's Jewish population. Most of the Hungarian Jews were Orthodox, and together with some Polish Orthodox formed a strong Agudah representation in the camp.[9]

With the addition of a small number of refugees who managed to enter Bergen-Belsen despite British policy, this population mix contributed to a firm and healthy socio-demographic profile. Stability did not imply stagnation. On the contrary, there was a natural process of growth. Most of the survivors were young men and women who had lost all their relatives. Thus the drive to re-establish families was naturally very strong. Many weddings took place during the first months after liberation, as well as a significant number of births. By the end of 1947, 1,000 children had been born in Bergen-Belsen.[10]

To sum up, the presence of young people and children right from the beginning, the stability not only in terms of numbers but also in terms of inward and outward movement, and the active pursuit of family life – all helped to consolidate the development of a solid organisational system. This, as we shall see, enabled the survivors of Bergen-Belsen to engage in a highly sophisticated network of cultural and political activity.

Living Conditions and British Policy

In order to understand how the survivors were able to construct a social and cultural system, and to explain the active national character of that system, one must look into the background and conditions prevailing after liberation. In one sentence, let us say that it was clear from an early stage that liberation was to be only partial. It would not be complete until a new homeland was found for all those who had been uprooted by the war and who refused to go back to their former countries of residence. What was meant to be a provisional situation after displacement thus prevailed for several years, until emigration was allowed and the camps closed around 1950.

The occupation authorities had not been prepared for the long-term management of a large DP population (the Jews were only a very small proportion of this population, which in the British Zone accounted for over 500,000 people). They would not force people to return to their home countries, but neither could they risk letting them out of the camps for fear of a breakdown of the legal and administrative system. Things were further complicated by the deteriorating economies of both Germany and Britain.

The situation was particularly difficult for Jewish survivors, who had gone through such extreme sufferings in wartime, and who had no anchor in the outside world. They had no idea when or how they could start a new life. Worst of all was being 'liberated but not free' as the survivors put it – forced to live in a camp under semi-military regulations, in over-populated barracks, with no privacy (though housing facilities were improved somewhat during 1946). Connections with the outside world were hampered by the fact that for a long period there were neither postal services, nor transportation facilities.[11]

Living conditions were very poor. There was a shortage of beds, blankets and sanitary equipment. The meagre diet of 2,000 calories provided by the military authorities was not sufficient even for healthy people, let alone people who had starved for years and had just begun to recover from typhus, dysentery and other diseases. Later, the situation worsened even more. The winter of 1946/7 was very harsh, and as late as the spring of 1947 basic commodities such as food and clothing were in short supply.[12]

One of the worst problems was unemployment. The possibilities for creating jobs by establishing workshops or factories in the camp were limited by the shortage of raw materials. Most DPs refused to integrate themselves into the German economy as a matter of principle, and some even found a way to take a form of revenge, by forcing Germans to work as their servants. The majority, dependent on welfare, with little hope for a productive occupation, lapsed into idleness and resorted to dealings on the Black Market.[13]

But above and beyond the difficulties of the general situation, there was yet another, created by the British who refused to view the Jews as a separate entity. They insisted that Jews remained a part of the national groupings to which they had belonged before the war. Without discussing here the possible reasons for that policy, the result was that Jews had to live in the same camps as the Poles, Ukrainians and Lithuanians who had not long ago been their enemies and persecutors, a situation which led time and again to violent incidents.[14] There was no preferential treatment for Jewish DPs, although they had suffered more under the Nazis than anyone else, and were in a far worse situation than the non-Jews. The same attitude shaped the British policy towards German Jews. Those who were camp survivors were considered victims and received special treatment. But those who survived by hiding, by joining the underground or by escaping, were considered German citizens.[15] Any rehabilitation programme earmarked for Jewish survivors, or encompassing all the Jews in the camps and outside communities alike, was thus met with restrictions and obstacles by the British authorities.

One of the results of British policy was the conspicuous absence of Jewish emissaries in the camp, apart from army chaplains, and later, soldiers of the Jewish Brigade. The Jewish Relief Unit from Britain and the workers of the American Joint Distribution Committee arrived only in August 1945, and confronted many difficulties.[16] While the Americans adopted a separate policy toward the Jews following the recommendations of Earl G. Harrison's report in the summer of 1945, the British stuck to their integration principle. They even refused to appoint a special adviser on Jewish affairs; Colonel Robert Solomon was assigned this task only in the spring of 1946.[17] This situation presented a challenge of the first order, the only answer for which was the establishment of a united Jewish national organisation which would overcome these obstacles and formulate a rehabilitation programme that offered the Jews a new and autonomous future.

Spontaneous Organisation

Scarcely ten days after liberation a Jewish committee was elected in Bergen-Belsen on the initiative of three block-committees. Yosele Rosensaft was elected Chairman. The moving force was a large group of Zionist youngsters, many of whom had belonged to pioneering *Halutz* movements in the past. They knew Hebrew, sang Hebrew songs and were prepared to go immediately to Eretz Israel. The impact of this group was decisive for several reasons. First, they constituted a large part of the survivor population; second, they were in relatively good health and their morale was high; and third, and most importantly, they had a clear aim and acted together as a group. These factors enabled them to serve as the leadership of the weak and exhausted survivors, to offer a vision for the future and to establish an organisational model.[18]

Zionist enthusiasm characterised this provisional committee although it was pluralistic and represented all parties and trends: Rosensaft himself had been a Poalei Zion activist; Ber Laufer was a member of Gordonia; Paul Treppman belonged to the Revisionists and Rafael Gershon Olevsky was a member of the General Zionists; religious liberal Jews were represented by Rabbi Zvi Helfgott-Asaria, who arrived in Belsen after being liberated from captivity as a Yugoslavian officer; and the Orthodox Polish Agudah was represented by Rabbi Israel Moshe Olevsky, the brother of Rafael Gershon. Most members of the committee were Polish, but the German Jews were represented through Norbert Wollheim, who arrived in Belsen a few weeks after being liberated near Luebeck. He continued to live in Luebeck as the leader of the group of survivors there. The one missing interest group from this early committee was the Hungarian Agudah group, and eventually this would become a source of conflict and friction.[19]

The broad representative character of this committee did not minimise its devotion to Zionism. Against the background of harsh conditions and hostile policy toward Jewish cohesiveness, spontaneous Zionism provided a strong basis for the establishment of an active framework which united all Jews in the British Zone. Their struggle was conducted on three fronts: on the political front, to achieve the Zionist goal in collaboration with the Zionist emissaries and leaders; on the organisational level, to consolidate a national leadership for all the Jews in the Zone – DPs, German Jews, Zionists and non-Zionists, secular and Orthodox; and on the cultural-educational front, to create a framework for healthy and normal life in the camps while preparing the inmates for their future as free individuals.

The foundations for this concerted national struggle were laid at the first Congress of *She'erit Hapleta* in the British Zone, which met in Belsen in September 1945 under the Zionist flag and represented all the Jews in the camps and nearby communities. A British-Jewish delegation was present, headed by Selig Brodetsky of the Board of Deputies of British Jews, with Sidney Silverman and Alexander Easterman of the World Jewish Congress. The Bergen-Belsen Congress was united in its call to open the gates of Palestine and to preserve Jewish unity as the main instrument to achieve this goal. A

Central Committee of 17 members was elected to represent the whole region, with its headquarters in Belsen. Rosensaft was the President and Wollheim his deputy and the head of the Communities Department. A whole series of departments was established: health (under Dr Hadassa Bimko, later Rosensaft); culture and education (under Olevsky, Rosenthal and Treppman who had already begun to publish the bi-weekly newspaper *Undzer Stime* two months before); theatre (under Sami Feder who directed Belsen's first theatre performance during the Congress); religion (under Rev. Helfgott as the head of the Zonal Rabbinate); and economics (under Samuel Weintraub of Hapoel Hamizrahi and Karl Katz of the Bremen community). The economics department was responsible for the allocation of food, clothing and accommodation.[20]

The Political Front

The Congress set the stage and gave direction to the survivors' struggle for freedom, which was closely bound up with the Zionist struggle for independence. On both fronts Britain was the source of antagonism, as the occupation authority in Germany, and the mandatory power in Palestine. There was one goal: to open the gates of Palestine. The restrictive immigration policy of the mandate and the battle to put an end to the Jewish DP problem in Germany were clearly interrelated, especially in the light of the fact that the alternative destinations for immigration, mainly the United States, were virtually closed. There is no doubt that the Americans had their own interests at heart in pressing the British to open Palestine to immigration. Such a step would lift the burden off American shoulders and ease their consciences. Nevertheless, this show of support was welcomed enthusiastically by the Jewish DPs, especially in the British Zone, where confrontation with the British authorities was a daily occurrence.

The Anglo-American Commission affair further highlighted the Zionist determination of the survivors. The Commission, appointed by Britain and America to investigate the possibility of solving the DP problem through immigration to Palestine, visited Belsen on 10 February 1946. At a meeting with representatives of the Central Committee, who were chosen very carefully by the military commander of the camp to represent all segments of the DP population, the message was very clear; after Auschwitz there was only one solution: Palestine. Rosensaft emphasised the disappointment of the Jews at being denied the only assistance they needed – the opportunity to rebuild their lives: 'After these years, in which the Jewish people has sacrificed 6 million Jews we have the right to build a new life in the land which is our only homeland: Palestine.' Norbert Wollheim accentuated the fact that he was a German Jew and that he had been far from Zionism before being deported to Auschwitz. His Zionism, he said, emerged as the only possible response to Auschwitz, for him as much as for any other Jew. He explained that there were only two small groups of Jews who might say no to Palestine – German Jews who were old and sick, or partners in mixed marriages, and those who had relatives overseas with whom they wished to reunite. Both groups, he said, comprised no more than 15 per cent of the Jews in the British Zone. Another representative, Ms Kleinman, who headed Bergen-Belsen's Jewish school, told the Commission that she had refrained from preaching or disseminating Zionism in her school. Nevertheless, Zionism had risen spontaneously in the educational context. Hebrew was the only common language, and Palestine was the only hope shared by all. Random encounters with camp inmates elicited the same response. The answer to all questions was unanimous: If we can not go to Palestine then our only alternative is to return to Auschwitz.[21]

Soon afterwards, when it became clear that the Anglo-American Commission's recommendations to permit immigration to Palestine were rejected by the British, Zionist militancy intensified. On the first anniversary of liberation day, 15 April, 1946, which fell on the first day of Pesach, a circular issued by the Central Committee called upon all the DPs to voice their demands for free *aliya* and to express their unanimous support for the *Yishuv* and its struggle against British Mandatory policy.[22] Indeed, the ceremony which took place on that day, to unveil a memorial to the victims of Bergen-Belsen was turned into a pure Zionist protest against the British for failing to complete their mission as liberators.[23] In the course of time, as the survivors began to despair of the prospect of freedom, their militancy increased, reaching a peak with the *Exodus* affair. The British Zone became involved when the ship arrived in Hamburg, having been turned away from Palestine on orders of the British government. However, this was to be the last battle in the national struggle of *She'erit Hapleta*. Soon thereafter the state of Israel was established and the gates were opened to the DPs at last.

Organisation, Centralisation and Self-government

From the very beginning of its work, the Central Committee insisted on exclusivity. It regarded itself as the only governing body of the Jews in the British Zone, and responsible for both internal affairs, and liaison with Jewish organisations around the world and the British authorities.

Internal co-operation between the Belsen camp and the Jewish communities was achieved mainly through personal contacts between Rosensaft and Wollheim.[24] Centralisation was highly developed, even autocratic. At one and the same time, the Central Committee governed the Jewish affairs in the whole of the British Occupation Zone as well as in Belsen (although officially there was a separate sub-committee for the camp).[25] The Central Committee insisted that everything done by voluntary organisations such as the Jewish Relief Unit, the (American) Joint, the Chief Rabbi's Religious Emergency Council, and the Jewish Agency for Palestine should be channelled through its offices. This included allocation of food, clothing distribution and the provision of housing. The aim was to prevent various organisations from obtaining preferential treatment for their protégés in the camp. Nevertheless, there were always complaints about discrimination, corruption and misuse of supplies. A Jewish police force had been appointed by the Committee to deter thieves and activity in the Black Market. This force was successful in exerting authority in daily affairs and establishing a sort of autonomy which minimised the intervention of the British authorities. But it did not really solve the problems which were caused by the economic situation described above.[26] Misunderstandings and objections were common amongst the DPs, hampering not only the efficiency of welfare operations but also the amount of material support received.

As already mentioned it seems that relations with the Hungarian Orthodox were not very smooth. There were rivalries and conflicts between the various Orthodox groups too, mainly between the Polish

Agudah and the Hungarian Agudah, and between the Agudah as a whole and the Mizrahi. The Central Committee was accused of neglecting the needs of the Orthodox, while the Orthodox were accused of unfairly demanding preferential treatment, challenging the Central Committee by appointing a body of their own, and not accepting the authority of the Committee. Repeated attempts to arrive at some agreement between the Orthodox groups within the framework of the Central Committee were not very successful.[27]

As for external relations, in the course of time the Central Committee acquired the status of the sole leader of the Jews in the British Zone. It gained the full support of the Jewish world and welfare organisations who recognised the Committee as a sort of 'German Board of Jewish Deputies', and won the respect of German Jews as well as DPs.[28] In the global Jewish community, Rosensaft and Wollheim were recognised as political leaders and acted as such. They travelled abroad for meetings and propaganda work, mainly to London, but also to the United States, and no one would ever have guessed that they were living in Germany as DPs. Rosensaft appealed directly to Jewish leaders as an authentic representative of the Yiddish-speaking masses in Germany. Wollheim was more of a diplomat, with the background and the languages (German as well as English) needed for liaison with external parties.[29]

The Central Committee was less successful in gaining the status of quasi-government in the eyes of the British authorities. Its demand to be recognised officially was rejected for a long time. The British saw no difference, and rightly so, as we have seen, between the endeavour of the DPs to form a centralised Jewish body and the Zionist cause. Recognising the Central Committee, would have meant the recognition of a Jewish entity encompassing all the Jews in the Zone, Germans and DPs alike, organised on a national basis. Moreover, this would have legitimised the Zionist demands and established the Central Committee as a partner for negotiating the future of the DPs and the future of the British Palestine mandate. This of course was unacceptable to the British.[30] Recognition of the Committee was thus denied until 1947, and this attitude only fuelled the fire of national struggle that went hand in hand with the struggle for a centralised Jewish organisation.[31]

Cultural Activity and Education

As we have seen, a cultural department was formed at the Congress in September 1945, but in this field much effort was invested even before the Congress. Culture and education were recognised as the main channels to recovery, but the obstacles were many: the shortage of facilities and school supplies, the scarcity of persons who could function as spiritual guides and teachers, and, above all, the lack of books. As people who had starved not only physically but intellectually, however, no obstacle could stand in their way. In June 1945 the first school was established and in July, the Yiddish newspaper *Undzer Stime* was first published, initially handwritten. This paper was to become the main Jewish organ in the British Zone and the mouthpiece of the Central Committee. These initiatives developed into a full-blown cultural enterprise that included Yiddish theatre, a library – a poor one but a library nevertheless – sport clubs, regular public lectures, entertainment programmes and various courses.[32]

By February 1946, there was already a network of educational institutions in Belsen, including a primary school for about 200 children and a Hebrew Gymnasium for 100 pupils which opened in December 1945 through the efforts of a survivor, Dr Helen Wrubel and a Jewish Brigade soldier, David Littman. There were also two Beth Jacob schools attended by about 200 children, one Polish and the other Hungarian, as well as a Yeshiva with 100 pupils and a vocational school teaching a variety of trades which was developed with the help of the local ORT organisation. There were also various Zionist youth groups and a Hehalutz centre with hundreds of members.[33] The atmosphere in the secular schools was Zionist; Hebrew and the study of Palestine were emphasised. Most of the teachers were themselves DPs, and were assisted by Jewish Brigade soldiers and the *shlichim* (Jewish emissaries). The welfare organisations enthusiastically joined the project, mainly helping with supplies and facilities.[34] Their co-operation was not hampered by the Zionist trend of the schools (an outlook which was shared by many of the relief workers as individuals). On the contrary, these organisations were supportive of the curriculum and recognised the value of Zionism as a tool for uplifting and preparing for the future.

Nevertheless, the problems were many and even a year after liberation there was a notable scarcity of books, paper and other equipment.[35]

Conclusion: Bergen-Belsen as a Centre of Zionism

The clearly Zionist character of the Belsen DP camp organisation was manifest from the outset. Zionism was a spontaneous response to circumstances and became a central issue, a compass directing all activities in the social and cultural spheres. The Zionist orientation was further strengthened by the establishment of *Histadrut Zionit Ahida*, a federation of all the Zionist political parties in Belsen, at the beginning of 1946.[36] Activity intensified all the more from the spring of that year when Kurt Levin opened the Palestine Office in Belsen.[37] Illegal *aliya* was going on all the time, with DPs taking advantage of the close borders with Holland and France. It was organised by all kinds of *sclichim* – Brigade soldiers, Jewish Agency emissaries and also JRU workers, many of whom were Zionists.[38] *Hachshara* and illegal *aliya* were pivotal issues, around which a whole network of social and cultural activities developed, in addition to and complementing the formal, centralised programmes of the Central Committee. Actually, the Zionist organisation and the Central Committee worked closely with one another, and most political as well as social, educational and cultural activities were carried out in full co-operation and agreement.

This does not mean that the camp was exclusively Zionist, as illustrated by the disagreement with the Hungarian Agudah. Neither are we saying that everything was harmonious, the impression one may get from the co-operation between the parties in the Central Committee. The fact is, when Bergen-Belsen was liquidated in 1950, many of its former inmates found their future in Israel. However, this was not true for all, or even most of them. Quite a number of devoted Zionist leaders ended up in America. Nevertheless, in Bergen-Belsen, Zionism reigned supreme. Conflicts and disagreements were put aside, and the Jews joined forces in the struggle to implement the only possible solution for the *She'erit Hapleta*. This was the case even among the many individuals who would not adopt Zionism as their own way of life. At the time, the whole Jewish world reacted in this way to the

Holocaust and the plight of the survivors, but this attitude was more evident among *She'erit Hapleta*, and especially in Bergen-Belsen. Zionism was the name of the game as long as the survivors remained homeless. It was the essence of their political struggle, as well as their social and spiritual guide throughout the long process of rehabilitation. The Zionism of *She'erit Hapleta* was shaped by their continued captivity following liberation. It was strengthened in response to mounting obstacles on the road to freedom, and encouraged by the pro-Zionist consensus of the Jewish world in the post-Holocaust period. The plight of *She'erit Hapleta* was the focus of this consensus, and through the story of Bergen-Belsen one may gain some understanding of how it was activated into a national revival.

NOTES

1. Hagit Lavsky, 'The Day After: Bergen-Belsen from Concentration Camp to the Centre of the Jewish Survivors in Germany', *German History*, Vol.11, No.1 (1993), pp.36–59, here: pp.52–3.
2. *Konzentrationslager in Hamburg – Ansichten 1990* (Hamburg: Hamburg-Portract, 1990); Werner Johe, *Neuengamme, Zur Geschichte der Konzentrationlager in Hamburg* (Hamburg: Landeszentrale für politische Bildung, 1984); Detlef Garbe and Sabine Homann, 'Juedische Gefangene in Hamburger Konzentrationslager', in Arno Herzig (ed.), *Die Juden in Hamburg 1590–1990* (Hamburg: Wissenschaftliche Beiträge der Universität Hamburg zur Ausstellung, 1991), pp.545–59; Reiner Froebe *et al.*, *Konzentrationslager in Hannover – KZ-Arbeit und Ruestungsindustrie in der Spaetphase des Zweiten Weltkriegs* (Hildesheim: Lax, 1985), Vol.2, pp.285, 331–69, 407–564; *Konzentrationslager in Hannover 1943–1945* (Hanover: Ausstellungskatalog, 1983); Klaus Mlinek *et al.*, 'Deutsche und Juden nach 1945', in *Reichskristallnacht in Hanover* (Hanover: Historiches museum, 1978), pp.97–104.
3. Lavsky, 'The Day After', pp.49–50. The initial numbers though must be viewed with caution: for quite a while after the liberation there was no attempt to compile lists of survivors. The first book listing the names of Jewish survivors was prepared by the Central Jewish Committee only in September 1945. Also, no records were kept of those buried in the mass graves, due to the race against death in the first weeks after the liberation.
4. Ibid., pp.50–51.
5. Information on Jews in the British Zone, Jan.1946, Public Record Office (PRO), Foreign Office (FO)/945/655; Statistics on Jews in the British Zone in Germany, living outside DP camps, 31 Jan. 1946, Board of Deputies Archives (BD), C11/13/16/4; Volks- und Berufszaehlung vom 29 October in den vier Besatzungszonen und Berlin (Berlin–Munich).
6. Hagit Lavsky, 'Displaced Persons, Jewish', in *Encyclopedia of the Holocaust*, Vol.1, pp.377–84, here, p.377.
7. Lt.-Col. Sir Brian H. Robertson, Control Commission for Germany British Element (CCG (BE)) to Sir Arthur Street, War Office (WO), 7 May 1946, PRO FO/945/384; Central British Fund (CBF), *Annual Report 1947*, pp.2–9; Internal note of the FO, 13

Aug. 1947: PRO FO/371/61821; FO to Paris Embassy, 11 Sept. 1947: PRO FO/371/61826.

8. Derrick Sington, *Belsen Uncovered* (London: Duckworth, 1946); Leslie Hardman, *The Survivors. The Story of the Belsen Remnant* (London: Vallentine Mitchell, 1958); Isaac Levy, *Witness to Evil: Bergen-Belsen 1945* (London: Halban, 1995); Letters of Rabbi Isaac Levy to the *Jewish Chronicle* (JC), 4 May 1945, p.1, and 8 June 1945, p.1; Interview with Yosele Rosensaft, 2 July 1964, Institute of Contemporary Jewry, The Hebrew University, Oral History Division (OHD); Hadassa Bimko-Rosensaft, 'Children in Belsen', in *Belsen* (Tel Aviv: Irgun Sheerit Hapleita Me'haezor Habriti, 1957), pp.88-97.

9. Letter by Rabbi Klein from Belsen to the JC, 22 June 1945, p.14; Letter by Rabbi Levy to JC, 4 May 1945; Sington, *Belsen Uncovered*, p.202; Klein was the Rabbi of the Hungarian Orthodox community. Many other Hassidic Polish Jews formed a separate community in the nearby town of Celle, after being brought there by the British in an effort to persuade them to go back to Poland. See Zvi Asaria, 'Eine Chassidische Gemeinde in Celle (1945–1950)', in *Zur Geschichte der Juden in Celle* (Celle: Der Stadt Celle, 1974), pp.103–7; *Celle '45 – Aspekte einer Zeitenwende* (Celle: Begleitpublikation zur Ausstellung, 1995).

10. Interviews with Zvi Asaria (Helfgott), March 1964 and Norbert Wollheim, July 1990, OHD. See also Bimko-Rosensaft, 'Children in Belsen'.

11. Reports by Jane Leverson, 6 June and 25 June 1945, Wiener Library, London (WL), Rose Henriques Collection (RHC)/Leverson Reports; Interviews with Isaac Levy, Bertha Weingreen and Sarah Eckstein-Grebenau, July 1992, OHD.

12. Circular by the Jewish Committee for Relief Abroad (JCRA) and the Chief Rabbi's Religious Emergency Council (CRREC), March 1947, WL, RCH/Bad Harzburg; Sarah Eckstein to Professor Brodetsky, 4 March 1947, BD, C11/13/17/1; Interview with Henry Lunzer, March 1993, OHD.

13. Letter by Kudish to friends, 17 May 1945, Yad Vashem Archive (YV), 0-37/19/1; memoranda by Shalom Adler-Rudel: 11 June 1945, Central Zionist Archives (CZA), A140/154; 28 June 1945, CZA, A140/272; 23 July 1945, CZA, A140/650; JTA bulletin on Bergen-Belsen, 16 Sept. 1945, and British newspaper clippings, 2–3 Oct.1945, YV, 0-37/19/1; Report by Alexander Easterman and Sidney Silverman to the World Jewish Congress (WJC), in a letter to the Under Secretary of State, Henderson, 12 Oct. 1945: PRO FO/1049/195.

14. CGE (BE), Prisoners of War and Displaced Persons Division (PW&DP) on formation of a Jewish committee, 2 May 1946, PRO FO/1049/367; Robertson, CCG (BE) to Street (Control Office for Germany and Austria, London), 2 May 1946, PRO FO/945/384; Norbert Wollheim, on the murder of a Jewish Blockaelteste, 6 May 1946, YV, 0-70/70/7.

15. Ursula Büttner, *Not nach der Befreiung – die Situation der deutsche Juden in der britischen Besatzungszone 1945–1948* (Hamburg: Landeszentrale für politische Bildung, 1986).

16. Hagit Lavsky, 'British Jewry and the Jews in Post-Holocaust Germany: The Jewish Relief Unit, 1945–1950', *The Journal of Holocaust Education*, Vol.4, No.1 (Summer, 1995), pp.29–40; idem, 'Liberated but not Free: The Foundations of Jewish National Organization in Bergen-Belsen', *Hazionut*, 18 (1994) (Hebrew), pp.9–37, here: pp.19–23.

17. Robertson to Street, 2 May 1946 (note 14, above); Lavsky, 'British Jewry', pp.35–6.

18. Lavsky, 'Liberated but not Free', pp.23–6.

19. Ibid., pp.26–31.

20. Ibid., pp.32–6.

21. Report by Wollheim, 15 Feb. 1946, YV, 0-70/1.

22. Circular by the Central Committee, 14 April 1946, YV, JM/10.375/1608; Report by Major D.H. Murphy, 15 April 1956, PRO FO/1030/307.
23. Report by Murphy, 15 April 1946; Lt.-Gen. A. Galloway to Robertson, 21 April 1946, PRO FO/1030/307.
24. See, for example, 'Protokoll über die Tagung der jüdischen Comitees und Gemeinden Nordwestdeutschlands am 9 May 1946 in Bremen', Zentral Archiv zur Erforschung der Geschichte der Juden in Deutschland, Heidelberg (ZA), Hanover Community Archives.
25. Memorandum by Col. R.J. Solomon, Adviser on Jewish Affairs, May 1946, PRO FO/1049/367.
26. Confidential report of the Höhne (Belsen) Jewish Civil Police, April 1946, BD, C11/13/17/1; Memo by Wollheim, 6 May 1946, note 14, above.
27. Office of the Dep. Mil. Gov. to Control Office, 16 April 1946, PRO FO/945/731; report of the Jewish police, April 1946; report by Rev. Rosen, 20 June 1946, Southampton University Archives (SUA), Schonfeld Papers (SP)/576/1.
28. Jewish Survey meeting, 1 April 1946, PRO FO/1050/1491 (Nurock's words are quoted).
29. CCG (BE) to N. Barou, 26 June 1946, YV, 0-70/16; Rev. Rosen's report.
30. CC to Welfare Dept., 8 Jan. 1946, YV, 0-70/30; Report on a visit of a Parliamentary commission headed by Chancellor Hynd, 20 Jan. 1946, YV, 0-70/5; Dep. Mil. Gov. to Control Office, 16 April 1946; Galloway to Robertson, 21 April 1946, note 23, above.
31. CCG (BE), 2 May 1946, note 14, above, recognition still denied. For eventual recognition see: Copy of a brief for the Chanellor's meeting with Solomon, 29 July 1947; and Brodetsky and Solomon meeting with Lord Pakenham, 30 July 1947, PRO FO/945/384; Barou to Rosensaft, 1 Aug. 1947, CZA, WJC 9/A; FO to Berlin, 14 Aug. 1947, PRO FO/1049/891; Meeting of the Chancellor with Solomon, Brodetsky, Brotman and others, 30 Sept. 1947, PRO FO/945/384.
32. Report of the Kultur-Abteilung, 2 July 1946, YV, JM/10.374/1578.
33. Report on Belsen by Rabbi Rev. Greenbaum, 22 Feb. 1946, WL, RHC/Belsen Reports; *Undzer Stime*, No.1, 12 July 1945, p.10; M. Lubliner, 'Jewish Education in Belsen', *Belsen*, pp.139–40; Edna Elazary, 'The Hebrew Gymnasium in Bergen Belsen' (M.A, thesis, The Hebrew University of Jerusalem, 1989) (Hebrew); Report of the Kultur-Abteilung, 2 July 1946.
34. Survey report by Brotman and Viteles, 29 March 1946, YV, 0-70/6; Report of the Kultur-Abteilung, 2 July 1946; Report by Rev. Rosen, 20 June 1946, note 27, above; Lavsky, 'British Jewry', p.34.
35. Brotman and Viteles, 29 March 1946; CBF, *Annual Report 1946, 1947*; Reports by Bertha Weingreen, 24 April 1946 and 15 Oct. 1946, WL, RCH/Belsen Reports; Jacob Wiengreen, 'Survey of Educational Work in Belsen', 14 May 1946, WL, RCH/ Wiengreen Reports; JCRA Volunteers' Newsletter, No. 20, Oct./Nov. 1946, SUA, SP/440/2.
36. Histadrut Hazionit Haahida Bergen-Belsen, circular on foundation, 5 March 1946; and letter from Weintraub and Giteles to the Jewish Agency (JA), 20 April 1946; letter from the Histadrut Zionit to the JA, 8 Aug. 1946, CZA, L10/232/1.
37. Weintraub and Giteles to the JA, 20 April 1946.
38. As for illegal *aliya*, see: Jewish illegal immigration to Palestine, March 1946; and minutes of a meeting at the WO, 27 April 1946, PRO FO/945/655; interview with Henry Lunzer, March 1993 (and his private documents), OHD; Maj. Gen. Sugden to Wilberforce, 8 July 1946, PRO FO/945/381; As for the Zionist inclinations (and even transformation) of the JRU emissaries, see Lavsky, 'British Jewry'.

PART IV: CONCLUSION

The Memory of Belsen

TONY KUSHNER

Bergen-Belsen concentration camp is saturated with memory. The nature of that memory is complex, diverse, contradictory and dynamic. It is a place of contested memory between those that experienced it as victim, perpetrator, bystander and liberator as well as within those groups. The power of these memories is such that they have acted as a barrier rather than a stimulus to the writing of Belsen's history. Indeed, the first and only major history of the camp was written in 1962.[1] Its unique role within the Nazi concentration camp system has been lost with its more emotive use as crude metaphor. Belsen has become a multi-layered and frequently contradictory symbol representing, firstly, the universal horrors of war or man's capacity for mass evil, secondly, the more particular atrocities carried out by the Nazis *or* the German people, thirdly, the damage inflicted on the Jewish people during the Holocaust and lastly, the reflected glory and decency of those who liberated its survivors in April 1945 and exposed to the outside world its undisguised and indescribable horror. It is only now, 50 years after its liberation, that it is conceivable that the various strands of memory of the camp (if the blatant anti-Semitism of neo-Nazis is ignored) can be reconciled and, furthermore, that the history and memory of Belsen can be brought together, if not in harmony, then in constructive debate.

> They say that nothing interests me
> That nothing moves me any more
> That with cold indifference
> Blows my deadened soul.
>
> And that now we've soup forevermore
> With all its pros and cons
> That never again will my thoughts fly
> To roads burning with stars.

This poem was recited by Mina Tomkiewicz in a literary evening at Belsen in October 1944. The author was a Warsaw Jew kept in Hotel Polski amongst the few thousand with foreign visas to Palestine, Switzerland and Latin America. She was deported to Belsen in August 1943 when it acted as a privileged camp for so-called exchange Jews. These Jews served a variety of purposes for the Nazis. On a pragmatic level they brought in money and served as a way of extorting payment from Jews locally and internationally. They could also be used to release German citizens interned by the British and others. More generally, these Jews, tiny in number compared to the millions murdered, were valuable propaganda proving to the Allies that the Jews were still alive and could be held as a ransom to the free world. That most of these exchange Jews, for all their privileged status, would still die, is a reflection of the determination of the Nazi regime to wipe out ultimately all Jews.[2]

Embarking on a policy of total genocide was, in fact, compatible with the short-term advantages that might be accrued from keeping a few alive, if in the most brutal circumstances, for work or bartering purposes. Nevertheless, Belsen, as Tomkiewicz's poem suggests, was until the latter stages of 1944, a place where Jews were not purposefully exterminated – however appalling the reality of its day-to-day existence. Its relative freedom until its transformation with the arrivals from the eastern extermination camps, followed by the chaos that reigned as the Nazi regime fell apart in the last months of the war (although it became increasingly difficult to maintain any form of record in the atrocious conditions of its last days), enabled a recording of memory unmatched by victims of other camps in the KZ system with the exception of Theriensenstadt. As a result, there are detailed diaries and reports that survive from Belsen dating as early as 1943 and extending to the weeks following its liberation.[3]

Thus, well before the liberation of Belsen and prior to it having resonance in the outside world, a battle raged within the camp not just between the Jewish and other victims' desire to survive and the Nazi imperative to kill all its inmates, but also over the memory of the offence. On the one side there were those in control of Belsen who wanted to disguise or distort the camp's complex connection to the 'Final Solution'. On the other, there were the few that were prepared to take the risks to write down their experiences and the many who desperately clung to life in the hope that their testimony would somehow find a place in a post-Lager world. In this war, the odds were, of course, stacked against the camp prisoners.

Life was still cheap, even when Belsen was, in the words of the Nazis, 'one of the most humane camps'. The chances of contemporary material surviving along with the writer were minimal. Moreover, those in the camp realised that 'it would be hard to share a common language with people who hadn't experienced on their own backs the horrors of "our" war'. Yet the Nazis' desire to remove all traces of their extermination campaign and the abandonment of the eastern camps with the Soviets' western advance ultimately had the opposite result of that intended. Ironically, the huge and monstrously brutal movement of survivors through the death marches to the western camps was to provide the western world with images that confirmed the essential evilness of Nazism. In the process, the difference between concentration and extermination camp was largely lost – a confusion that still reigns 50 years later. Nevertheless, the images of mass death, the dying and those struggling for life in the liberated western camps were to be some of the most enduring of the Second World War.[4]

It would be easy to assume that in the battle over memory, the immense western media coverage of the liberated camps would swing the pendulum in favour of the tens of thousands of survivors liberated by the United States and Britain between Buchenwald on 11 April and Mauthausan on 8 May (technically, Theresienstadt was the last camp to be liberated when it was taken over by Soviet forces on 12 May, but it had been handed over to the International Red Cross ten days earlier). Compared to the coverage of the eastern camps liberated by the Soviets, with the partial exception of Majdanek, camps such as Buchenwald, Dachau, and particularly Belsen received massive publicity in British and American press, radio broadcasts and newsreels. It is the quality as well as the quantity of these reports that is noteworthy. The photographs, in particular, of Belsen which 'were published at the time in the press throughout the world ... have come to symbolise the horror which existed in National Socialist concentration camps'.[5]

All those involved in communicating the scenes of mass death, misery, dirt and stench realised that here was something special, that what they had discovered was destined to become part of the memory and history of the Second World War. Reporters such as the outstanding broadcasters Ed Murrow and Richard Dimbleby at Buchenwald and Belsen respectively felt enormous responsibility to choose their words and images with immense care. The newspaper reporters, broadcasters, photographers and camera-crews, as well as the various individuals involved in liberation, would shape the memory of the Nazi concentration camps for generations to come. After the attempts of the Nazis to destroy the record of their extermination campaign and the brave attempt of the victims to preserve it, the devastating military victory also brought the western Allies instant and almost total control of the representation of camps such as Belsen to the free world, initially through the media coverage and then, war crimes trials.[6]

The western representation of Belsen was shaped by the ideologies of liberalism and nationalism as well as real politics which distorted the first post-war memories of the camp. The initial accounts varied in their portrayal of the perpetrators. They were seen, firstly, as satanic monsters. For example, Irma Grese, a leading SS figure who had come from Auschwitz to Belsen became the 'bitch of Belsen' and Josef Kramer, the commandant who had also come from Auschwitz, was known as the 'beast of Belsen'. The latter was 'depicted in caricatures in the shape of a shambling gorilla – a sadistic beast in human form thirsty for the blood of his tortured victims'. Secondly, these individuals were perceived as the evil results of the Nazi regime. Thirdly, they were dismissed as typical Germans, the products of a warped and diseased nation. The first memorialisation within Belsen, alongside the mass graves with their stark messages of 'Here rest 1,000 dead', was that erected by the British troops which combined elements of the second and third categories:

> This is the site of the infamous Belsen concentration camp liberated by the British on 15 April 1945. 10,000 unburied dead were found here. Another 13,000 have since died. All of them victims of the German new order in Europe. And an example of Nazi Kultur.[7]

As the new logic of the cold war advanced and the need to cultivate friendship with the German people increased, the third category disappeared in official if not in popular British memory. Thus the film sponsored by the Ministry of Information on the liberation, directed by Sidney Bernstein and completed in late summer 1945, which had a fiercely anti-German focus, was never released. The questions posed by Bernstein's documentary, and particularly the involvement of ordinary Germans in Belsen, were never answered. The closing off with regard to official debate at such an early stage was partly responsible for the residue of popular anti-Germanism that lies only partially buried in popular memory in post-war Britain.[8] The career of the outstanding goalkeeper Bernhard (Bert) Trautmann is a particularly good example of the nature of the ambivalent British reactions to Germans after 1945.

Trautmann was born in Bremen during 1923. His childhood was unremarkable and it appears that he joined the Hitler Youth movement in the 1930s more for the sporting possibilities it offered than out of any great ideological conviction. He had a brutal war, surviving the eastern front before being taken a prisoner by the British in France during the last months of the conflict. He was moved to Lancashire, based in a prisoner of war camp in St Helens where his talents as a footballer soon became apparent. After four years linked to various camps, and on the verge of his repatriation to Germany, Trautmann was signed as a goalkeeper in 1949 by Manchester City Football Club. The signing was massively controversial not only in Manchester but also throughout Britain. Protests were bitter, particularly from some local Jews and those who had been in the forces:

> When I think of all those millions of Jews who were tortured and murdered I can only marvel at Manchester City's crass stupidity.
>
> As a disabled servicemen from the last war I am writing with bitterness in my heart. To think that after all we in this country went through and are still going through due to that war, Manchester City sign a German.[9]

There were some who saw the irony of labelling all Germans as evil: 'Racial antagonism ought not to be perpetuated like this ... One would think that the player was the Belsen Camp commandant.' Yet although Trautmann eventually became a folk hero at Manchester

City (their largest stand is now named after him), his German origins and his service in the German army hung over him in his treatment by the club and even in his own marriage. The intelligent, humorous, and courageous player, who developed a deep love for the north of England, could still be transformed, when matters became difficult, into that 'bloody Nazi' decades after the conflict. Ordinary Germans, even those who played on in a Cup Final with a broken neck, it seems, were never that far removed in nature from the 'beast of Belsen'.[10] The important but essentially isolated film *Frieda* (1947) was probably the only major British cultural product in the immediate post-war years in which unwavering anti-Germanism was at least questioned. The possibility of good Germans is allowed for, but not before the full horrors of Nazism are exposed. The film utilised Belsen footage for this purpose but also to differentiate the ultimately redeemable *Frieda* from her evil, concentration camp guard brother. Only after a major interrogation of the nature of 'Germanism' is even the possibility of a different Germany, past present and future allowed for in the film.[11]

But it was not only the image of the perpetrators and bystanders which was distorted in the post-liberation period. That of the victim was also contoured by the liberators' ideology, in this case the limpet-like adhesion to the liberal imagination. After the opening of a major permanent exhibition at the site of Bergen-Belsen concentration camp in 1990, the Minister for Federal and European Affairs in Lower Saxony, Jurgen Trittin, commented that 'Remembering the crimes of National Socialism is first and foremost a moral obligation towards the victim, an issue of humanity'. This has been the dominant, if not exclusive official German attitude in recent years, although it was one that took a long time to develop.

It has been suggested in the British case by the commentator and novelist Sebastian Faulks that 'we have learned to endure the footage of the concentration camps, more or less at the insistence of survivors, and we all humbled by it'.[12] Faulks' reading, however, is rather inappropriate when the image and description of the victims from 1945 in British culture and many other western cultures are examined. Various features stand out. First, there is the emphasis on death represented by naked bodies piled up or scattered without any hint of individuality. This lack of differentiation is particularly pronounced in the recurring filmic image of the British army bulldozers pushing the marbled, expressionless bodies into one of the massive pits. Newsreels, followed by Resnais' *Night and Fog* ten years later, and the Hollywood *Judgment at Nuremberg*, released in its cinema version at the time of the Eichmann Trial, all use the Belsen bulldozer-pit imagery. The focus on the victim is simply to indict the Nazis/German people. Such imagery was used with similar lack of sensitivity at the time of the fiftieth anniversaries in 1994 and 1995 of the last stages of the Second World War.[13]

It is perhaps inevitable that in this concentration on mass death, the particularity of the victims would be lost, especially for those producing the images so quickly and without time to assimilate the trauma of what they had seen. For example, at least one of the major British cameramen involved in recording the scenes at Belsen was unable to confront his own work. Yet it is still striking how few references there are to the Jewishness of the survivors and victims of Belsen in contemporary accounts.

Belsen was, as a result of its unique history in the Nazi system by the time of its liberation, of all the western camps, essentially a Jewish camp. The large majority of those murdered there, those dying in the weeks following liberation and those surviving were Jewish. Belsen had an intimate relationship to the death camps in the east, especially Auschwitz both in terms of many of its inmates and perpetrators. Its multi-national Jewish prisoners represented in their life stories a fair cross-section of experiences of what would later be known as the Holocaust. Some reports, most obviously in the case of the Jewish press, but also outside it in the case of the *Manchester Guardian* and to a far lesser extent, the *Daily Mirror*, did emphasise the Jewishness of the victims and connect Belsen to a bigger programme of extermination that had succeeded in murdering millions of Jews across Europe. These exceptions indicate that the silence of most of the media on this subject was not accidental or due to a shortage of information.[14]

To stress the Jewishness of those who had suffered in Belsen was seen to be against liberal principles when dealing with minorities within the nation state. Emphasising minority particularity, even in mass death, was seen as dangerous leading to the risk of further anti-Semitism. At its worst, to highlight Jewish difference was, in the words of the British state, to 'perpetuate the very Nazi doctrine which we are determined to stamp out'. In contrast, liberal universalism was benevolent to all concerned. Although this was the official British line, no direct pressure was brought on the media to carry out this policy and the downplaying/ignoring of the Jewish aspect of Belsen which was presented to the British public in April 1945 was essentially voluntary. Not surprisingly, hardly any of the several hundred Mass-Observers at this time refer to Jews as specific victims of the Nazis, even though the western camps and especially Belsen received enormous attention in their diaries.[15]

Several clear themes emerge from the reports and broadcasts of the western concentration camps and the reception to them by the British public. First, camps such as Belsen are seen as the worst of the Nazi regime. A mass-circulated 'The War in Pictures', covering the last year of the conflict and published in 1946 was insistent on that point: a photograph of the open pit grave at Belsen was accompanied with the following commentory:

> Nazi cruelty exposed to the world: As the Allies advanced deeper into the Reich they overran some of the infamous Nazi concentration camps at Dachau, Belsen, Buchenwald, Nordhausen, Ohrdruf and elsewhere. All these camps revealed horrors and bestial cruelty on a scale that far exceeded those found in the former Nazi-occupied countries.[16]

The absence of awareness of Auschwitz throughout, and way beyond 1945, is remarkable to us today, especially in light of the immense media coverage in January 1995 of the fiftieth anniversary of its liberation. It is therefore crucial to stress that in contrast at the end of the Second World War Auschwitz simply had no popular resonance in liberal culture. Indeed, chronologies created of the Second World War in the years following provide no mention of Auschwitz whereas the liberation of the western camps were given special prominence – further indication that the camps had become part of western Allied war history rather than being connected to any specific Jewish disaster.[17]

When information about the processes of extermination, and particularly the use of gas chambers, did gain in popular recognition (especially through the post-war trials), it became logical to connect them to the western camps where they had in fact never been employed (although there was a small, essentially experimental gas chamber in Dachau which was hardly utilised. It was, moreover, very different in purpose to those used in the eastern camps). The confusion or merging of western and eastern camps was a common feature of the Nuremberg and International Military Tribunals and was a remarkable aspect of the film *Judgment at Nuremberg*. In this film the impression is given that the mass movement of peoples and their murder occurred at Buchenwald – there is footage from the Soviet's liberation film from Auschwitz but it is never referred to by name.

The confusion that Belsen had gas chambers as well as crematoria is still widespread today, even amongst some of those who were involved in the liberation of the camp. Belsen remained, particularly in Britain, in the words of a cheap paperback on the subject published as late as 1959, 'Hitler's most infamous Death-Camp'. There was thus a curious combination in which Belsen has a special place in British culture but where ignorance of its real history was almost total.[18] It was shown at a popular level as late as the last years of the 1970s when the punk rock group 'The Sex Pistols' attempted to exploit Belsen's memory.

Many of the punk groups that emerged on both sides of the Atlantic from the mid-1970s revealed a fascination with Nazi symbolism. In Britain particularly, these could be used to shock an older generation for whom the Second World War was central in the formation of their identity and national sense of belonging. In contrast, some in the punk movement believed that the constant reference to Britain's 'finest hour' was the cause of the country's general complacency. The use of swastikas and other Nazi regalia was hardly neutral, however, especially in an atmosphere of growing racial harassment and right-wing extremism.[19]

The specific interest of the 'Sex Pistols' in Holocaust imagery can be put down to a mixture of their growing nihilistic tendencies; their xenophobia/racism; and lastly and perhaps most importantly, their desire to cause as much offence as possible at the same time as seeking commercial success. Belsen, especially, featured in the lyrics of the group – most notoriously and vilely in 'Belsen Was a Gas'. The song was not by any means unambiguously pro-Nazi (there is, for example, no hint of Holocaust denial in the 'Sex Pistols' work in contrast to the contemporary skinhead neo-Nazi 'Oi Bands'). Nevertheless, it is significant in the context of this article because the sick joke of the title could not work in a popular culture unless the name Belsen was important for both the younger and older generations. Moreover, the pathetic pun could have resonance only if the function of Belsen was totally misunderstood:

> Belsen was divine
> If you survived the train
> Then when you get inside
> It's Aufiedersein [sic].[20]

It is now popularly assumed that the liberation of the western camps, and especially Belsen, 'brought home the reality of the Holocaust'. With the assumptions that Belsen represented the limit of Nazi evil, the widespread confusion concerning the function of the concentration camps of the 1930s with those liberated in spring 1945 (for example, the News Chronicle provided the headline late in April 1945 of 'HORROR CAMPS: Facts we told before the war'), and the downplaying of the Jewishness of the victims, this was far from the case. Although many of the Jewish survivors were interviewed by the media and then by those collecting evidence for the following war trials, this material was rarely used.

Even in the Belsen trial, the first war crimes trial which began in September 1945 and, unlike the International Military Tribunals and Nuremberg Trials, did not rely so much on documentary evidence, there was only passing reference to the testimony of Jewish survivors. At the Belsen Trial it was especially the evidence of British liberators such as Brigadier Hughes and Captain Sington or the few British victims of the camp that predominated. Likewise in the film Frieda, the rather unlikely victim of the concentration camp who confronts his former persecutor is a British soldier. In such processes, the ownership of the memory of Belsen was passing from the Nazis to the British. Once again, the Jewish victims were bypassed.[21]

Making the memory of Belsen 'British' had its problems. Camps such as Dachau and Buchenwald were at least familiar to the public as there was a continuity in name with the pre-war era. Belsen, however, to all but a tiny minority of the free world had no resonance in the war. The few activitists working on behalf of the persecuted Jews would have been familiar with the camp as a centre for the exchange Jews from the second half of 1944, reflecting the complex operations involving visas and funds to assure their release. It is also possible that British intelligence sources knew about the camp – there were aerial reconnaisance photographs taken by the RAF in September 1944. Yet, despite of the unfamiliarity of its name, Belsen (rather than the full Bergen-Belsen) very quickly became part of the day-to-day language and popular culture of Britain, facilitated by the word's simple phonetic quality. Through the intimate connection brought about by both the military and the medical liberation of Bergen-Belsen, it became 'our', that is, Britain's camp. The timing of its liberation was perfect in terms of rounding off neatly the narrative of the war. This was symbolically shown at Belsen itself in the weeks following liberation. The last hut was ceremonially burnt down by British forces on 21 May 1945. A portrait of Hitler and an Iron Cross flag (again showing the frequent blurring of Nazi and German) were burnt whilst the Union Jack was raised. British proprietorship of the camp was now confirmed for all to see.[22]

It was fitting that the country, which had, in its own popular mythology, fought alone against the Nazis at great sacrifice, was responsible for liberating the victims of the regime at its most barbarous. Yet the British government was anxious that although the Britishness of the liberation should be emphasised, such particularism did not extend to the victims. References to Jewishness were seen as dangerous at a time when Zionists were claiming the nation-bondedness of all Jews in opposition to British policy in Palestine, but also because, as we have seen, to stress Jewishness was against liberal universalism. In the running of Belsen as a Displaced Persons' camp for the five years following liberation, it was deemed wise to follow the same policy: the Jewishness of the Displaced Persons, other than on a religious level, was downplayed by the British military authorities. Moreover, the name Belsen (its shorter name helping to make it more accessible to the British), was limited in the official British mind to the camp when it was part of the Nazi system and not to its new function as a DP centre. As Joanne Reilly has pointed out, they referred to it as Höhne camp whereas the survivors continued to call it Belsen.[23]

The odds were thus still stacked against the survivors with regard to *their* memory of the camp predominating. Yet the Jews of Belsen organised quickly: three days after liberation a Jewish camp committee, eventually to become the Central Jewish Committee, British Zone, was established. But however skilled and persistent they were in their negotiations with the British authorities at Belsen, there was little they could do at this stage to change the image of the camp victim that had permeated the western mind in spring and summer of 1945. Survivors were met with not only indifference but, often, antipathy as they attempted to relate their experiences.

Guilt in many of the formerly Nazi-occupied countries such as France and Holland and, in the British case, a form of annoyance that their sacrifices paled, comparatively, into insignificance, meant that it was hard for survivors to have their voices heard or their work published. Moreover, the images from the camps were too powerful and limited to be easily reconstructed. On the one hand, it was hard to imagine from their skin and bone representation that they would have any future or had any past in the rich pre-war life of European Jewry. On the other, the camp films, exhibitions, postcards and other pictorial representations of the victims had more than a voyeuristic element. The pictures of naked women particularly were prone to exploitation as pornography, starting a trend of the female victim as a titilating sexual plaything of the Nazis which is still alive in cultural representations of the Holocaust today. The idea of survivors as decent people able to recover from their Holocaust experiences was hard for many, even the most sympathetic witnesses at Belsen, to accept. Josef Rosensaft, who emerged as the major leader of the Belsen survivors after liberation, recalled later that for the 'free Jews' who came after the war to Belsen, 'they looked upon as objects of pity'. He added that

> They had forgotten that we were not brought up in Belsen, Auschwitz and other concentration camps, but had, once upon a time, a home and a background and motherly love and kindness; that before the calamity we, too, had our schools and universities and Yeshivot.[24]

Within Belsen DP camp, however, the Central Jewish Committee, which had been able to win some autonomy of its own affairs from the British authorities, was able to begin the process of Holocaust commemoration that was so lacking elsewhere. A year after liberation, it erected the first permanent memorial at Belsen. With its prominent Stars of David and its admonition (in Hebrew and in English) that 'Israel and the world shall remember thirty thousand Jews exterminated in the concentration camp of Bergen-Belsen at the hands of the hands of the murderous Nazis. Earth conceal not the blood shed on thee!', this was a very Jewish memorial. The date of 15 April was used for commemorative services which became universally remembered by the Jewish survivors of Belsen beyond 1946 across the world.[25]

Thus after the war, to both the British and the Jewish survivors, Belsen had become 'our camp'. The ongoing battle over the site of Auschwitz is now familiar, but that regarding Belsen is less well known. As has been related, at Belsen all the camp buildings were ceremoniously burnt down by the British for health reasons, with only the mass graves left as an initial reminder of its murderous history. The separate cemetery for the tens of thousands of Soviet prisoners of war who died through disease and neglect at Belsen in the first years of the camp from 1941 was complemented by a memorial erected in June 1946, two months after its Jewish equivalent was unveiled. The Soviet memorial, however, was away from the main site, symbolising the marginalisation of these soldiers in the history and memory of Belsen – victims, perhaps, of cold war logic. In 1947 work began on a large obelisk and memorial wall with inscriptions: a more general project overseen by the British military government.[26]

These few memorials remained in the late 1940s and early 1950s, along with the mass graves, alone in the barren landscape of the former concentration camp. In the years after the end of the DP camp in 1950 they were visited by Jewish survivors, ex-British soldiers and a few Germans in relative harmony and without much attention. In 1952 the regional government of Lower Saxony took responsibility for managing the obelisk and memorial wall, but there was little attempt to provide the visitor with information about the site as a whole. By 1956 a correspondence raged in the *Daily Telegraph* over the neglect of the memorial with one British liberator writing in disgust that 'Old soldiers may never die, but the causes for which they fought are very soon put quietly to death'.

On a personal level, a bond could and did develop between survivors and liberators, both of whom found their traumatised memories marginalised or subject to partial amnesia in a world that did not want to remember that aspect of the war. No help was on offer on a therapeutic level to allow these individuals and groups to come to terms with the past and its never-ending memory.[27] This was particularly marked in the 1950s when in film and literature the war was being reconstructed more as an old-fashioned military struggle as in the successful Anglo-American production *The Desert Fox* (1951) based on the career of Rommel. Such films and television documentaries on the war were reassuring for a British and, to a lesser extent, an American audience in that victory was always guaranteed. Returning to the career of Bert Trautmann, one such series on the allied invasion of Europe in 1944 shown in the early 1950s prompted the following locker room conversation at Manchester City:

> 'Did you see the TV last night?'
> 'Yes, we won again, did you see it Trauty?'
> 'No I bluddy didn't you bastard'.[28]

'Trauty' could and did become 'at moments of tension', as his biographer suggests, 'Krauty', and there were still supporters who would chant 'Seig Heil' at the opposing goalkeeper. But the angry British anti-Nazism/anti-Germanism of the immediate post-war years, with the images of the concentration camps at its central core, began to fade as the 1950s progressed. There was also a move in some quarters towards the ideas of reconciliation, particularly in the church. In Germany, the immense success in 1956 and 1957 of the theatre version of *The Diary of Anne Frank* prompted a march of 2,000 young Germans to Belsen to pay homage to the place of her death. The march took place under the auspices of the Hamburg Society for Christian and Jewish Co-operation and was widely applauded by the British Council of Christians and Jews (CCJ). Significantly, however, the CCJ rejected any memory of the concentration camps that did not lead to reconciliation. Underlying such approaches was the message of Christian forgiveness (and the implied Jewish inpetus towards Old Testament revenge). The combination of Belsen and the memory of Anne Frank would again be used for such reconciliation purposes at the time of Ronald Reagan's visit in 1985.[29]

The Christian impetus was also present when controversy broke out between the Jewish survivors and those who wanted to create an international monument to its victims. A new international memorial was added to the Belsen landscape challenging the specifically Jewish one. Although, because of the campaigning of Jewish survivors, it had a small Hebrew–Yiddish inscription alongside many others, the international memorial was overshadowed and dominated by the massive cross erected by the French. Jewish groups were unable to stop this development which provided a link with an earlier cross erected by Polish Catholic survivors of Belsen. As with Auschwitz, a site that was fundamentally dominated (as a concentration camp as opposed to its earlier days holding prisoners of war) by Jewish death and suffering, had effectively been internationalised and Christianised. Further dispute emerged in the late 1950s and early 1960s when attempts were made by the French government to remove its own nationals from the mass graves of Belsen. It was at this point that the growing influence of Holocaust survivor groups, and particularly the World Federation of the Bergen-Belsen Associations, was shown. The German government, facing massive Jewish protests, refused to bow to French pressure and the bodies of the dead remained undisturbed.[30]

Although the international legal battle over the graves of Bergen-Belsen extended into the late 1960s, the memory of the camp in that decade became increasingly privatised. As a site, survivor groups (who now began to write aspects of Belsen's history, including its post-war years as a DP camp which were seen as providing a Zionist model for Jewish self-determination), Germans and British army groups did visit the site, but it was a minor centre of commemoration on the European scene, even with the addition of a small documentation centre there in 1966.[31] In the 1960s it was still a symbol for mass evil, but Auschwitz, especially after the Eichmann trial, was beginning to achieve the notoriority and metaphor for mass evil that it possesses today. References to it started to surpass those to Belsen. In this respect, Sylvia Plath's poem 'Daddy', written in the early 1960s, is an important cultural guide in which Belsen and Auschwitz are accorded equal weight.

James Young has argued convincingly with regard to the heated
debate about Plath's use of Holocaust imagery that 'rather than
disputing the authenticity of her figures, we might look to her poetry
for the ways the Holocaust has entered public consciousness as a
trope, and how it then informs both the poet's view of the world and
her representations of it in verse'. Young points particularly to the
influence of the Eichmann trial on Plath: 'a time when images of the
camps flooded the media and commanded world attention as they
had not since the war'. But it should be added in relation to Plath
that, yet again, western and eastern camps are merged with little
regard or understanding of their respective functions:

> An engine, an engine
> Chuffing me off like a Jew.
> A Jew to Dachau, Auschwitz, Belsen.[32]

In 1965, the year these lines were published in the posthumous
collection *Ariel*, apart from Richard Dimbleby's moving return to
Belsen, the liberation of the camp was almost universally ignored in
the twentieth anniversary of the ending of the war. The image of the
western concentration camps still lingered in the minds of many who
could remember where they were when they saw the newsreels, but
they almost totally lacked a context in which to operate other than as
atrocity material. For example, the British novelist and writer
Frederic Raphael was known after the war at his school as 'Belsen'
not as a way of attacking his Jewishness, but simply because he was
thin. It was done, he recalls, 'without any thought of Hitler's real
aim'. It must be suggested that for the latter part of the 1960s and
through the 1970s, there was little that was new in the
commemoration of Belsen. For those that had liberated the camp,
painful memories remained but there were few opportunities to come
to terms with them. The individuals involved remained isolated in a
society that with only rare exceptions lacked understanding of their
massive and lasting impact. Some survivors of the camp were active
in Bergen-Belsen associations across the world, but perhaps the
majority continued on with their lives without such mutual support
mechanisms. The outside world remained, in essence, indifferent.[33]

It is ironic that the change in the memory and commemoration of
Belsen from the private to the public realm, which took place

particularly in the 1980s, should have its roots not, given its past history, in Britain, or Germany, or Israel, but in the USA. It is true that American imperialism had sometimes extended in the realm of concentration camp liberation so that it is occasionally GIs who exposed Belsen. *Judgment at Nuremberg* (1961) almost moves in this direction, thus Auschwitz becomes Buchenwald in the need to Americanise the Holocaust.[34] This was particularly important at the time of greatest rivalry and tension between the USA and USSR, when the contribution and enormous losses of the latter to the Allied victory in the Second World War had to be conveniently ignored. Nevertheless, there is just about an acknowledgment in the film that Britain liberated Belsen. But it was, from the very late 1970s until the present, the USA, and particularly American Jewry that was anxious to preserve the memory of the Holocaust. For the Holocaust to be Americanised initally required some direct link with the events in Europe. The American troops liberating the western concentration camps provided that connection. Throughout the 1980s, the fledgling organisations in Washington that were to become the Holocaust Memorial Museum, put together events and publications that brought together survivors and liberators. There was revived interest in the experiences of those who had entered the camps and perhaps for the first time serious attention paid to the survivors themselves.[35]

The interest in Britain was not as intense but, with the lead given across the Atlantic those survivors and a few others inside and outside the Jewish community who had campaigned ceaselessly for Holocaust commemoration, new possibilities emerged. In 1985, at the time of the fortieth anniversary of the end of the war, Bernstein's forgotten film was rediscovered and shown for the first time to a British audience. In an important documentary put together by Bernstein's Granada Television, the testimony of survivors and liberators was added to provide the first bringing together of such memory undertaken in Britain. Nevertheless, progress beyond this documentary was slow. It took further campaigning and negotiation with the Imperial War Museum, the official keeper of Britain's war memory, to create the first permanent exhibition on Britain and Belsen, installed in 1991. It, and its printed counterpart are, perhaps, still biased towards the representation of Belsen as a British rather than a Jewish camp but the two are at least brought together in a form unthinkable for many years after the liberation. The more recent move of the Imperial War Museum towards a separate Holocaust museum also reflects the positive change in attitude that has taken place in British society with regard to the Jewish experience in the Second World War.[36]

In conclusion I want to deal briefly with the possibilities offered with regard to the future memory of Belsen. The recent memorialisation of the camp has been less controversial and politicised than ever before. It was this that prompted Ronald Reagan to visit Belsen after his disastrously planned tour to Bitburg at the time of the fortieth anniversary of the ending of the Second World War. Having earlier rejected going to Dachau, Belsen was seen as less problematic to his administration. Reagan feared that visiting Dachau would open old wounds and bitternesses. Furthermore, Dachau, the first Nazi concentration camp, was perhaps particularly unappealing to Reagan as its initial function was to deal with political opponents of the Third Reich (and essentially those on the left). Two weeks earlier, Helmut Kohl, Chancellor of the Federal Republic of Germany, had made a speech at the site of Belsen when he had remembered all those who had been killed by the Nazi regime (including Gypsies and the mentally handicapped). In a similar, if less extensive manner, Reagan referred to the 'Christians – Catholic and Protestant' as well as the Jews who had died at Belsen.

On the one hand, therefore, Kohl and Reagan universalised the camp (the French cross and the International Memorial enabling such an approach).[37] On the other, by stressing the memory of Anne Frank who died at Belsen, Reagan preached hope for the future and, to an extent, forgiveness. This was a crude reading of Anne Frank, almost as limited as the Hollywood film of her diary with its happy ending released in 1959.[38] But if nothing else, the almost accidental visit of Reagan to Belsen exposed the poverty of the information available at the site. Work then began on an improved visitor centre which led to the creation of a permanent exhibition and extended documentation centre which opened in April 1990, 45 years after the camp had been liberated. As a result of this new approach and the tremendous efforts of those involved at the Bergen-Belsen Memorial, the site is now receiving up to half a million visitors every year. The permanent exhibition covers all aspects of Belsen's complex history. It in no way minimises the horror associated with the camp but the exhibition, in contrast to that at the Imperial War Museum, still manages to re-establish the individuality and humanity of its victims.[39]

Finally, there is a need, in total contrast to Reagan's Bitburg and Belsen visit, to remember Belsen in a way that does not minimise the suffering of its victims (it will not do, for example, to suggest as Storm Jameson did in the early 1950s that Anne Frank died with 'a profound smile ... of happiness and faith') but also recognise their courage and strength in bearing witness.[40] It is also essential to recognise the efforts of those who liberated the camp and have had to live with those images throughout their subsequent life. Only if the particular history, the particular experiences and the particular memories of Belsen are acknowledged, further complicated by age and gender as well as race and nationality, should we even begin to think of universalising from it – a feat at least partly accomplished at the Bergen-Belsen Memorial since 1990.

As we move closer to a world without the witness of those who experienced Belsen directly this need is ever more important. The memory of Belsen has been abused too readily in their lifetime. There is now no excuse for it to be distorted in the future. It is thus fitting to finish with Josef Rosensaft, Jewish leader of post-war Belsen, writing in the 1950s, but whose words are as relevant today as this murderous century draws to a close:

> We are often told on all sides that it is time to forget Belsen. True, we cannot remember every hour of the day. We are only human and tend to forget from time to time. But we cannot accept the advice to cut Belsen out of our memory. *Belsen will always remain part of us.*[41]

NOTES

1. Eberhard Kolb, *Bergen-Belsen* (Hanover: Verlag für Literatur und Zeitgeschehen, 1962); idem, *Bergen-Belsen: From 'Detention Camp' to Concentration Camp, 1943–1945* (Göttingen: Niedersachächische Landeszentrale für politische Bildung, 1985; second edition). Kolb has been the only major historian of the camp and little sustained academic research was produced between his first and second editions.
2. Mina Tomkiewicz, *There was Life Even There ...* (Warsaw: Polska Fundacja Kulturalna,

1991), poem 'My Warsaw' reprinted on inside cover; one of the most thorough accounts of Belsen as 'exchange camp' is A. Oppenheim, 'The Chosen People: The Story of the 222 Transport', unpublished typescript, Wiener Library, London. See also the documents reproduced in Rolf Keller *et al.* (eds), *Konzentrationslager Bergen-Belsen: Berichte and Dokumente* (Hanover: Niedersächsische Landeszentrale für politische Bildung, 1995).

3. Daniel Goldhagen, *Hitler's Willing Executioners: Ordinary Germans and the Holocaust* (London: Little, Brown, 1996), Part IV on the extermination through work campaign; Monika Godecke *et al.*, *Bergen-Belsen: Explanatory Notes on the Exhibition* (Hanover: Niedersächsische Landeszentrale für politische Bildung, 1991), p.76 comments on diary writing and art in Belsen. Hanna Levy-Hass, *Inside Belsen* (Brighton: Harvester Press, 1982); Renata Laqueur, *Bergen-Belsen Tagebuch 1944/45* (Hanover: Fackeltrager-Verlag, 1989, 2nd edition); H.G. Adler, *Theresienstadt 1941–1945* (Tubingen: J.C.B. Mohr, 1955).

4. On the last stages of the Holocaust see Yehauda Bauer, 'The Death Marches, January–May 1945', *Modern Judaism*, Vol.3 (Feb. 1983), pp.1–21 and Goldhagen, *Hitler's Willing Executioners*, Part V; the Nazi description of Belsen as a 'humane camp' was used in the exchange negotiations. See *Jewish Telegraphic Agency Daily News Bulletin*, Vol.XI, No.160 (13 July 1944), pp.1–2; Tomkiewicz, *There was Life*, p.45 on the problems of communicating the world of Belsen to the outside world.

5. Jon Bridgman, *The End of the Holocaust: The Liberation of the Camps* (London: Batsford, 1990) provides a starting point but lacks vigour. The approach adopted by Joanne Reilly, *Belsen: The Liberation of a Concentration Camp* (London: Routledge, forthcoming) is far more multi-layered and complex even if concerned largely with the one camp. On coverage of Majdanek see *The Times*, 12 Aug. 1944; *Illustrated London News*, 14 Oct. 1944 and Deborah Lipstadt, *Beyond Belief: The American Press and the Coming of the Holocaust 1933–1945* (New York: Free Press, 1986), pp.261–2; Godecke, *Bergen-Belsen*, p.67.

6. Jonathan Dimbleby, *Richard Dimbleby: A Biography* (London: Hodder & Stoughton, 1975), Ch.5; Murrow's broadcast reproduced in Brewster Chamberlin and Maria Feldman (eds.), *The Liberation of the Nazi Concentration Camps 1945: Eyewitness Accounts of the Liberators* (Washington, DC: United States Holocaust Memorial Council, 1987), pp.42–5; Alexander Kendrick, *Prime Time: The Life of Edward R. Murrow* (Boston, MA: Little, Brown, 1969). For the account of one British cameraman at Belsen see Paul Wyand, *Useless if Delayed* (London: George Harrap, 1959), Ch.8. For a classic early account by a liberator see Derick Sington, *Belsen Uncovered* (London: Duckworth, 1946).

7. Raymond Phillips (ed.), *Trial of Josef Kramer and Forty-Four Others (The Belsen Trial)* (London, Edinburgh and Glasgow: William Hodge, 1949), p.xxxix; a photograph of the temporary British memorial can be found in the Fred Kirby collection, 1985/502 Manchester Jewish Museum.

8. On the Bernstein film see Public Record Office (PRO), INF 1/636, *Sunday Times*, 19 Feb. 1984 and *Observer*, 8 Sept. 1985. 'Two World Wars & One World Cup', an 'Everyman' documentary produced by Christopher Salt and shown on BBC1, 25 April 1993, provided a nuanced account of the persistence of anti-Germanism in the lives of a variety of people in Britain during the 1990s. As a woman broadcaster of German-Russian origin who had lived in London for many years put it: 'When you say German, a lot of people think Nazi immediately'.

9. Alan Rowlands, *Trautmann: The Biography* (Derby: Breedon Books, 1990) and Bert Trautmann, *Steppes to Wembley* (London: Robert Hale, 1956). For the local press debate, see the *Manchester Evening News* and *Manchester Evening Chronicle*, Oct. 1949.

10. Rowlands, *Trautmann*, pp.96–7, 107–8 and 231. The Bert Trautmann stand was opened in the 1995/96 season. The controversy over treatment of Trautmann was in marked contrast to the signing of Uwe Rossler by Manchester City from Dynamo Dresden in the 1993/94 season. Rossler was one of the first of many German footballers to come to Britain in the 1990s and apart from very quickly becoming a 'fully fledged terrace hero', he appears to have faced very little anti-Germanism from opposing fans. See *The Big Issue in the North,* No.85 (5–11 Dec. 1995), pp.10–11.

11. *Frieda* was directed by Basil Dearden. On the film more generally see Terry Lovell, 'Frieda' in Geoff Hurd (ed.), *National Fictions: World War Two in British Films and Television* (London: British Film Institute, 1984), pp.30–34. Ultimately, the taunt of Frieda's brother that 'we are one ... I embrace war' is rejected.

12. Trittin in the foreword to Godecke, *Bergen-Belsen*, p.5; Sebastian Faulks, 'Back to the Front with Tommy', *The Guardian*, 15 Sept. 1993.

13. The newsreels and the British liberation film are available at the Imperial War Musuem. The first thorough analysis of such material is in Marie-Anne Matard-Bonucci and Edouard Lynch (eds.), *La Liberation des camps et le retour des deportes: l'histoire en souffrance* (Paris: L'Editions Complexe, 1995); On *Night and Fog*, released to mark the tenth anniversary of the camp liberations, see Andre Pierre Colombat, *The Holocaust in French Film* (Metuchen, NJ and London: Scarecrow Press, 1993), Ch.6. *Judgment at Nuremberg* was originally a television series and then transformed into a film released in 1961. See Judith Doneson, *The Holocaust in American Film* (Philadelphia, PA: Jewish Publication Society, 1987), Ch.3. On the 1995 commemorations, see Tony Kushner, '"Wrong War, Mate": Fifty Years after the Holocaust and the Second World War', *Patterns of Prejudice*. Vol.29, Nos.2 and 3 (1995), pp.3–13.

14. This was true of Fred Kirby whose photograph album from Belsen is now deposited at the Manchester Jewish Museum. Kirby did not talk about his experiences at Belsen and later suffered a nervous breakdown. Conversation with the author, Manchester, spring 1986. For a similar example, see Godecke, *Bergen-Belsen*, p.67; *Jewish Chronicle, Zionist Review* and *Manchester Guardian*, April–May 1945; *Daily Mirror*, 21 April 1945. A good cross-section of British press cuttings on the liberation of Belsen can be found in Josef Rosensaft papers, 070/27, Yad Vashem Archive, Jerusalem.

15. For a more extensive development of this argument, see Tony Kushner, *The Holocaust and the Liberal Imagination: A Social and Cultural History* (Oxford: Blackwell, 1994); for the government line on de-emphasising Jewishness see PRO Lias to Grubb, 30 Aug. 1942, FO 371/30917 C7839 and similarly FO 371/42811 WR457, 1944 and Dixon to Martin, 16 May 1944 in PREM 4/51/8; Mass-Observation Archive, University of Sussex, D 5390, 23 April 1945 and D 5447, 1 Aug. 1945 for rare exceptions which do refer to the Jewishness of the victims.

16. *The Sixth Year of the War in Pictures* (London: Odham Press, 1946), pp.194–5.

17. Tony Kushner, '"It's a Bastard When You Come to Think Of It": Anglo-America and the End of Auschwitz', *Jewish Quarterly*, Vol.41, No.4 (Winter 1994/5), pp.10–14.

18. Donald Bloxham, 'The Representation of Operation Reinhardt at the Nuremberg Trials' and 'The Represention of Auschwitz at the Nuremberg Trials' (unpublished typescripts) on confusion about types of Nazi camps. See also Gitta Sereny, 'The Men Who Whitewash Hitler', *New Statesman*, 2 Nov. 1979; Abby Mann, *Judgment at Nuremberg* (London: New English Library, 1961), pp.92–6; Brian Cathcart, 'The Man Who Found Belsen', *Independent on Sunday*, 15 Jan. 1995; Joseph Schrieber, *Belsen* (London: Brown, Watson, 1959), cover and inside page.

19. Jon Savage, *England's Dreaming: Sex Pistols and Punk Rock* (London: Faber & Faber, 1991), esp. pp.108, 135. The racist context within which such music operated is dealt with great subtlety in Paul Gilroy, *There Ain't No Black in the Union Jack: The Cultural*

Politics of Race and Nation (London: Hutchinson, 1987), pp.122–30.

20. The original lyrics are reproduced in Savage, *England's Dreaming*, p.249. The desperate attempt to shock with this 'song' were revealed when it was performed in Brazil with the notorious train robber in exile, Ronnie Biggs. It was recorded on the Sex Pistols' appropriately named album 'The Great Rock'n'Roll Swindle' (1979–80). Belsen also appears in their 'Holidays in the Sun', 1977. See *Searchlight*, 1980s and 1990s for neo-Nazi rock bands and similarly, *The Guardian*, 11 Sept. 1992.

21. Kushner, 'Wrong War, Mate', p.4; *News Chronicle*, 27 April 1945; Phillips, *Trial of Josef Kramer*, esp. pp.30–65. In *Frieda*, Tom, a British soldier with a massive facial scar, confronts Frieda's brother who inflicted the injury at 'Brandenberg Concentration Camp'.

22. See, for example, the diaries of Ignacy Schwartzbart, 25 Jan. and 1 Feb. 1945 in Yad Vashem archive, M2/775, Jerusalem. The RAF picture taken on 19 September 1944 is located in University of Keele and is reproduced in Paul Kemp, *The Relief of Belsen* (London: Imperial War Museum, 1991), p.9. Joanne Reilly has personal postcards from Belsen which depict the burning of the huts along with the flag and Hitler portrait. A photograph with the raised Union Jack prominent in the front is reproduced in *The Relief of Belsen*, p.16, highlighting the Anglocentric tone of this publication.

23. See Joanne Reilly, 'Britain and Belsen' (Ph.D. thesis, University of Southampton, 1995), Chs.3 and 5.

24. Sam Bloch (ed.), *Holocaust and Rebirth: Bergen-Belsen 1945–1965* (New York: Bergen-Belsen Memorial Press of the World Federation of Bergen-Belsen Associations, 1965); *Belsen* (Tel Aviv: Irgun Sheerit Hapleita Me'Haezor Habriti, 1957, hereafter *Belsen*) on Jewish politics in Belsen which perhaps understates non-Zionist activities; Tony Kushner, 'Holocaust Survivors in Britain: An Overview and Research Agenda', *The Journal of Holocaust Education*, Vol.4, No.2 (Winter 1995), pp.147–66. Even Leslie Hardman, who became as the first Jewish chaplain in Belsen, a key figure in the re-building of shattered lives, found it hard at first to believe that the survivors had any future. See his *The Survivors: The Story of the Belsen Remnant* (London: Vallentine Mitchell, 1958) and Rosensaft in *Belsen*, loc. cit., pp.25–6. Richard Dimbleby was likewise pessimistic when he made his famous radio broadcast from Belsen.

25. The photograph of the unveiling of the Jewish memorial is reproduced in Godecke, *Bergen-Belsen*, p.85; see also Bloch, *Bergen-Belsen*, for post-war commemoration.

26. Rosensaft, 'Our Belsen', in *Belsen*, pp.24–49. At the Wiener/Parkes Library 'The Liberation of Belsen' conference, London, April 1995, an informal and non-hostile conversation between two (non-Jewish) British liberators commented on how Belsen's memory had become Jewish; Andrew Charlesworth, 'Contesting Places of Memory: The Case of Auschwitz', *Environment and Planning D: Society and Space*, Vol.12 (1994), pp.579–93; for the Soviet memorial and inscription see Keller, *Konzentrationslager Bergen-Belsen*, p.261 and Godecke, *Bergen-Belsen*, p.84 for the obelisk.

27. Keller, *Konzentrationslager*, pp.246–56; *AJR Information*, Aug. 1956 for the *Daily Telegraph* debate. On the lack of support, see the articles by Judith Hassan and Howard Cooper in *The Journal of Holocaust Education*, Vol.4, No.2 (Winter 1995), pp.111–30 and 131–45, issue devoted to 'Family/History: Survivors and their children'.

28. Andy Medhurst, '1950s War Films' in Hurd, *National Fictions*, pp.35–8; Rowlands, *Trautmann*, p.112. As late as the 1990s, Germans based in Britain complain that 'The war, the war seems to be the one subject on their minds, its always on television'. Quoted in 'Two World Wars and One World Cup', BBC1, 25 April 1993.

29. Rowlands, *Trautmann*, pp.107–8, 112; *Common Ground* Vol.11, No.2 (Summer 1957), p.24 and Lawrence Graver, *An Obsession with Anne Frank: Meyer Levin and*

the Diary (Berkeley, CA and London: University of California Press, 1995), p.128. *Common Ground*, Vol.8, No.5 (Sept.–Oct. 1954), pp.27–8 and Vol.8, No.6 (Nov.–Dec. 1954) on the Council of Christians and Jews, *The Diary of Anne Frank*, concentration camps and reconciliation; Geoffrey Hartman (ed.), *Bitburg in Moral and Political Perspective* (Bloomington, IN: Indiana University Press, 1986).

30. See Bloch, *Holocaust and Rebirth* and Josef Rosensaft, 'Our Belsen', in *Belsen*, pp.48–9 for Jewish protests about the attempt to universalise/Christianise the site. For the earlier Polish cross, see Godecke, *Bergen-Belsen*, p.84; Isabel Wollaston, 'Sharing Sacred Space? The Carmelite Controversy and the Politics of Commemoration', *Patterns of Prejudice*, Vol.28, Nos3–4 (1994), pp.19–27; Sam Bloch, 'Is There to be No Peace for the Martyrs of Belsen?', *Midstream*, Vol.15, No.6 (June/July 1969), pp.56–60 and Menachem Rosensaft, 'The Mass-Graves of Bergen-Belsen: Focus for Confrontation', *Jewish Social Studies*, Vol.41 (1979), pp.155–86. Rosensaft concludes (p.178) that 'While short-term political interests might have influenced the German authorities toward an accommodation with France in this matter, ... the moral pressure exerted by the Jewish survivors served as an effective counterweight'.

31. On the 1966 centre, see Keller, *Konzentrationslager Bergen-Belsen*, pp.257–8. Richard Dimbleby, in returning to Belsen in April 1965, was struck by the quietness and desolation of Belsen. See Robert Rowland, 'Return to Belsen 1965', in Leonard Miall (ed.), *Richard Dimbleby Broadcaster, By His Colleagues* (London: BBC, 1966), pp.47–9. See particularly Bloch, *Holocaust and Rebirth* and *Belsen* for Zionist readings of Belsen's post-war history. For a more recent analysis on similar lines see Hagit Lavsky, 'The Day After: Bergen-Belsen from Concentration Camp to the Centre of the Jewish Survivors in Germany', *German History*, Vol.11, No.1 (1993), pp.36–59.

32. James Young, *Writing and Rewriting the Holocaust: Narrative and the Consequences of Interpretation* (Bloomington, IN: Indiana University Press, 1988), p.132; Sylvia Plath, *Ariel* (London: Faber & Faber, 1955), pp.54–7. It might also be suggested that the filmic influences from Belsen shaped the description of 'Daddy' as a 'Ghastly statue with one grey toe'. On the literal confusion of Auschwitz for Belsen, see *Times Higher Education Supplement*, 27 March 1992 and comment by Edmund Morris, 10 April 1992. The list provided by *Roget's Thesaurus of English Words and Phrases* (Harmondsworth: Penguin, 1968 edition), p.300 under the category 'Prison', is also revealing: prison camp; detention camp; internment camp; stalag; oflag; concentration camp; slave camp; Belsen; Auschwitz; Buchenwald; penal settlement; convict settlement; Botany Bay; Devil's Island.

33. Rowland, 'Return to Belsen 1965', pp.47–9. The film was repeated on BBC2, 9 Jan. 1995. The return was made more significant because Dimbleby was by then dying of cancer. Although Rowland reports that Dimbleby when walking round the camp was particularly moved by the epitaph on the Jewish memorial, it is Christian symbolism that frames his short Panorama documentary. The film ends with the French cross at Belsen dominating, accompanied by words of Christian forgiveness from a message left by a woman prisoner in Ravensbrück. The word 'Jew', as with Dimbleby's famous broadcast from Belsen, was not mentioned in this documentary, a fact that Jonathan Dimbleby failed to comment on when introducing the programme on BBC 1, 9 Jan. 1995.

Colin Richmond comments in 'Diary', *London Review of Books*, 13 Feb. 1992, that he is 'one of the many' who recalls where and when he saw the Belsen images: 'I sat in about the tenth row (in an aisle seat on the left-hand side) of the circle, the Regal Cinema, High Street, Sidcup, Kent. It was either late April or early May 1945. I was not yet eight years old.' The novelist Alan Sillitoe remembers the Belsen images from the newspaper photographs in 1945, though he confirms that he, at that stage a young man in Nottingham, did not connect them at that stage with a specific Jewish disaster:

Coming home from work one evening, my mother, before bringing in my food, opened the Daily Mirror to show a double page spread of photographs of Belsen. She leaned over my shoulder, and said: 'Just look what the rotten Germans have done to people.'

I saw what few could have imagined, and from then on we were to learn that the Germans and their all too willing helpers had deliberately murdered millions of men, women and children because they happened to be Jews. Poles, Russians and Gypsies, also considered less than people, had been starved, butchered and done to death as well, telling everyone on the Allied side, if they weren't already convinced, that the war could not have been fought in any better cause.

Looking at those pictures, I did not take in at that time that the heaps of bodies, and the survivors, were Jews. I soon learned, from many other sources. The main impression from seeing those photographs was one of sorrow for the victims, and anger at what had been done, though I was not naive because I at least knew that it was beyond all reason. (Alan Sillitoe in Parkes Centenary Lecture, 'Memoirs of a Philo-Semite: Jewish Influences on My Writing' and in conversation with the author, 6 March 1996).

It is also the lasting impact of the scenes from Belsen that is crucial in terms of the formation of individual as well as collective memory in post-war memory: 'Images of the liberation of the camp, seen on the cinema when I was a child, still live with me, and many others.' Rhoda Atkin, letter to the author, 19 Feb. 1996. Similarly Sillitoe adds in his Parkes Centenary Lecture that: 'I have lived with those revelations ever since, and will for as long as I live. If such a thing is possible, I am more affected by it the older I get, and one doesn't need to ask why, because it is obvious that one would be.'

For Frederic Raphael, see his 'The Worst of Times', *Independent*, 2 March 1993 and *Jewish Chronicle*, 4 May 1990.

On the liberator side, the liberation and relief of Belsen was generally part of other duties. Yet rather than act as a continuum, their experiences at Belsen could not be assimilated, it was too phenominal even within the context of a total war. This is well-expressed in Joy Trindles' 'Until Belsen', in Victor Selwyn (ed.), *More Poems of the Second World War: The Oasis Selection* (London: J.M. Dent, 1989), pp.265–6. Trindles was a nurse in Belsen after its liberation. For those liberated, the relative isolation of survivors in countries such as Britain (in contrast to the USA, Israel and Germany) made organisation difficult. It is perhaps the case that very young survivors from Belsen have been particularly marginalised. See *Jewish Chronicle*, 6 July 1990 for the getting together of a young Belsen survivor, Paul Oppenheimer, with a Belsen liberator, Harry Drummond, in the Midlands after a press feature on the former. It would have been hard before the 1990s for such encounters to take place other than by sheer coincidence – there was an equal lack of interest within British society in either 'group'.

34. *Judgment in Nuremberg* (1961); on the Americanisation of Holocaust memory on an international level see Judith Miller, *One, By One, By One: Facing the Holocaust* (London: Weidenfeld & Nicolson, 1990), pp.220–75.

35. See Chamberlin and Feldman, *The Liberation of the Nazi Concentration Camps*. See also Robert Abzug, *Inside the Vicious Heart: Americans and the Liberation of Nazi Concentration Camps* (New York: Oxford University Press, 1985). The intricate dynamics of the United States Holocaust Memorial Museum, especially with regard to the liberation, are superbly analysed in Edward Linenthal, *Preserving Memory: The Struggle to create America's Holocaust Museum* (New York: Viking, 1995). See also James Young, *The Texture of Memory: Holocaust Memorials and Meaning* (New Haven, CT: Yale University Press, 1993), Part IV.

36. The documentary was shown on ITV, 8 Sept. 1985. See *Observer*, 8 Sept. 1985 and

Jewish Chronicle, 13 Sept. 1985; Kemp, *The Relief of Belsen*. See Kushner, *The Holocaust and the Liberal Imagination*, p.264 for further comment on the Imperial War Museum. The current debate within the Imperial War Museum is no longer about the need for the Holocaust to be covered but in which context it should be placed. It is now clear that the early plans of the Imperial War Museum for an emphasis on comparative genocide has been modified with greater attention to be paid to the European Jewish historical, cultural and religious background.

37 Hartman, *Bitburg in Moral and Political Perspective*, pp.244–50, 253–5 and 256–61 for the speeches of Kohl (21 April and 5 May) and Reagan (5 May) at Bitburg and Bergen-Belsen. On Gypsies at Bergen-Belsen, see Wolgang Günther, *'Ach Schweister, ich Kann nicht mehr tanzen ... ' Sinti und Roma im KZ Bergen-Belsen* (Hannover: Satz, Druck und Verlag, 1990) and Sybil Milton, *In Fitting Memory: The Art and Politics of Holocaust Memorials* (Detroit, MI: Wayne State University Press, 1991), p.321 on the inscription for Gypsies installed at Belsen in 1982. More generally, see M. Schaller, *Reckoning With Reagan: America and Its President in the 1980s* (New York: Oxford University Press, 1992), pp.63–4 for Bitburg.

38. Reagan referred to the faith of Anne Frank and her hope for the future and mankind. The memory of her, argued Reagan, 'beckon us through the endless stretches of our heart to the knowing commitment that the life of each individual can change the world and make it better'. Speech reproduced in Hartman, *Bitburg in Moral and Political Perspective*, p.255; *The Diary of Anne Frank* (produced by George Stevens, 1959). More generally, see Alvin Rosenfeld, 'Popularization and Memory: The Case of Anne Frank', in Peter Hayes (ed.), *Lessons and Legacies: The Meaning of the Holocaust in a Changing World* (Evanston, IL: Northwestern University Press, 1991), pp.243–78.

39. Godecke, *Bergen-Belsen* for a full catalogue of the permanent exhibition. The Imperial War Museum exhibition 'Belsen 1945' has little sensitivity in its use of victim images whereas at Bergen-Belsen emphasis is put on the pre- and post-war lives of the victims and survivors of the camp.

40. Storm Jameson, preface in *The Diary of Anne Frank* (London: Vallentine Mitchell, 1952), pp.9–11 and her autobiography, *Journey From The North,* Vol.2 (London: Collins, 1970), p.257. This, however, was a very rare slip from Jameson who was more than aware of the full horror of the Nazi concentration and death camps. She knew its victims, had campaigned in the 1930s and during the war itself on their behalf and visited the sites after the war.

41. Rosensaft, 'Our Belsen', *Belsen*, p.24.

APPENDIX

BELSEN TESTIMONIES:
THE CAMP AND ITS LIBERATION

Many of the essays in this volume have made extensive use of personal testimony, whether it be in the form of contemporary diaries and reports from Belsen or post-war accounts and oral history. Many survivors fear, not without reason, that the Holocaust could, in the hands of insensitive academics, lose its human dimension. As editors, we believe that the contributors to this book have avoided treating their subject matter as 'just another historical issue'. The final section in *Belsen in History and Memory* stresses even further the need for historians and others involved with writing on the Holocaust to listen to the voices of those who suffered the brute force of Nazi racialism, and to those who were witness to it, as in the case of the liberators of Belsen. The accounts in this section provide a cross-section of testimony and attempt to achieve a variety of perspectives – Jewish and non-Jewish; women and men; a range of nationalities; children and adults; and survivor and liberator. Through these different voices, we hope that the reader will be provided with another standpoint from which to confront Bergen-Belsen which supplements and sometimes challenges the perspectives offered by earlier sections of this volume.

HELEN BAMBER

The stories told to me in Belsen poured from people like the ferocious process of vomiting rather than the recounting of a story. I began to understand the importance of testimony and the bearing witness that I was forced to personally undertake. The truth was so stark, so naked that the only honourable way to receive it was to be naked too, bereft of all familiar values. I remember sitting on the ground with a woman and as we clung to each other she recited the sadistic excesses of one notorious woman guard in which the eye of one young man was destroyed as the whip lashed and lashed at the group selected for punishment. She continued to tell me of her husband's death too. If only, she said, and these words were repeated many, many times, if only I had stayed with him I could have saved him. She repeated it over and over again until I realised that she felt, *she felt*, responsible for his death.

Another story may have come from another camp but it was told
to me in Belsen. And it is not actually very important to me whether
it happened in Belsen or not. Belsen became the depository for many
such stories as people came to the camp, searching for family,
clutching minute pieces of what was generally cigarette paper with
the names of their loved ones. This is the story. A group of women
were being marched along in a line with guards and dogs; a line of
men were passing in the opposite direction. One man recognised his
wife and turned and called out. He was pushed forward by the guards
and the dogs were set on him. He was torn apart and made no sound
so that his wife should not turn and see him die. And yesterday, I did
ask myself in this room [at the 'Liberation of Belsen' conference], do
we have the right to ask questions about resistance in the camps?

Unfortunately, in the situation that I found myself there was no
mechanism for the systematic recalling of testimony. And as is so
often the way we tended to what we believed to be the most
immediate needs: establishing a search bureau, manning the hospital,
arranging treatment for young people suffering from tuberculosis and
introducing basic schooling for the children.

I know a number of former British soldiers whose lives were
deeply affected by what they saw at the liberation of Belsen. But there
is no doubt that over time there was a hardening of attitudes towards
the survivors. Even that title changed from former inmates or
survivors to Displaced Persons. As people began to recover they
produced spokespeople who demanded justice and recognition, and
while fraternisation between some servicemen and Germans became
commonplace the Displaced Persons remained in a bureaucratic
nightmare unable to obtain travel permits. They were viewed in fact
as a nuisance and the very essence of all that is created in survival and
recovery, so marvellous to witness, a privilege to see, became a source
of criticism and control.

This miserable state of affairs was personified for me by one of a
number of incidents. Many Polish Jews left the camp illegally to
return to their villages and homes desperate to see if any of their
family members had survived. I am sure that it is well known that
they were driven back by the Poles. Some lost their lives in the
endeavour. Most had no alternative but to face a hazardous and
exhausting journey back to Germany. They arrived in Wupperthal

hungry and seriously debilitated. In the changing climate the Jewish Relief Unit was inevitably brought into an advocacy role, and on this occasion I went with another to negotiate with the commander of the military government, for food and essential resources. The officer was at first very angry: 'They are here illegally and as far as I am concerned they don't exist'. Much later in the negotiations as his humanity was called upon, he said in true and obvious desperation 'My God, these people must have done something terrible to deserve this'.

There are many such distortions and much counter-brutality and it will always be so. But there are some who are willing to listen, and who continue to tell. And I think it would be very sad if we were to sit back after the 50-year commemorations and let the world forget. People have roles. There are teachers here who are asking how best to teach the subject and there are sympathetic journalists and interviewers, even if there are some who are somewhat ignorant. Is it possible, perhaps, that out of this conference we could establish a working party to look at the strategies for using oral testimony more effectively. I have in mind a title for this endeavour: 'Memory for Action'. I don't know, perhaps it sounds naive but I think we have to do something, we have to begin to do something.

Sometimes I go out on to my patio and deliberately smell the geraniums. When I told this to a group of former Far East British prisoners of war, in the context of my work with the Medical Foundation for Victims of Torture, one elderly man came to me after the event. He took my hand and he said 'I know why you smell the flowers. You need to remember Belsen, you need to remember'. Now I take my hope from this man but I do believe we have to work very hard to remember the past.

ESTHER BRUNSTEIN

It can happen any time anywhere but mostly it happens at night when sleep so often eludes me. I lie awake very much aware of my comfortable bed and clean linen. It is then that Belsen and Auschwitz creep into my thoughts and the agony returns. My body starts to itch as if still infested by lice and the dreadful nauseating, unspeakable stench of decaying corpses coupled with excreta, fills my nostrils; I am transported back in time and feel trapped.

Language fails me. Try as I might I know I am incapable of expressing and transmitting the trauma, fear and despair which were the norm of our existence there – on another planet, far, far, away from anywhere.

Elie Wiesel said some years ago that before Auschwitz no-one could imagine Auschwitz, and now, after Auschwitz, no-one can retell Auschwitz. This, of course, applies to Belsen, Majdanek, Treblinka and all other death and concentration camps.

I think it a pointless exercise for this conference to establish whether Belsen belongs to the category of death camps or concentration camps. As far as I know there were no gas chambers in Belsen but thousands upon thousands died there from starvation, disease and killings. Belsen most certainly belongs to the category of horror camp in an inhuman era where decency, reason and compassion were absent among the rulers of this hell where terror reigned supreme.

Many books have been published in which the authors analyse and evaluate all that happened in those dark days and, no doubt, a discourse on the subject of extermination of European Jewry will go on for many years to come. I can throw no new light in that direction and leave this task in the skilled hands of professional researchers, historians and sociologists. What qualifies me to stand on a platform to speak is my experience and the unwritten 'degree' I earned for miraculously surviving the Lodz Ghetto, Auschwitz, a labour camp and Belsen.

The memory of those days has left me with a feeling of total madness. I am an eye-witness to a world which became temporarily unhinged and sunk into an abyss of apocalyptic proportions.

I came to Belsen in January 1945 after the labour camp I was in near Hanover was liquidated. We marched to Belsen quite unaware of the place and what might greet us there. On the way I remember seeing neat little red-roofed houses. It seemed another world, one in which we had played no part for so long and I was surprised to find it still existed. We could see children and adults peeping through the curtained windows, looking on at the throng of skeletal creatures in striped concentration camp garb. I wondered then and still wonder today what thoughts went through the minds of these onlookers. Were they really unaware, as so many later claimed, of what did go on in their Fatherland? This will forever occupy my thoughts.

The memory of my arrival in Belsen is hazy. There were 400 of us and we were herded into different barracks which were already overcrowded with the living and decaying corpses. As we made our way I tried to keep close to my friends from the camp where, despite the harsh conditions, the inmates had shared a strong sense of camaraderie and the daily routine had some kind of structure.

Total chaos and the stench of decaying bodies everywhere, that is how I remember Belsen; a living 'Inferno' which almost renders me speechless to this day. I see myself, this skinny, bewildered 16-year-old, running from hut to hut, looking, searching, hoping to find a friend, a cousin, or maybe an aunt still among the living. Rumours were going round that somewhere in the camp there was a sectioned off area for children and people with foreign passports who were getting preferential treatment. Everything seemed so unreal. So much went on in that vast camp of which the majority of inmates were unaware.

One day a friend told me to come very early next day to a certain point where a few women would be chosen to work in the kitchen peeling potatoes and vegetables. I got very excited at the mere thought of maybe having a little extra food. Luck was with me. I was chosen. I worked in that kitchen barrack for a few days and it was there, one day, sitting with my cold feet deep in mud that I felt a fever taking possession of my body. I was quite aware that it was probably the end of the road for me.

Typhus and dysentery were rampant in the camp and I recognised the symptoms. Two friends helped me by holding me up to march back to our section of the camp and somehow got me inside a so-called Isolation Block. I remember slipping slowly into an unconscious state of mind with occasional moments of lucidity. I knew that I was lying on the lowest bunk next to the bucket, the only receptacle for our bodily needs. There were four women to each two-foot wide bunk. The three women who shared my bunk were in the last throes of death and would soon join the heap of corpses just outside the barrack. Indeed, that lower bunk which I occupied was meant for those for whom there was no hope of survival.

When moments of consciousness returned, I vividly remember feeling hollow and devoid of emotion. To experience emotion requires some physical effort of which I was no longer capable. I was resigned to my fate but just felt deep regret that after so much suffering and the struggle I had put up that I would not make it after all. I recalled the images of all that was dear to me bidding farewell to my loved ones and my young life.

When I awoke from a dreadful nightmare there were friendly, smiling faces around me telling me it was all over. I was too numb and confused to make sense of what they were saying. However, on seeing four chunks of black bread and four cans of Nestlés condensed milk on my bunk it dawned on me that the longed for moment had come and we were free at last. I remember looking at the bread and bursting into uncontrollable tears.

For five-and-a-half years I had dreamt of one day being given the opportunity to eat and eat without the limit of time until I burst. I was robbed of that satisfaction for I was too ill to swallow a crumb. It most likely saved my life for it is well known that many people died after liberation due to eating the wrong foods after years of starvation. I also feel cheated for not having the memory of experiencing the initial exhilarating moment of liberation.

The first few days were joyous and yet sad, confusing and bewildering. I did not know how to cope with freedom after years of painful imprisonment!

Looking out of the window I could see German soldiers being made to clear the mountain of corpses – the fruit of their labour. The inmates had to be restrained from attacking them. There was murder in all of us and it scared me. I remember praying silently. I did not really know to whom to pray but I never prayed so fervently in all my life. I prayed not to be consumed by hatred and destroyed for the rest of my days.

M.R.D. FOOT

There were not many British prisoners in Belsen. Among the 1,875 death certificates reported at the Belsen trial,[1] only 15 were down as 'English', beside 403 French, 349 Dutch, and so on; these figures presumably refer to deaths after the camp had been cleared of German guards. One cannot readily conceive of Kramer or his colleague Dr Klein spending time in signing death certificates. Out of my profound ignorance of detail, I can bring to historical notice one or two in person.

One was a schoolmaster from the Channel Islands, Hugh Le Druillenec of Jersey, who had been arrested on 5 June 1944. That was bad luck: the very eve of operation 'Neptune', the assault phase of 'Overlord' the operation that was to set western Europe free. His crimes were two: he possessed a wireless receiver; and his family had helped, 18 months earlier, to hide a Russian who was on the run from the occupier – and remember that on the Channel Islands there were 36,000 occupiers and only 60,000 civil inhabitants, so control was not light. There was no nonsense about a trial; he was sent, after some French prisons, to Neuengamme, the camp where prisoners' morale was broken before they were moved to be worked to death elsewhere.

He had retained, even after Neuengamme, shreds enough of his past character and intellect to think of Dante on first entering a hut in Belsen.[2] He was put to labour on his second day – hauling corpses to the crematorium, or rather, to be stacked in piles close to the crematorium, which had run out of fuel. Emaciated though the corpses were, it took four men to shift each – on a diet of nothing at all: not even turnip soup, let alone dry bread. For five days on end Le Druillenec was driven out to this work, for a 12-hour day, with nothing either to eat or to drink.[3] By this time, early April 1945, such sanitation system as there ever was in the camp had broken down; in the almost inconceivably cramped huts into which the prisoners were huddled over night, one had to splash and wade through excrement, and I only do not call the stench unbearable because people bore it: what else was there to do but die? Le Druillenec survived, to be the first witness from inside the camp heard at the Belsen war crimes trial in September 1945.

He made so profound an impression on the court, with his conclusion that Belsen was 'probably the foulest and vilest spot that ever spoiled the surface of this earth'[4] that they overrode the plea by Colonel Smith, professor of international law at London University, that they were a military court trying war crimes: concentration camps, Smith argued, 'have nothing to do with the war at all'[5] because Hitler had set them up on coming to power, perfectly legally under German law, so that they were outside an English court's reach. They turned out not to be quite outside the reach of English common sense; moreover, as Smith remarked, 'Public opinion, sound or unsound, has lashed itself up into a fury over this case',[6] and the forename of Irma, at least, seems in Irma Grese's iniquitous memory to have disappeared from English christening ceremonies. It is worth remembering that this court at Luneburg, inquiring into the affairs at Belsen, finished its two months' proceedings on 17 November 1945, three days before the grander tribunal at Nuremberg opened. But we must get back from legal theory to individual fate.

Keith Meter did not survive. About him I happen to know a certain amount, by a fluke. He took part in a combined operation – a sort of commando raid – on Haugesund on the south-west coast of Norway, for which it had been my task to provide the intelligence. Indeed, I briefed his commander, Sub-Lieutenant John Godwin, RNVR, with whom I had an odd bond – we were born on the same day. A moment's excursus on John Godwin may be allowed.

He was born in Argentina, and took ship to England with his twin brother to join up when the war began. He was trained in small boat work, and took to Norway with him on 29–30 April 1943 a commando sergeant, a naval petty officer, and four ratings (of whom Meyer was one). They lay up on an island that he and I had spotted on air photographs, and attacked shipping with limpet mines, with some success; till they tackled a little warship that was too big for them. They were overpowered and captured. They were all in uniform, on a legitimate operation of war; they were held to come under Hitler's notorious commando order of the previous October,[7] and were handed over by the German navy to the SS.

Under the 'Nacht und Nebel' regulations, they were not reported as prisoners of war.[8] They were sent to Sachsenhausen, where Meyer was presumed Jewish on account of his surname and was put into solitary. The rest of the party spent 14 hours a day, for 14 months, testing boots for the German army. On 1 January and 20 April (Hitler's birthday) they had a day off; otherwise they worked a seven-day week, marching round and round a cobbled track; till it came to their turn to fall in with a larger party to go to the execution ground.

At a momentary hitch at one of the steel gateways in the camp, Godwin reached over, took the pistol out of the belt of the SS lad in charge, and shot him dead.

He only survived a few seconds; and the best the decorations system could do for him was a posthumous mention in dispatches, because nobody senior to himself was present to testify to his bravery.

If I ever find myself face to face with St Peter, both those lives will be on my head; for Godwin was acting on the principle I had taught him – if you are taken prisoner, the war is not over for you, you must seize any chance that offers to make trouble for the enemy.

Shortly after Godwin's end, Meyer was sent – who can say why? – to Belsen instead. There he caught the prevalent typhus. In mid-March 1945, as he lay wrestling with that dread disease, an SS man walked up to him, asked him if his name was Meyer, got a nod in reply and shot him through the forehead.

One other name deserves mention: Yvonne Rudellat's – not an English name but she had been working for a British secret service, the Special Operations Executive. She was in fact an enemy national when SOE took her on, for she was married to (though separated from) an Italian waiter in Soho. She was French by birth, and could pass easily for the Frenchwoman that she was. She had been a receptionist at a small hotel in Ebury Street, between Eaton Square and Victoria Station, occasionally used by SOE officers; one of whom offered her the chance to volunteer. She parted from her grown-up daughter, did the usual paramilitary training, and had spent some useful months in the middle Loire, receiving parachuted stores and distributing them locally, before she was arrested in a scuffle in mid-June 1943, badly wounded.[9] She was among the many prisoners who were marched into Belsen from elsewhere in Germany, during the insensate shuffling that accompanied the collapsing Third Reich, arriving about 1 March 1945. By mid-March, as I have said elsewhere,

> she was then as well as any one could be amid the prevailing lack of food, fuel, clothing, decency, privacy, what civilised communities call 'the necessities of life'. She [I quote her friend Vera Atkins] 'was not in bad health, she suffered occasionally from loss of memory, but she remained in good morale and she

looked neither particularly drawn or aged'. But she soon fell dangerously ill [– she had typhus on top of dysentery.] When she was captured she was too far gone in her diseases, or too steeped in her cover story, or both, to tell a soul what she had been; unnoticed to the last, she died on 23 April 1945 or the day after, and her body was huddled with 20,000 others into one of the huge mass graves.[10]

I have an uneasy feeling that there may have been other British prisoners who, like Meyer, were executed in Belsen because they had been on some operation outside the conventional fighting fronts; and that they belonged to the brigade which I had the honour to serve in 1944, the Special Air Service Brigade. I have not succeeded in digging out details that attach any of the victims to this particular camp; but can never forget that a 100-odd members of this brigade were taken prisoner in north-west Europe in 1944–45 – all, like Godwin, in uniform, and all, like Godwin, on legitimate asks of war; of those 100-odd prisoners only six (of whom, again by fluke, I am one) came back to tell any tale at all. Those of the rest who were not shot on the spot were sent to concentration camps.

NOTES

1. Raymond Phillips (ed.), *Trial of Josef Kramer and Forty-Four Others* (London: Hodge, 1949), p.140.
2. Ibid., p.58.
3. Ibid., pp.60–61.
4. Ibid., p.65.
5. Ibid., p.494.
6. Ibid., p.489.
7. *The Trial of German Major War Criminals* [at Nuremberg] (London: HMSO, 23 vols., 1946–50), pp.iv, 2–3. This order laid down that any members of the Allied forces found operating behind the German lines were to be shot out of hand, or handed over to the SS for special treatment.
8. Under the Nacht und Nebel (Night and Fog) system, no questions put to German authorities about prisoners held under it were ever acknowledged, let alone answered. Its prisoners could receive no mail, let alone parcels; they were kept in strict isolation, except from each other. See Helmut Krausnick *et al.*, *Anatomy of the SS State* (London; Collins, 1968), pp.471–2.
9. See Stella King, *Jacqueline* (London: Arms and Armour Press, 1989), her biography, *passim*.
10. M.R.D. Foot, *SOE in France* (London: HMSO, 1968), pp.431–2.

ALFRED GARWOOD

David Faber was 17 years old when sent to Auschwitz arrived in Bergen-Belsen from Buchenwald, at the beginning of April 1945. He tells the following story:

I woke on my bunk. Dead men lying on either side of me the stench of death was all around. Boach typhus. Delirious and shivering with fever I knew I had to get out of there or I would die with them. Somehow I dragged myself into the fresh air and sat propped against the side of a barrack warming my body in the sun. Gradually as my vision cleared I saw on the other side of the barbed wire, a few feet away, a sight which seemed unbelievable. A man was standing looking at me. Not dressed in camp pyjamas but in proper clothes with a yellow star. He was carrying a small blond child in his arms and [holding] another, a little older, by the hand. I could not believe my eyes. He asked me to look for his mishpucha, his family, and he would give me bread. He threw some bread over the barbed wire and I struggled to reach it in the scramble it created. I hung on to a piece which I ate lovingly. He returned the next day and threw over another piece of bread even though I had not been able to find any of his family. The following day, when I looked, that part of the camp was empty. I thought it must have been a delirious dream as my fever had worsened and I had become increasingly ill and too weak to leave the barrack. Some time later, I cannot tell how long, I heard the voices of British soldiers.

Many weeks later when I had been nursed and fed back to health a British soldier came to find me. He told me he was my brother-in-law having married my sister who had gone to England before the war. He would arrange for me to come to London. Eventually, he did and we lived in Black Lion Yard, just off the Whitechapel Road.

Walking along Black Lion Yard one afternoon I saw a man coming towards me holding a child. He looked just like the man who had saved my life in Belsen. I approached him cautiously, asked apologetically so as not to offend him, 'Excuse me, but a man who looked just like you saved my life in Belsen'. The man confirmed that it was he who had thrown the bread. We embraced, wept and walked arm in arm to the man's tiny flat in Old Montague Mansions, on the corner of Black Lion Yard amazingly only a few yards from my sister's flat.

The man was my father and I was that child. Many years later I asked my father why, when we were starving and so close to death had he given away precious bread. He replied, 'although we were starving, David was in a terrible, much worse state'.

The story contains the essence of what I wish to briefly discuss. Defiance and resistance. The maintenance of compassion and integrity. The importance and survival of completely or nearly complete families. Survival and miracle of chance.

Those of us who were there will not have to be told that to throw bread over the barbed wire was to risk being shot on sight by the guards in the watch towers. This was one of many acts of defiance and courage reported to me.

The inmates of the Stern Lager may not know that the Greek Jacques Albala, the Judenältester or Jewish administrator, devised a scheme to 'sweeten' Joseph Kramer, the commandant sent from Auschwitz, and the notorious guard Irma Grese. Grese had a ferocious killer Doberman which she would set loose on us, for her pleasure. My father was multilingual and a lager friseur, a camp barber, and thus allowed to move around the camp. Albala asked him to buy some costume jewellery brought in mainly by the French women. The fake jewels together with some genuine stones were used by the Jewish goldsmiths to make jewellery which looked of great value. These were given to Kramer and Grese and did indeed please them. Thus Jewish ingenuity, better known as a Yiddisher cop, fooled two of the most notorious of the Nazi butchers. A small victory but a very important act of defiance and courage, as it saved lives; discovery would have meant hanging for my father and all the others involved.

The Nazis made great efforts to get their hands on the diamonds of Amsterdam. Many Dutch diamond workers with their families were brought to Belsen under a scheme the Nazis cooked up to set up a diamond cutting factory there, trying the old ploy of making us believe that if we were useful to them they would let us survive. The diamond-cutting equipment was shipped to Belsen and prolonged negotiations took place with the diamond workers to get them to disclose where the diamonds were hidden. Eventually the Nazis lost patience and gave them a deadline. If they did not disclose the location of the diamonds they would all be sent to Auschwitz. For the whole night the diamond workers discussed what they should do. In the morning, showing great courage, knowing their fate, they refused. The next day they were shipped out to Auschwitz and were murdered in the gas chambers. Their wives followed soon after, leaving some 50 orphans in Belsen.

Compassion for our fellow sufferers and integrity were not totally lost in the camps, as some would have you believe. Bruno Bettelheim was a German psychoanalyst and spent a year in Dachau and Buchenwald in 1938. His description of behaviour in the camp was unremittingly negative and denigratory. He implied survivor collaboration by stressing identification with the aggressor as a key behaviour pattern in which camp inmates adopted the values of the Nazis and were moulded into 'useful subjects of the Nazi state'. 'A prisoner had reached the final stage of adjustment to the camp situation when he had changed his personality so as to accept as his own the values of the Gestapo'. This is a gross distortion and denial of so much that happened.

Dr Sevy Koretz, born in Rzeszov Galicia, was Chief Rabbi of Salonika. In Belsen he maintained his compassion and integrity, comforting and supporting those that came to him in need and despair. My mother describes many occasions when he listened patiently to her and found words with which to comfort her, in contrast to the reports I have received, of his actions in Salonika. Dr Jean Allaluf was a distinguished surgeon from Salonika. Despite immense difficulties he performed surgery including an appendectomy on a young Dutch boy who survived and now lives in New York. Hanna Levy Hass, a teacher from Sarajevo, secretly created a school at great risk and taught the children.

Ariella Lowenthal Mayer, born in my town of Przemysl, orphaned at nine years of age and transported to Belsen with my family after interrogation at Montelupich Gestapo Headquarters in Cracow, tells of my father, a year after our arrival in Belsen, dropping bread on her bunk and rushing off before she could thank him. He was risking severe punishment, perhaps death with this act of kindness. I am sure most survivors could tell similar stories.

Luck is a terrible and wonderful thing as we survivors know only too well. Jacques Albala, the Judenältaster had been transported from Salonika to Belsen with his young wife and infant son Siegurd. By a twist of fate Siegurd and I were born on the same day. This seemed to have a special meaning for Albala and he took a special interest in us. When Siegurd died on the Trobitz transport a few days before we were liberated, Albala asked my father to bury him. At what emotional cost did my father carry out this compassionate act when I, too, was close to death. A few days earlier when the transport had stopped at a Berlin station, my mother begged for a little milk for me. The reply that she received from the German woman in the restaurant was 'why waste milk on him when he is going to die anyway'.

Jose Kramer appointed a German communist named Hanke to the position of Lager älteste, camp administrator and superior to Albala. Hanke's wife and daughter had been murdered in Auschwitz. My sister Leonie, six years old, reminded him of his beloved daughter and was allowed to play in his office at any time, except when a red light indicated she was not to enter. Leonie rarely left his office without being given a piece of bread or a little jam. Although starving Leonie never ate the food but always brought it back where it was shared between us.

Although I have not researched this, it is my impression that more complete families or nearly complete families survived Belsen than any other camp and may nearly match those who survived in hiding. Survivors struggled and fought to keep precious family members alive. In my view the most consistent single reason for survival was to stay alive for, or to keep alive, a precious family member and the greatest wound was their loss.

Which brings me to my last subject. The Holocaust was one of the most important and incomprehensible events of an apparently civilised age. It is essential that it is studied by academics of all relevant disciplines. Professor Yehuda Bauer, Sir Martin Gilbert, Claude Lanzmann and many others have made important contributions to our understanding and gained some degree of well-deserved fame and recognition. However, we survivors are becoming increasingly aware of the large and rising numbers of Holocaust specialists and experts. It has become an industry. If the result is that the Holocaust will never be forgotten, you might say all well and good. But that it should not be forgotten *is not good enough*. *How* it is remembered is what is of the greatest moral importance. What made the Holocaust so unique and important was the ferocity of the onslaught, the unimaginable suffering and the enormity of the losses inflicted on us the Jewish people. While specialists and experts make careers and achieve fame and fortune, we survivors fear that what is being forgotten or overlooked is the fact that the unimaginable suffering and bloodshed was our suffering, our blood, real people, sitting among you. The losses were not just numbers in history books but were our bubbas, zaidas, fathers, mothers, brothers and sisters. The communities destroyed were our homes, our birthplaces.

The losses and suffering of the Holocaust are too great to be fully mourned or healed in one generation. Sadly we survivors must bare the unwanted burden of those losses as must our children. For when we lost our mothers, they lost their bubbas. Too many have never known their bubbas, zaidas, uncles or aunts.

We survivors expose our suffering and scars willingly when we believe it serves to ensure our loved ones' suffering and death will not be forgotten. When we do so we are striking a bargain, for there is always a high price to pay when we remember. The specialists must always be careful to maintain a sensitive balance. For if we detect that the fame and the careers of the specialists are becoming more important than the Holocaust and the survivors, as has recently been observed, than the bargain will be one-sided and we survivors will be left feeling used and betrayed. If the Holocaust is to be understood then, above all else, it must be understood in terms of human suffering and loss – and if this is achieved then, truly, it will never be forgotten.

ERYL HALL WILLIAMS

I am speaking on behalf of the many civilian relief workers who joined in the combined operation to clear the camp of its inmates alive and dead, set up a hospital in the 11 blocks of the nearby Panzer barracks, and arranged for the able-bodied to be repatriated or to move on to another destination.

The British Red Cross Commission was the umbrella organisation under which we worked. Teams of 12 members, of both sexes, including teams from the Scouts and Guides and The Salvation Army, provided a variety of services in the six weeks before the rather spectacular burning ceremony which took place on 21 May 1945 in Camp I, when the last hut was ceremoniously set on fire by the British army.

I was a member of the Quaker Relief Team, and drove an ambulance. I spent most of my time on the so-called 'dry run' ferrying inmates from the Human Laundry, where relays of German nurses under medical supervision were bathing and cleaning up the DPs, to the impoverished hospital blocks in the 11 squares of barrack buildings, or working in the clothing store, nicknamed 'Harrods', or transporting inmates from the hospital blocks to the clothing store. In this situation while waiting for the inmates to be ready, I became a sitting target for members of the press, and gave many interviews (the journalists were discouraged from visiting Camp I). Other members of my team worked in the hospital organising the nursing and catering service, or were engaged in organising the messing arrangements for all the relief teams, providing transport for the Hungarian guards still guarding Camp I, foraging in the German countryside for additional food supplies and useful items like toilet necessities, making a hopeless attempt to get the drains running again in Camp I, purifying the water supply or providing a primitive first-aid clinic with the help of inmate doctors.

Apart from a brief visit to Camp I when we evacuated in our ambulances the 200 surviving children who had been cared for as far as possible by kindly women drawn from the inmate population, and a few days spent there assisting the 'walking cases' to be evacuated (one day we evacuated 17 Hungarian and Polish women whom I described as a terrible group of sad and feeble women, many of them half dead – this was on 11 May), my duties rarely took me to Camp I. But as I mentioned, I attended the burning ceremony.

My principal impressions were, apart from the grief and despair of those who had lost loved ones and did not know where to turn for their futures, was of the survivors' surprising resilience and the speed at which they recovered, so far as they could, their spirits, their desire to live a new life, (the girls were soon dating British soldiers!), and the way in which the relief workers responded to the difficulties they faced without being in any way 'phased' or affected by their experiences or what they were called upon to do. The phrase in Jung Chang's book *Wild Swans,* the history of those brave Chinese women who over three generations survived all the cruelty and hardships that the political regime in China could provide, struck me as summing it all up very well: 'amid suffering, ruin and death, [she] had above all known love and the indestructible human capacity to survive and to pursue happiness' (p.671).

I have since been asked many times how I could bear the experience, and my usual reply is that we were so busy we did not have time to think of it.

I also came to live with the almost daily disorganisation and frustrations of the role we tried to fulfil, and the frequent and unwelcome difficulties and disappointments involved, with some fortitude and calmness, not expecting anything to go right. This served me in good stead later when we got to work with the difficult task of caring for and arranging the repatriation of Poles from the Brunswick area. I remained in Germany another year until flying back with the RAF to Farnborough and my discharge from the civilian relief service. I must admit some pride in what was achieved by the Team and all the others involved in this magnificent effort.

REV. LESLIE HARDMAN

As one of the early liberators of the Belsen concentration camp on 15 April 1945, I have been invited to address this conference as to what, as an eyewitness, I saw and experienced during those early dark and devastating days in coming to the aid of those thousands of men, women and children, whom the Nazis barely left alive. So far as the 10,000 or so were concerned, whom they had already murdered and whose bodies remained unburied nothing else could be done but to say Kaddish over them.

But before doing so, let me say, despite the fact that we are commemorating the 50th aniversary of the liberation of this infamous camp and that, all things after 50 years tend to perforce to recede from the memory. I wish to underline that, owing to the horrendous manner in which our people suffered and were put to death, there must be no such thing as forgetting at least not this side of the next 50 years. As long as a single survivor lives and as long as every verbal and evidential record remains intact memory must remain indestructable. And men and women, young and old born after 1939, must be eternally vigilant to the recrudence of neo-Nazism and all racial discrimination, which at this moment in time I should have thought would have been far removed from people's behaviour, if not totally obliterated. But it is not.

Let me add an additional preamble which anticipates the question many people will want to ask if there is time for questions. In the book of Leviticus Ch.10 v 3, the Torah narrates the incident which led up to the death of Aaron's two sons; he took such a tragic blow with stoic resignation. He simply remained silent: *'vayidom aharon'*. In a word, Aaron accepted God's judgement without question. On the other hand, King David who suffered considerably more in my opinion, both in personal matters and in matters of statehood, of him it is written: *'V'lo Yidom'* (he was not silent). On the contary, he continued to sing praises to God, as it is written: *'L'maany'zamercha chavod, v'lo yidum, hashem elokai l'olom o'deka'* (My glory will sing praises to you and will not be silent O Lord my God; I will give thanks to you forever) Psalm 30.

Commenting on the different reactions of Aaron and David, one scholar says, 'It takes great courage and inner strength to be "silent" in the face of stark tragedy. But it takes a spiritual giant to transcend silence and to continue singing praises to God.' Let me declare that at the very beginning of coming face to face with the Belsen scene I could neither be Aaron nor a David. I do not know how anyone else could have, or would have reacted differently. I could not remain silent like Aaron. That is to say, I could not say *'mah d'avid rachmona, l'tave Ovid'* (What God does is done for the best), nor could I bring myself to say 'They must have sinned most grievously and God's will must be done'. I could not accept with perfect faith and equanimity as Aaron did, nor could I sing praises to God at that very moment as I usually do when I conduct a funeral service which opens with the words, 'The Rock, His work is perfect, for all His ways are judgement, Just and Right is He'.

Well, having said that, let me tell you how I became involved in that blessed moment of the liberation of the camp. It was on a Sunday late afternoon, on my return to my Headquarters in Celle from visiting troops, that I was told to go see the Colonel. He did not look the picture of sound good health. When I enquired, he replied, 'we have uncovered a concentration camp not far from here and it is horrible, ghastly, sickening. Most of the inmates are Jews, your people, and I think you should go there; they will need you.' He tried to describe some of the conditions. Yet, however vivid my imagination, not in my wildest dreams could I have imagined the terrible scenes which were to confront me. On the way to the camp, the colonnade of trees astride both sides of the road, were marked with notices: 'Keep away, Typhus'. I still could not picture what I was soon to see.

On entering the satanical inferno, the first person I met was a female who seemed to be wandering aimlessly, but I could not determine her age. When she saw the Magen David emblems on my uniform, she attempted to throw her arms around me. Her appearance was so repulsive, she was so emaciated, that I instinctively stepped back, although I immediately regained my balance to prevent her from falling. She said, *'farr loss mir nisht'* (please don't leave me). We then walked further into the camp.

Now before I proceed on this track, let me say this. Whatever and however many speeches you may have heard during the past 50 years about Hitler and the Nazi party and whatever books you have read or films or photographs you have seen about them, I maintain that far too many people have hardly scatched the surface of the enormity of the satanical evils the Nazis perpretrated against our people. Unless we become more acquainted with the real evils of Nazism and not just with its political and economic policies but the cruel, inhuman, barbaric and brutal savage manner in which these Nazi fiends physicaly and mentally tortured Jews and subsequently killed them, the possibility exists therefore of submitting to the cry: 'Now that 50 years have passed and Hitler is dead and Nazi Germany is defeated let us try to forget all about it.'

In future we must become more knowledgeable about the manner in which the Nazis tried to dehumanise us. They set out to destroy every vestige of human dignity in their victims, weakening their resistence so as to make it simpler to get rid of them without difficulty. I will give you some examples of this type of satanical behaviour. In one town they killed Jews like animals by cutting the throat, They disembowelled them and cut the bodies into chunks and sent them to feed the wild animals in the circus visiting in the town. A man was shot in Belsen by the SS. One eye was gouged out and a young man was forced to keep it between his lips, with his hands held high. As soon as he dropped his hands, and that often happened, he was beaten until he was eventually killed. There was a high heap of shoes in the centre of the camp, belonging both to the living inmates but mostly to their dead relatives and friends or compatriots. Every so often the inmates were forced to walk around this huge heap of shoes, which was already eaten into by lice and vermin. If they closed their eyes or tried to look away, they were beaten by the SS.

As we walked further into the camp, I suddenly froze, for in front of me several bodies were lying on the ground. Admittedly, the weather was good and quite sunny but still I asked her why they were sleeping there, instead of going into the hut quite close by? She replied in a tone of voice, as if she were referring to a heap of cast-off dolls, they are dead. It was then that I recalled a speech the late Jabotinsky made. He was the founder of the Zionist Revisionist party, later known as Herut, and now in Israel, the Likud Party. It was late autumn in 1938 in Leeds, England where he addressed a meeting of some 1,500 people, during which he urged Anglo-Jewry through its leaders to have the Jews of Poland dumped on the shores of Palestine, 'before it was too late'. I objected to the term 'dumping human beings'. He replied 'I agree with you' young man, but I repeat dump them now before it is too late'.

The spell which until now had appeared to have numbed all my senses, suddenly broke and the foul stench of the thousands of dead and decaying corpses reached my nostrils, with the words of Jabotinsky ringing in my ears '… dump the Jews of Poland now on the shores of Palestine, otherwise!' Here I was witnessing the otherwise. It was the girl's presence that prevented me from being violently sick. Within a few more minutes, a group of people looking like a number of bones held together with transparent skin, came tottering towards me. I let out a cry, 'O my God, the dead are walking'. My escort looked at me without the slightest emotion, 'they are not dead but they soon will be and so will we all if more food and medical help are not forthcoming'.

I cannot remember if it was the same day, or a few days later, again I was walking through the camp, when I noticed a very large screen was straddling part of the enclosure. I came closer, only to find that on it American films were being shown with beautiful actresses in beautiful gowns. I was quite puzzled as to why such films were shown especially when some of the victims said to me 'we know that we look like something that came out of the ground, but we are intelligent, cultured people, many of us are university graduates, solicitors, academics, medical practitioners and bankers. Is this your method of trying to rehabilitate us?' We soon removed the screen.

In this regard and in many other matters let me admit that whilst I could not help criticising the military authorities, I am sure the Army was doing its best under the prevailing conditions and circumstances, but not quickly enough for me. One officer said to me: 'we are here to kill bloody Germans and the quicker the better'. Another officer suggested, 'would it not be better were we to let them die, since having undergone so much suffering, mentally and physically, they will be a blight on humanity if they ever survived?' At first sight it was not easy to disagree with such a suggestion, but I insisted they must be given every chance to recover. It was then I prayed for a sign that they were fit to be saved.

The very first sign that faith had not passed them completely, was when I visited a hut on Friday night. When I got there, another shock greeted me. At one end of the hut were several corpses; and sick people were using the dead bodies as mattresses and cushions. At the other end were a number of women and one young girl sitting on the lap of her mother, all apparently waiting for me. Shabbat candles were lit, I must have supplied them a few days earlier. I made Kiddush and was invited to partake of some food. I could not refuse such g'filte fish, as they called it. I put it down to that when I went down with acute diarrhoea for two days. Several years later I met the mother and daughter in better circumstances.

A further good sign was forthcoming when I took Yosele Rosensaft, the Jewish leader of the camp, to Army HQ to meet Rabbi Brodie. On the way I passed a prosperous looking farm. I stopped the car and asked Yosele if he would try to get some eggs for the sick people. I gave him a few marks to pay for them. I waited at the end of the drive but was able to see the door of the house. I was nervous as to what might happen, but I hoped for the best. He knocked at the door and a few seconds later a woman appeared. I saw them gesticulating and realised what they were talking about. She then went back into the house with Yosele waiting outside. I breathed a sigh of relief. She handed him a box of eggs and he handed her the money. When I asked him why so few eggs he replied she was under strict orders to supply the British authority with a certain number each week. The eggs she gave him were from her own personal supply. Another sign.

After hundreds of letters began to arrive in the camp from all over the world in reply to those the DPs had sent, I suggested that a postman be appointed to deliver them. I met a youngster about 15 years of age coming into the camp from outside. I asked where he had been and he replied 'I have been outside walking around the streets and without being molested'. 'This is how it should be', I said. He grew solemn. 'I saw German children playing outside their homes but I couldn't kill them.' 'What do you mean?' 'Haven't you heard of the gas chambers, the crematoria?' I didn't reply. 'They murdered my parents. Even children like those I met in the street used to beat us, kick us. But I couldn't do that to them. I just couldn't do it.' After relating the story to the officer in charge, the boy became my postman.

Another sign was this. It was a Friday morning. I was busy in my office when there was a knock at the door. A middle-aged man, or so he seemed to me, stood hesitantly before me. On asking him what he wanted, he replied, 'Rabbi, could you give me something to eat?' Are you not getting sufficient food, I asked him. 'Oh yes, but I would like something tasty for Shabbos'. I went over to the cupboard where I kept a stock of canned foods. His eyes followed me and watched as I took a tin of sardines and handed it to him. He accepted it but when I was about to close the cupboard door, he placed his hand on my arm and then I heard the words, 'Rabbi, please wait'. He had seen the tephillin and said that it was three years since he had last worn them. I brought them down from the shelf and he put down the tin of sardines. He then took hold of the plush bag with shaking hands and with tears running down his puffy cheeks. 'Please may I use them?' I opened the siddur at the meditation page and his lips stirred. He recited the words, 'I am here intent upon the act of putting on the tephillin ... may the evil inclination not mislead or entice us, but may we be led to serve the Lord as it is in our hearts to do'. Then, still with shaking hands he took the tephillin out of the bag and as he prayed I looked at him and thought 'even through the three long dark years that had at last come to an end, this man had always sought to walk close to his God'.

In those very early days the problem of feeding the inmates gave everyone considerable discomfort. I personally felt that hundreds, if not thousands, of lives might have been saved if sufficient food and the right kind could be obtained. At first, there was little but German black bread and vegetable soup of a sort. The British troops offered their own rations of bully beef which in many cases was too heavy for the DPs. I would not like to put a figure on the number who died from such causes. The fact was that most of them had already reached such a serious physical condition that they would have died, whatever food would have been brought at that moment.

After a few days following liberation we found several cases of tinned milk, bearing the words 'to be consumed by Jan. 1945' (four months previously). These cases had been brought in by the Swedish Red Cross in December 1944 on the understanding they were for the inmates. My information is that a number of the inmates saw the arrival of the Red Cross officials, who were not allowed to see the horrible scenes of suffering and death in the camp itself. The Germans accepted the gift to show the world their own 'goodness' but their duplicity came to light when we discovered these cases. I did not consider it advisable to use this canned milk but the doctors among the inmates were of the opinion that it could be taken without any ill effects. And thank God they were right.

However well organised the Army was in getting in more food of the right sort, it was still insufficient. The officer in charge had to go a hundred and more miles for constant replenishments. A Jewish RAF chaplain came in, as so many other officers did as sightseers, and I urged him to help. Within a couple of days he took me to a Canadian Royal Air Force base which supplied me with truck loads of light foods, medicines and millions of cigarettes. A well-known American chaplain, Rabbi Shubov, came in and I asked him for help. He brought in an ambulance filled with white loaves of bread and then took back to an American hospital five women who were very sick at the time. I met them again alive and well several years later in Israel.

These few instances and there are many more, clearly indicate that the Jew is born civilised and nothing will ever totally dehumanise him, and by Heaven, the Germans did their damnedest to achieve it. I read the other day a statement purporting to come from the pen of Mr John Adams, President of the United States who wrote a letter on 16 February 1809 to a Mr F. A. Vanderkemp. He wrote: 'I will insist that the Hebrews have done more to civilise man than any other nation. If I were an atheist and believed in blind eternal fate, I should still believe that fate had ordained the Jews to be the most essential instrument for civilising the human race.'

It is related of the late Henry Springer, the German owner and publisher of the largest chain of newspapers in post-war Germany, that he took his son to Bergen-Belsen to place flowers at the grave of Anne Frank. Before they left he told his son to dig the earth with his fingers until he found some bones of human bodies. He told him to take one of these bones and place it where he could always see it, where he would never be able to forget what the Germans had done to the Jewish people. Mr Springer did this because, as a father, he was concerned with finding a concrete way of wakening his son's conscience to oppression and human cruelty of the extreme kind.

We are, I maintain, constantly in search of moral heroes. Heroes who keep us from falling prey to the defeatist assumption that little can be accomplished against evil. Such moral heroes exist today. Among non-Jews, for example, is Axel Springer who taught his son how the Third Reich denied liberty and life to Jews. Beatte Klarsfeld alerts the world to Nazis who have escaped punishment. Among Jews, Simon Wiesenthal is a genuine moral hero, because of his conviction that the world must being Nazis to justice.

I do not believe we are entitled just to ask God to save us without doing something for outselves. Just to cry: 'hoshiah et amecaha' is not enough. I agree with the Jewish preacher who says: 'It is not God alone who saves, but human beings who are his moral agents on earth.' It is written 'atem aydai' (ye are my witnesses). Only when you are my witnesses am I God. But when you are not my witnesses I am nor your God. In other words, God's reputation rises or falls in relation to our own deeds. Professor Rabbi Herschel said, 'The souls of men are candles of God.' Man 'in-deed' is God's most important need. We are not videos recalling the past. We are the children of prophets creating conditions for a better future. Our faith is not in what has happened but in what yet will be.'

ANITA LASKER-WALLFISCH

I will give a brief account of what happened to me and how I came to be an inmate of Belsen. I was born in Breslau which was a German town at the time but is now Polish. My father was a lawyer and my background typically Jewish middle-class. I had two sisters; we all learned to play musical instruments and looking back, I cannot think of anything other than a very happy childhood.

The clouds gathered in the 1930s with all the implications that I do not have to go into here, because they are so well known. All our efforts to emigrate failed miserably, partly because of the insurmountable difficulties put in place by the governments of countries which might have saved my parents from their ultimate fate.

The inevitable happened, my parents were deported. On 9 April 1942 they were sent to a place called Isbica near Lublin. There the Jews were murdered – but first they had to dig their own graves. They were forced to undress and were shot into these graves.

At that time I was working in a paper factory, making toilet rolls. My sister and I were arrested by the Gestapo in 1942 and sent to prison because we had been trying to escape with forged papers. After a year in prison we were sent to Auschwitz and after a year in Auschwitz we were sent to Belsen. In Auschwitz I had the great good fortune to be a member of the camp orchestra, which gave me at least a temporary chance of survival.

We have seen a great deal of Auschwitz-Birkenau following the commemorations of its liberation 50 years ago, and there will be few people who have not at least an inkling of the horror which reigned in this place. When in May/June 1944 thousands upon thousands of Hungarians poured into the camp, the death machinery was totally unable to cope. Gassing, burning, murdering. The crematoria worked around the clock. At the end, people were thrown into the flames alive.

We had hardly any information about events outside the camp and had no conception of how the war was going. We existed from day to day, always wondering how long this *status quo* could continue. And then one day, I think it was the beginning of November 1944, the dreaded moment came. We were ordered to line up, Jews to one side, Aryans to the other. This could only mean one thing: *gas chamber*. However, it transpired that we were not going to be gassed, but, believe it or not, we were going to be sent to another camp. To *leave* Auschwitz, not by way of the chimney, but actually to put distance between oneself and this murder factory, seemed nothing short of a miracle. Of course we did not know what was awaiting us at our destination.

We were issued with different clothes. In other words, all the relatively acceptable garments which we had managed to 'organise' by that time were taken away from us and we were given some really atrocious outfits, certainly most inadequate for the temperatures of the time of year. I managed with great cunning to retain my red jumper which I had been wearing day and night in Auschwitz. I continued wearing it day and night until my liberation six months later, and one can now see what is left of it at the Imperial War Museum. We were loaded into a cattle truck and began our journey westwards. Some rumours had been circulating that we were going to a convalescent camp, and that it was called Bergen-Belsen. Nobody had ever heard of it.

By this time, I was a vintage prisoner with a great deal of experience in the art of survival. We were no longer an orchestra, of course, but we were a group of people who had already survived against impossible odds, and it was obvious from the beginning that we were going to stick together come what may. And that was the first key for survival, to stick together, not to be alone. We kept ourselves going through these freezing days and nights in the train by singing our respective orchestral parts and by blowing on to each other's backs in order to create some warmth.

One day the train stopped and we were ordered to get out with the usual: *Schnell! Schnell! Schnell!* We were at a small station and there was not a living soul about. We were ordered to group ourselves in rows of five and started marching. We marched for a considerable time and then to our dismay we heard continuous shooting. Further on we passed a sign which read : 'ZU DEM SCHIESSTAND' [To the firing range]. In the gothic script I misread it as 'JUDEN SCHIESSTAND', and was sure that was exactly where we were going. I was marching in the front row and one thing that I clearly remember thinking was that I was glad I was going to be shot first, and that I would not have to see my sister and my friends being shot. However, we kept marching. No-one shot us and we arrived at the entrance of the camp.

Belsen did not look then as you have come to know it. We did not see heaps and heaps of corpses, that was yet to come. We saw some dishevelled creatures milling about. We saw someone with a 'Kapo' armband scraping out an obviously empty soup vat. My sister remarked drily: 'If a Kapo needs to do that, things must be pretty bad here.' Well, things were pretty bad, but not as bad as they were to become.

We entered the camp and it was soon evident that there was simply no room for us. I think we were some 3,000 people, and there were no barracks for us. In fact, we were herded into vast tents and, completely exhausted, flopped down on the bare earth. One of the things I knew only too well was that it was imperative to create gangways so that people could leave the tent if they had to relieve themselves. With a friend of mine I tried to achieve this, but to no avail. We were all too tired and just sat there on the bare ground, waiting for God-knows-what.

Then came the famous storm, and the tents collapsed on top of us in the middle of the night. How we survived that night, I shall never understand. Somehow we managed to scramble free and stood there in the dark, in the pouring rain and howling storm. The next morning we were led to a store bunker. We remained there for some days, with hardly any room to move, but happy to have a roof over our heads. And then suddenly and inexplicably there were empty barracks available for us. We did not know how this was achieved, but we all had our suspicions. After some weeks of sitting around and doing nothing we were put to work in what was called the *Weberei*. We made a sort of ersatz rope by platting strips of cellophane.

I remember the first body in our block. The first body! I also remember that I helped to remove it from the block. Then the death marchers arrived. This was a sight which it is not possible to describe, simply because there are no words in any vocabulary to come anywhere near it. Conditions deteriorated more and more. Corpses became so commonplace that one just simply ignored them.

The watery so-called soup we were given became irregular and eventually stopped altogether. Typhus raged and people dropped dead like flies. The mountains of unburied corpses grew higher and higher, and nobody could deal with them. We were ordered to drag the corpses to the end of the camp, out of the way so-to-speak. We tied string round the hands and tried to drag them along the Lagerstrasse. This exercise, however, did not last long. We were all too weak and one just could not keep up with the ever-growing mountains of bodies. By now it was April and very hot. We had stopped being cold but now we had another hazard, the corpses were decomposing. The stench must have been horrendous, but we did not notice it.

One day, it was April, there was a lot of noise coming from outside the camp. We had a feeling that something unusual was happening, but had no idea what it was. We saw fewer and fewer SS men and felt somehow that the end must be near. But what this end would be, we could not know. All I remember now is that we greatly feared that the Germans would blow up the camp before it was liberated. Some people said that the rumbling noises outside the camp might be tanks belonging to the Allies. I did not want to hear this and I was furious most of the time. I could not face any disappointment. I was more familiar with thoughts of death than with thoughts of possible 'liberation'.

Yet, it actually happened. I was weak by then, and my sister tells me that she dragged me outside the block and that we sat down on the ground – surrounded by corpses – and waited. And there it was, the first British vehicle rolled into the camp and the nightmare had come to an end.

It is very regrettable that 50 years had to go by before we could have a serious dialogue. This is, of course, the reason why there is such general ignorance about the Holocaust, not necessarily among this audience but among the majority of young people nowadays. I am thinking here of a young newspaper reporter whom I came into contact with; he is 30 years old and did not learn one single word about the Holocaust at his school. Even more shattering for me was a meeting only last week with a young Jewish lady of about 40. In the course of a conversation she told me that her mother had been in Auschwitz. When I asked her for some details she admitted she knew nothing, because her mother does not want to talk about it. I asked her if she had ever asked any questions and her answer was no.

This lady had lived in Israel when she was a teenager. I do know that some Israeli youth, with their guns at their side, used to maintain that *they* would not have gone like sheep to the slaughter. They would have done something about it. To me this is the final insult. It also casts a sense of shame on we survivors. Yes, there was shame, but the shame was not ours. We do not deserve this, I assure you. Let us not forget the uprising in the Warsaw Ghetto, and in Sobibor, and many individual heroic acts. The bottom line is, however, that we were defenceless.

Maybe, we the survivors should not be all that upset [over the lack of knowledge about the Holocaust] because part of it is our own fault. But if you have survived the Holocaust, it is not easy to talk about it. In fact it is almost impossible, because whatever you might say or tell, never comes anywhere near the reality. Apart from that, and I speak for myself only, when I came to this country some 49 years ago, nobody but nobody asked me any questions. There seems to be a taboo about this subject. People on the whole, and English people in particular, do not like to ask personal questions, and let us face it, somehow this theme does not lend itself to casual conversation. Now, however, we have reached a point when the ranks of survivors are shrinking rapidly, and many of us have started to talk or write. Anniversaries are, of course, very helpful here. We have an excuse to talk and you have an excuse to ask questions.

We have to be very vigilant because there is a great danger that historians will lump the Holocaust together with all the other extremely regrettable acts of genocide, which the human species should be ashamed of, and conveniently overlook the essential uniqueness of this particular event. Thus, here I am 50 years later telling you about my own personal experiences during this sorry episode, hoping that you can relate more easily to what happened to me during the war in the middle of Europe, and to all those people whose only crime was to be born as a Jew. And if you fail to see any purpose in trying to learn about the Holocaust, try to think of it as a debt which we owe to the millions of people who disappeared without trace.

REV. DR ISAAC LEVY, OBE, TD

The 50th anniversary of the liberation of Belsen re-awakened a consciousness of the horrors perpetrated by the Nazis on their hapless victims. The press, radio and TV all played their due role in giving prominence to the suffering inflicted by a ruthless and merciless regime. All too little attention, however, was directed by the media to the conditions which prevailed in the immediate aftermath of the liberation. It is on the problems which these conditions created that I wish to dwell for they were my major concern throughout the last months of my military service.

In the immediate post-liberation period there were only two Jewish chaplains in the British Zone of Occupation, Leslie Hardman and myself. We were desperately in need of assistance but none seemed to be forthcoming. The Jewish Committee for Relief Abroad was training teams for welfare work overseas and was eager to assist us but the authorities at Supreme Headquarters Allied Expeditionary Force (SHAEF), who alone could authorise the admittance of such teams to Belsen, were all too hesitant to grant such permission. By chance I had heard that a Jewish team was stationed in Rotterdam and was far from overworked.

In order to submit my claim for their services I called on the Headquarters of the Civil Administration in Brussels, there to be interviewed by an officer of equal rank to myself. He showed me a map on which were pinned a number of places which, he stated, were camps within the Zone. To my utter chagrin he told me that as far as he was concerned it was an academic problem! My reply was couched in non-clerical language and in no uncertain terms I told him what I thought of a man who could sit and enjoy the luxuries of Brussels while in Belsen they were dying like flies and he had the gall to say that this was academic. I could only threaten to take the matter up with higher authorities.

Fortunately, such action was not taken for during my absence and unbeknown to me, the Chief of Staff of 2nd Army, who had seen me in Belsen, had left a message with my immediate superior in the Chaplain's Department, that I was to inform him of the number of chaplains I required to alleviate our desperate situation. My immediate reaction was to ask for five and in due course the War

Office was cabled to that effect and the request was passed to Rabbi Brodie, then the Senior Jewish Chaplain to the Forces, to make the necessary selection.

Five men duly arrived. Two were army chaplains and three civilian Rabbis dressed in Jewish Relief Team uniform. The selection was far from auspicious. One of the civilian Rabbis, Dr E. Munk was an excellent choice, capable, orderly and dedicated; of the other two, one proved to be a source of trouble to himself and to the inmates and ultimately was removed, the other was a well-meaning Chassidic Rabbi whose side curls were well hidden under his military beret.

Several weeks passed before the Jewish Relief Team arrived and when ultimately they joined us they proved a most welcome addition to our strength and performed superbly. In the interim, however, we were greatly assisted by a Quaker Relief Team who apparently had no difficulties in gaining admission to the camp. This team had one Jewish member, Jane Leverson, who had originally joined up with the JCRA and in her impatience to serve volunteered with the Quakers. I was indebted to her for much detailed information on the subsequent transfers of inmates from Belsen to other camps in the Zone.

With the passing of the first few weeks the inmates who showed some promise of life, thanks to the dedication of the army medical services, were removed from the infested huts and it was then possible to make some calculation in terms of survival rates. Hundreds of former skeletal apparitions now assumed human form. But with the restoration of health new problems had to be faced. Basic natural human desires manifested themselves. The women became more conscious of their femininity and their newly aroused maternal instincts combined with their passionate determination to perpetuate the Jewish name, presented us with a fundamental question – could we and should we conduct marriages in the camp. The religious implications were obvious. I therefore wrote to London Beth Din to obtain a ruling or at least some guidance. Too my utter astonishment the response I received revealed that our religious authorities were either completely out of touch with reality or were reluctant to commit themselves to a positive ruling.

'No marriages may be solemnised until a complete list of survivors is obtained' was their decision. To this my reaction was 'How long, O Lord, how long' would we have to wait for this to be achieved. It was obvious to us that those who wished to marry or, what was more probable, to cohabit, would not wait indefinitely. If proof of this were needed, here was a simple example. A man approached me and showed me a slip of paper on which was written in Yiddish 'I ... son of take ... daughter of ... to be my wife' and this was countersigned by two witnesses. A legal document clearly, a common law marriage maybe, but not legally binding in Jewish law. Were they eligible for marriage since both had been married before? Both were survivors of Auschwitz whose spouses, they were convinced, had been led to their death. Who was I to doubt their testimony? Those notorious selections for the gas chambers were too well known to be questioned. The expressed desire for marriage grew in such alarming proportions that the Chassidic Rabbi, one of the five dispatched to us, felt compelled to contact the authorities and even succeeded in obtaining the help of the Royal Engineers to build a *mikvah* for the use of potential brides. To what extent it was utilised I was not in a position to ascertain.

While the question of marriages might be high on the agenda, a more serious issue was developing of which I knew nothing until it was brought to my attention by a Jewish medical officer who gave me a copy of a memorandum which he had sent to the camp commander. Apparently, the number of pregnancies among single young women was considerable. Their was reason to be concerned for their state of mind. They were consulting army medical officers with the view to terminate their pregnancies and this exposed them to grave dangers. The author of the memorandum urged that these women be accommodated in separate houses where they could be cared for and their physical and mental health supervised. Unfortunately I was unable to learn of the authorities' reaction before my period of military service terminated.

By this time Belsen had become a vast multi-national Displaced Person's camp, the number of whose inmates, according to the authorities, had to be reduced for administrative and medical reasons. To achieve this a system of transfers to other camps had to be undertaken which, as it transpired, proved an utter failure. Thus, for example, over 1,000 Jews were transferred to a place called Lingen, on the Dutch border, a camp which was hopelessly ill-equipped to receive them and where conditions were worse than those of Belsen. This camp was also multi-national, containing Russians, Poles, Italians, Yugoslavs and Czechs. Such a mixture of nationalities could, under normal conditions, be bearable were it not for the activities of the Polish liaison officer who constantly harassed the Jews by persuading them not to renounce their Polish nationality. The adverse physical conditions plus the anti-Semitic hostility of the Russians and the Poles made the return to Belsen inevitable.

The only positive method of reduction of numbers was by the repatriation of the various nationals within the camp. The French, Belgians, Dutch and Hungarians were only too eager to return home. Only the Polish Jews remained adamant in their refusal. 'To what do we return? To the cemetery of our people?' was their response to all the overtures made to them. Their own desired destination was Palestine but the prospects of obtaining the necessary emigration facilities were dim indeed.

It was in this connection that whilst on a brief visit to London I called on Sir Herbert Emerson, the High Commissioner for Refugees, to place before him a first-hand report on the situation in Belsen and to plead with him to intercede on behalf of the inmates who wished to emigrate to Palestine. His genuine sympathy was clearly visible in his response but he could only express regret that it was beyond his capacity to persuade the mandatory authorities to issue the necessary certificates which were the pre-requisite for admittance to Palestine. As I left him I could only assure him that were I to return to Belsen and inform the younger element that the doors of Palestine were barred to them I might well find some of them hanging from the rafters of their huts. My own conviction was that these desperate young people would find the ways and means to reach their desired destination. We were even then aware of the 'underground route' through Europe to the ports where ships would convey them on their 'illegal' Aliyah.

If the repatriation of Polish Jews was problematic that of the German Jews gave cause for concern. The authorities were interested in political nationality not religious persuasion and, therefore, Jews were not to expect differential treatment. Hence an official ruling was issued that the German Jew, whilst in a camp, would be treated like a Displaced Person but on his return to his home would be treated like any other German civilian. The implication of this ruling was brought home to me when I visited Berlin and learned of the plight of the returnees from the camps. Food, clothing and housing were all distributed on the basis of ration cards issued on a varying scale of values. The highest card was given to workers and the 'victims of fascism'. Jews who returned from the camps, being unfit for heavy manual labour were deemed worthy of the lowest scale of ration card. I found this most disturbing and grossly unjust. I wrote a memo of protest to the British Military Governor to the effect that not to deem suffering in a concentration camp as a victim of fascism was monstrous and such Jews deserved to receive the highest scale of ration card. All I received was a sympathetic response and the suggestion that the matter be taken up in London, the perfect example of 'passing the buck'.

With the realisation that complete repatriation of Jews could not be achieved the inmates of the camp could have maintained some sort of mental equilibrium were it not for the fact that periodic outbursts of anti-Semitism disturbed the harmony of the Displaced Person's camps, for which Polish and Russian inmates were largely responsible. As a result some of us were convinced that for their safety and peace of mind, Jews ought to be housed separately. At various meetings with the authorities I proposed that Jewish transit camps should be established where inmates could receive some new form of training which would contribute ultimately to their future life.

This proposal received warm support from the American Joint Distribution Committee and the Jewish Committee for Relief Abroad but was never officially accepted by the Military Government. But meanwhile the Jewish Relief team did excellent work in Belsen. Schools were established and workshops opened. Belsen assumed the character of a vast transit camp, since by this time all its inmates were Jews. The Central Jewish Committee, a self-appointed and autonomous body, assumed responsibility for the enrichment of the inmates. It promoted cultural activities, established a theatre, created its own newspaper called 'Undzer Stime' (Our Voice) and undertook to maintain contact with camps in the American Zone in order to present a united Jewish front in negotiations with the military authorities. Under its own dynamic leadership the Committee displayed all the essential qualities of a government within a government.

L.G.R. WAND

The question of whether the British forces did enough, quickly enough in Belsen is almost impossible to answer. In the circumstances what possibly could have been enough?

What must never be forgotten is that the war was still being fought, that the Germans were still fighting fiercely. The German troops opposing 21st Army Group were numerically equivalent, although their morale was poor and a fuel shortage limited their mobility and accentuated Allied air superiority. Our Medical Services had the clear and unequivocal duty to provide medical cover to our fighting troops. The liberation of Belsen took place only two to three weeks after the Rhine crossings; we had suffered very many casualties and we were continuing to take many casualties. Our General Hospitals were fully committed. The priority was to finish the war.

Consequently only formations which were in reserve could be sent to Belsen. The 11th Light Field Ambulance after having been heavily committed was taken into reserve, but was taken out of reserve again a few hours later when a reconnaissance party had reported back the horror of Belsen. It was, incidentally, subjected to German air attack shortly after it had set up by the camp. Other formations sent to the camp – the 113th Light Anti-Aircraft Regiment, the squadron of Royal Engineers, the 35th Pioneer Group, the 102nd Mobile Laundry and Bath Unit were all reserve troops. They were all that could be spared from the order of battle and they arrived quickly. They were commanded by officers completely committed to doing their utmost to help and one cannot commend their work too highly. Brigadier Glyn Hughes, the Medical Commander at 21st Army Group gave his all to help from the time the situation in the camp was exposed.

With regard to the General Hospitals, these had been filled from the Rhine crossing and the subsequent fighting. To make a General Hospital available it was necessary to evacuate the wounded, dissemble and pack up and to transport to the new location. This sounds easy but the hindering factors were (i) they were still needed for our wounded; (ii) rail transport did not exist; and (iii) road transport was very difficult because of the damage of war. Further, the equipment that goes to make a General Hospital is vast – memory suggests that at least two goods trains were needed. It takes two to three weeks for a General Hospital to move from one location to another. Nos.9 and 29 General Hospitals came on the scene in Belsen in the first week of May. They did their best and moved as fast as they could when they could. By then, of course, we had begun evacuating Camp I to the improvised hospitals in the ex-Panzer barrack.

The 97 British medical students who went to Belsen is another story. We were already on stand-by, kitted-out and documented for relief in Holland after its liberation. The liberation of Belsen came before our departure so our role was changed. We were all volunteers and nobody backed out when the new instruction came. I arrived at Belsen on 1 May: three or four days were lost due to freak weather – snow, ice and fog prevented flying – and one day must be allowed for call-out and transport to the departure airfield in Gloucestershire. That still leaves nine or ten days unaccounted for between 15 April, the day that Belsen was liberated, and 1 May. Why the decision to send us out could not have been made earlier I simply do not know. The most charitable possible explanation is lack of aircraft - we needed eight or nine Dakotas. I rather fear it was lack of decision rather than lack of aircraft.

We were, obviously, not the first medically capable persons in the camp but we were the first to go into the huts to work. For whatever reason the daily death rate in the huts fell quite dramatically from the time we started work. My hut (we each took over the care of a hut) had 460 inmates on take-over. Forty died on the first day, the numbers dying each day progressively and quite dramatically diminished until by day nine I had no deaths. It is conceivable that lives might have been saved had we been able to start work a week earlier. Who can say? At the time we believed that those who had decided they were going to die, died and conversely, those who were determined to live, lived. Probably the belief was a mistaken one. In summary, I believe that the British Army did its very best with all that was available and with all speed.

MAJOR W.R. WILLIAMS, RASC

I have decided to write this report, nearly 50 years late, to put on record my memory of the first British troops to enter Belsen on 15

April 1945. At the time I was a Staff Captain S and T (Supply and Transport) at HQ 8 Corps, when I was called by Colonel Walter Blackie MC to go immediately to join up with Brigadier Glyn-Hughes DSO MC DDMS of 8 Corps (and later of 2nd Army) and representatives of the Royal Engineers, Military Government, a Padre and one other. The names of these officers elude my memory but I knew Brigadier Glyn-Hughes from HQ meetings at Worthy Priory leading up to D-Day and subsequently during the campaign from Normandy. We were to go forward as a reconnaissance party to ascertain the conditions in a camp the German army were anxious to pass on to us and to avoid the war going through the area.

The high level negotiations between British General Staff 8 Corps and the opposing German army command are well documented as 8 Corps were in operational command of 11th Armoured Division, Guards Armoured and 15th Scottish Infantry; the camp was in the line of march of 11th Armoured Division. As a recce party we met up in our jeeps, hoisted white flags and proceeded along a defined route which, towards the final reference point, was bordered on our left by a fir tree plantation from which a side road led off; there were no signs or directions indicating that there was anything ahead. However, only 30 yards along this side road there was a German striped sentry box with a lift-bar pole across the road. It was staffed by an armed Hungarian soldier who just lifted the bar without the slightest interest.

Inside, immediately on the right where the trees had been cleared, there was a two-storey building outside a high barbed wire fence of stranded wire and reinforced timber, with a double gate. Outside the building were grouped SS and German army personnel, fully armed; the senior SS officer came forward to meet the Brigadier (later we were informed that he was Kramer, with Irma Grese in support).

Brigadier Glyn-Hughes immediately ordered escorts for us to go into the camp through the main gate to carry out our specialised recce: I to study the catering facilities and any signs of food, the Engineers to do the same for water and electricity, Military Government to check administration and population and the Brigadier himself the medical conditions and facilities; all were told to report to him one hour later. We were instructed to use the term 'Displaced Person' (DP) in any reference to the people in the camp.

Going into the camp proper along a dry earth roadway, with not a blade of grass anywhere, the smell and stench of what lay ahead became increasingly apparent. The daylight was clouded over by a heavy acrid haze hanging in the air, fouled by the smoke of some fires started by the DPs attempting to rip and burn their soaking and infected straw palliasses and sodden boards from the huts. These abandoned skeletal humans from hell were even trying to burn their filthy clothing. The quietness throughout was oppressive.

The DPs had started to break out of their Lagers, wooden huts surrounded by ten foot high fences of stranded barbed wire; some had collapsed on to the bare earth inside the wire, more were hanging on the wire inside as well as outside for support. Others were stumbling outside the wire in the central concourse, and many more were lying where they had fallen and died. Freedom was a forgotten word but possibly the noise of the approaching battle had penetrated their dulled senses and extracted those impossible words – freedom from hell! The strain was too much, and they were embraced in the eternal peace of the Soul.

The two SS men escorting me had no compunction in shooting two DPs who had tried to approach me. I was most apprehensive and felt vulnerable at this uncalled-for action. The hundreds of DPs with their pleading sunken eyes in grey faces and hairless heads dressed in their filthy grey striped clothing were the living dead. They made an impression that will always stay with me. Never had I seen, apart from at the Falaise Gap, such desolation and carnage, accompanied by the smell of putrefaction, but that was war, this was deprivation.

Going into and around the camp I repeatedly saw the results of mass death. The horror of increasing numbers of corpses inside and outside the Lagers, together with the stench, added more and more to the spectacle and overwhelming task that had to be tackled. Outside the hospital area some of the dead had been collected into piles seven or eight high and about 50 feet long, all naked and decomposing. There were no gas ovens nor open graves, just rotting stacks of dry skin and bones.

In the first cookhouse, a brick building, there was no water, fuel or signs of food nor containers that could possibly be used for cooking or even heating water. In all I inspected five such cookhouses, all equally bare, except that in one there were about 50lb of rotting turnips.

I reported back to Brigadier Glyn-Hughes and he immediately ordered me to return to 8 Corps HQ to alert Colonel Blackie with the urgent demand to get food and water to the camp as soon as possible. I advised that the camp was about the size of three football pitches and that we had hundreds and hundreds of DPs to feed.

Colonel Blackie immediately set my colleagues at S and T to the task and by mid-morning the next day I was able to lead the first food convoy into the camp. The food consisted of British 12-man 'compo' rations and some USA army compo packs. The water was in tanker trailers and the lorries also brought in cooking equipment. The Colonel came with me but only stayed a sufficient time to add his personal assessment of the task ahead.

We, the RASC drivers, distributed the food to all the cookhouses but it proved too rich for those who were first able to stumble to collect their rations. The effect of trying to eat such food was too much for their pitiful strength and shrivelled stomachs. So we opened all the tins into large containers, added lots of water and made a thin gruel stew which was more palatable and digestible. Likewise with the tea, which we took to the Lager huts to those too weak to reach the cookhouses. I looked in the huts but never went in, unprepared for the sight of Hades where the living were lying with the dead in the stench-filled gloom.

Other arrangements had to be made. Milk was most obviously a suitable foodstuff for the DPs but an army on the march pursuing a retreating enemy does not carry such luxuries. I decided to widen my search of the surrounding area to try and find powdered milk or tins of condensed milk. By accident I discovered a deserted army tank barracks about one mile away which had a storehouse of breakfast cereals and, more importantly, a bakery in full working order. I took the surrender of the officer left in charge.

Meanwhile, more and more help arrived, water became available and the electricity supply was restored. Gradually more professional units from 2nd Army arrived and took over our RASC primitive arrangements. This gave me more time to look around at the awesome task undertaken by the Light Anti-Aircraft Gunners who were carrying out the clearance of the copses into mass pits excavated by the Engineers. I remember being so tired and drained of energy, as was everyone else engaged in this tremendous relief work.

I witnessed two occasions when the SS were used to lift the corpses on to the only transport we found in the camp, an old tractor and a two-wheeled trailer. Once, two SS attempted to escape through the barbed wire; both were shot and their colleagues were sent after them to retrieve their bodies and load them on to the trailer to be buried with the DPs. On another occasion, during the same operation, two SS men were loading a body on to the trailer when the head came away from the trunk. The SS man casually threw the head on the trailer and together they lifted the remains and added it to the load showing no signs of remorse or discomfort. How our Gunners managed to remain sane I shall never know.

[Letter written by W.R. Williams from Belsen in April 1945]

Weds. 18th April 1945   Captain W.R. Williams
                                         S.T. Branch
                                         HQ 8 Corps
                                         B.L.A.

Dear Tom,

You've read in the papers all about the horror concentration camp we've captured. Well, that's where I'm working from now. I came in with the first troops, and have been here ever since. So you know the reason for no letter lately.

Everything you've read and more are absolutely true. I've seen everything and can swear to it. Anyone you meet, pass it on. I never believed all the fantastic stories we've heard, read about, and the atrocities committed by the SS men and women. But after being here 4 days, boy – some experience.

The conditions, the dead bodies rotting in piles 6 and 7 high, no food or water – the rags which they wear. It's a miracle how many are still alive. 500 died the first night I was here.

I could rattle off innumerable stories for you, but they must be seen to be really believed. You would never think human beings, including Germans, could stoop so low, or have such low morals. Absolutely fantastic.

The first day I spent organising cookhouses and trying to cope with the hungry mobs. Now I have a complete platoon working for me doing the detailed [work in] the cookhouses, which are inadequate, and cannot properly cope. There are no skilled cooks, and there was no lighting or water.

Now we have both, and food for all who can walk to get in. Some are so weak they try and get up and fall back dead. Nobody takes the slightest notice, and the bodies are everywhere.

We have captured SS men and women on the job now, shifting the masses of rotting discoloured bodies to a central burial trench. If they try and run away they are shot. Two did today. They are in the trench too.

Every British and co ally citizen and soldier should see this place, or on the screen. It would help solve the Jerry problem.

In one part of the camp I found some British lads, all P.O.W.'s. I whisked them off back to B[ritish] lines. Since then I find more every day.

Not a very cheery letter son, but I feel it part of my duty to pass on this information.

I'm very tired, lousy, but happy to be doing my share of the final liberation of Poles, Greeks, Russians, French and all the rest. Women and men.

As ever Chum,

[signed] Dick.

Notes on Contributors

EDITORS

Tony Kushner is Marcus Sieff Senior Lecturer in Jewish/non-Jewish relations in the Department of History at the University of Southampton. He is currently co-writing a study of refugees in the twentieth century.

David Cesarani is Parkes-Wiener Professor of 20th Century Jewish History and Culture at Southampton University and Director of the Institute of Contemporary History and Wiener Library, London. He has written and edited several books on British Jewish history and the history of the Holocaust, including *Justice Delayed* (1992) and the *Final Solution: Origins and Implementations* (1994). His most recent publication is *Citizenship, Nationality and Migration in Europe* (1996) (edited with Mary Fulbrook).

Jo Reilly is the Education and Outreach Officer at the Institute of Contemporary History and Wiener Library and co-editor of *The Journal of Holocaust Education*. Her doctoral thesis 'Britain and Belsen', examining the liberation of the camp, was completed at Southampton University in 1995.

Colin Richmond is Professor of Medieval History at Keele University, where he also teaches courses on the history of the *Shoah*. He is joint editor of *The Journal of Holocaust Education* and has written several articles on the Holocaust period. He is author, most recently, of *The Paston Family in the Fifteenth Century: Fastolf's Will* (1996).

CONTRIBUTORS

Christine Lattek has taught at Washington University, St Louis and at Cologne University, where she worked on Bergen-Belsen. Her doctoral work, completed in Cambridge in 1991, was a study of

German socialist immigrants in London in the nineteenth century. She is currently working on radicalism in the nineteenth century.

Richard Breitman is Professor of History at the American University in Washington, DC. He is author of, among other works, *The Architect of Genocide: Himmler and the Final Solution* (New York: Knopf, 1991).

Thomas Rahe works at the Bergen-Belsen Memorial Museum. He has published work on the early Zionist movement and on the Third Reich period, including 'Judische Religiositat in den national-sozialistischen Konzentationslagern' in *Geschichte in Wessenschaft und Unterricht,* Vol.44, No.2 (1993).

Annette Wieviorka is a member of the Centre National de la Recherche Scientifique, University of Caen. Her published works include *Deportation et genocide: entre la memoire et l'oubli* (Paris: Plon, 1992).

Paul Kemp is the compiler of the Imperial War Museum's 1991 publication, *The Relief of Belsen, April 1945* and formerly worked in the department of photographs at the museum.

Hagit Lavsky holds The Samuel L. Haber Lectureship for She'erit Hapleta, at the Avraham Harman Institute of Contemporary Jewry, The Hebrew University of Jerusalem. She has published a number of articles on Bergen-Belsen as a centre of Jewish Displaced Persons after the war.

TESTIMONY CONTRIBUTORS

Helen Bamber is Director of the Medical Foundation for the Care of Victims of Torture, formed in 1985. Born into a Jewish family in London she trained for a year in the 1940s with the newly formed United Nations relief and Rehabilitation Association and worked with the survivors of Bergen-Belsen concentration camp after the war.

Esther Brunstein lives in London. She has an active interest in Yiddish language and culture, has taught in several London colleges, and now works as a volunteer at the Wiener Library translating Yiddish documents. She was born in Lodz, one of three children, into a working-class Jewish family. In 1940 she was forced into the Lodz ghetto and spent four years there before being sent to Auschwitz. From there she was taken to work in a women's labour camp near Hanover and in January 1945 was marched to Belsen, where she contracted typhus. After a period of convalescence in Sweden, Esther joined her one remaining brother in London in 1947. She married in 1949 and has two daughters and five grandchildren.

M.R.D. Foot served as an army officer during the Second World War and was awarded the French Croix de Guerre for work with the SAS in Brittany. He taught politics and history at Oxford and was Professor of Modern History at Manchester. He is author of several works on the Second World War period, including *SOE in France* (19966) and *Resistance: An Analysis of European Resistance to Nazism, 1940–1945* (1976).

Alfred Garwood is a psychoanalytic psychotherapist and GP and a founder of the Holocaust Survivor Centre in London. He is the youngest member of a complete family of four survivors of Bergen-Belsen. He was born in the ghetto of Przemysl, Galicia and he and his family were among the first group of Jews to be send to the Star Camp in Bergen-Belsen in July 1943. He was liberated on 23 April 1945 from a transport which left the Belsen camp on 5 April 1945.

Eryl Hall Williams, a qualified barrister and Professor of Law, retired in 1986 from a career in teaching, first at the University of Hull and then at the London School of Economics and Political Science. During the Second World War, as a conscientious objector, he joined the Friends of Relief Service and in 1945 he served as a member of the Quaker Relief Team which was sent to Belsen. He has published an account of the work of Friends Relief Service Team 100 at the end of the war under the title *A Page in History* (1993).

Leslie Hardman is now retired after long service as the minister at Hendon Synagogue and lives in London. He served in the British forces during the Second World War and he was the first Jewish chaplain among the liberators to enter Bergen-Belsen, where he worked tirelessly on behalf of the survivors during 1945. He is co-author of a book *The Survivors: The Story of the Belsen Remnant* (1958), an account based on his experiences in Belsen camp.

Anita Lasker-Wallfisch is a cellist and a founder member of the English Chamber Orchestra. She was born in Breslau, one of three children in an assimilated Jewish family. In December 1942, following a period of forced labour and imprisonment by the Gestapo, she was deported to Auschwitz-Birkenau where she was co-opted to play in the camp orchestra. In winter 1944 Anita and her sister Renata were among a transport sent to Bergen-Belsen where they were liberated on 15 April 1945. Anita has published her memoirs as *Inherit the Truth* (1996); the manuscript on which the book is based is available to researchers at the Wiener Library.

Isaac Levy is now retired, having been minister to the Hampstead, Hampstead Garden Suburb and Bayswater synagogues. In 1939 he volunteered for active service as a chaplain to the Forces and after serving in the Middle East was appointed Senior Jewish Chaplain to the British Liberation Army. He subsequently became Senior Jewish Chaplain to all H.M. Forces and worked in Bergen-Belsen concentration camp after the liberation. He is author of several books, including *Witness to Evil* (1945) about his experiences in Belsen.

L.G.R. Wand retired in 1990 following a career in medicine spanning more than 40 years. He trained as a doctor at Trinity College Cambridge and St Bartholomew's Hospital, London and in his second clinical year was called as part of a student relief team to Belsen, where he worked under the auspices of the Red Cross for five weeks. After the war he worked as a Medical Registrar before becoming a GP in 1951. An interview recorded by Dr Wand about the work of the medical students in Belsen is available to researchers in the Imperial War Museum's Department of Sound.

W.R. (Dick) Williams retired from a career in the motor industry in 1981, after working for Austin, later British Leyland, in export sales and as a personnel manager. Having joined the army in 1939 he later received a commission. In April 1945 he was a staff captain, Supply and Transport, at Headquarters 8 Corps and, thus, was among the first party of soldiers in Bergen-Belsen on 15 April 1945. He was responsible for organising the first British convey of food into the camp, where he worked for two weeks before returning to the front.

Index

The Library of Holocaust Testimonies

Have You Seen My Little Sister?

Janina Fischler-Martinho

A vividly-told account of the author's childhood experiences of the Krakow Ghetto, this work details the loss of all her immediate family, except her older brother, with whom she escaped from the Ghetto during its final liquidation, via the sewers. An important theme in this moving tale is that of memory and loss; whilst memory may be painful, it is the only memorial to many of those who have been consumed by the *Shoah*.

1997 c 288 pages
0 85303 334 X flapped paper £14.50/$19.50

Memoirs from Occupied Warsaw 1940–1945

Helena Szereszewska
Translated by Anna Marianska

These memoirs recount the struggle for survival of a middle-class Jewish family during the Nazi occupation of Poland. Inside the Warsaw ghetto, the author witnessed the daily battle against overcrowding, hunger and disease.

1997 512 pages
0 85303 313 7 flapped paper £17.00/$25.00

The Children Accuse

Maria Hochberg-Marianska and Noe Gruss

This most unusual book contains evidence collected by the author in 1945 in Poland from children and teenagers who surfaced from hiding in forests and bunkers, and told the story of their survival as it happened. The interviews, expertly translated from the original Polish, document life in the ghettos, in camps, in hiding, in the resistance and in prison.

1996 280 pages
0 85303 312 9 flapped paper £16.95/$21.00

Vallentine Mitchell

Newbury House, 900 Eastern Avenue, Newbury Park, Ilford, Essex IG2 7HH
Tel: +44 (0)181 599 8866 Fax: +44 (0)181 0984 E-mail: vminfo@frankcass.com

North America: Vallentine Mitchell, c/o ISBS, 5804 Hassalo Street, Portland OR 97213-3644
Tel: (800) 944 6190 Fax: (503) 280 8832 E-mail: orders@isbs.com

Website: http://www.frankcass@com/vm

My Heart in a Suitcase
Anne L. Fox

Immediately after Kristallnacht in 1938, the author, then aged twelve, was sent to safety in England. This book tells of her experiences in adjusting to an unfamiliar environment, living with Jewish and Gentile families on a primitive farm and at a progressive boarding school.

1996 reprinted 1997 170 pages illus
0 85303 311 0 flapped paper £12.50/$17.50

A Cat Called Adolf
Trude Levi

This is one Holocaust memoir which does not stop at survival but goes on to describe the lasting effects of the persecution, betrayal and suffering upon those survivors.

The author's wish in telling her story is that the lessons of the Holocaust are never forgotten and that the events she has recorded are never allowed to happen again.

'The reader cannot help but marvel at her resilience and adaptability.'
The Jewish Chronicle

1995 reprinted 1995, 1996 184 pages illus
0 85303 289 0 flapped paper £13.50/$19.50

A Child Alone
Martha Blend

This book describes the author's background in pre-*Anschluss* Vienna, through its annexation by Hitler, her passage to England as a *Kindertransport* nine-year-old and her gradual assimilation into England and English culture during and after the war years.

'...compelling detail, giving an insight into how the Kindertransport children transcended the horrors of separation, guilt and uncertainty to lead full, if not altogether happy lives.'
Riva Klein, *Times Educational Supplement*

1995 170 pages illus
0 85303 297 1 flapped paper £13.50/$16.00

Vallentine Mitchell

Newbury House, 900 Eastern Avenue, Newbury Park, Ilford, Essex IG2 7HH
Tel: +44 (0)181 599 8866 Fax: +44 (0)181 0984 E-mail: vminfo@frankcass.com

North America: Vallentine Mitchell, c/o ISBS, 5804 Hassalo Street, Portland OR 97213-3644
Tel: (800) 944 6190 Fax: (503) 280 8832 E-mail: orders@isbs.com

Website: http://www.frankcass@com/vm

An End to Childhood
Miriam Akavia

Written as fiction but based on fact, this book describes the efforts of a young Polish brother and sister to survive in secrecy and constant anxiety in Lvov, at a time when Jews were being rounded up and sent to the Ghetto – or worse.

'This deeply moving book vividly recreates the complex perils of occupied Poland. Fear is tangible.'
The Jewish Chronicle

1995 124 pages illus
0 85303 294 7 flapped paper £14.50/$22.50

I Light a Candle
Gena Turgel with **Veronica Groocock**

Out of the ashes of the Nazi concentration camps came an extraordinary love story which caught the public's imagination at the end of World War II. This autobiography tells how the author survived the camps and met her husband, a sergeant working for British intelligence, when he arrived to round up the SS guards for interrogation.

1995 160 pages illus
0 85303 315 3 flapped paper £9.95/$16.00

Breathe Deeply My Son
Henry Wermuth

The autobiography of a young German Jew who was deported from Frankfurt-am-Main to Krakow, and survived both the Plaszow camp (depicted in *Schindler's Ark*) and Auschwitz.

'This book is an epic account of physical strength, low cunning, pluck, luck and an indomitable will to live.'
The Independent on Sunday

1993 reprinted 1996 216 pages illus
0 85303 246 7 flapped paper £14.50/$19.50

Vallentine Mitchell
Newbury House, 900 Eastern Avenue, Newbury Park, Ilford, Essex IG2 7HH
Tel: +44 (0)181 599 8866 Fax: +44 (0)181 0984 E-mail: vminfo@frankcass.com

North America: Vallentine Mitchell, c/o ISBS, 5804 Hassalo Street, Portland OR 97213-3644
Tel: (800) 944 6190 Fax: (503) 280 8832 E-mail: orders@isbs.com

Website: http://www.frankcass@com/vmv

From Dachau to Dunkirk

Fred Pelican

Born in Upper Silesia, the author was imprisoned before the war for the 'crime' of being a Jew. He subsequently served in the British Army, was nearly captured in Dunkirk and ended the war as an interpreter at BAOR (British Army on the Rhine) Headquarters, helping to investigate war crimes.

1993 224 pages illus
0 85303 253 X £14.50/$19.50

My Lost World
A Survivor's Tale
Sara Rosen

An account of how a young girl from Krakow was able to survive the Tarnow ghetto and escape to Bucharest, this book tells the story of what was once the largest Jewish community in the world, in a country never to be the same again for the remnants of Polish Jewry.

'*The Holocaust wiped out not just a way of life, a tradition, and Rosen's story is in rememberance of this. She escaped through a series of risky adventures and was among one of the first survivors to enter Palestine.*'
The Jewish Chronicle

1993 reprinted 1996 320 pages
0 85303 254 8 flapped paper £14.50/$19.50

My Private War
One Man's Struggle to Survive the Soviets and the Nazis
Jacob Gerstenfeld-Maltiel

The author experienced the first 21 months of Soviet rule in the Polish town of Lvov and then, from June 1941, the nightmare of Nazi genocidal policies. He survived in a most unusual way, by disguising himself as a civilian auxiliary of the German Army.

'*His closeness to the events he describes enables him to provide a wealth of detail. He recreates the unbearable tension of life.*'
The Jewish Chronicle

1993 336 pages
0 85303 260 2 flapped paper £14.50/$19.50

Vallentine Mitchell

Newbury House, 900 Eastern Avenue, Newbury Park, Ilford, Essex IG2 7HH
Tel: +44 (0)181 599 8866 Fax: +44 (0)181 0984 E-mail: vminfo@frankcass.com

North America: Vallentine Mitchell, c/o ISBS, 5804 Hassalo Street, Portland OR 97213-3644
Tel: (800) 944 6190 Fax: (503) 280 8832 E-mail: orders@isbs.com

Website: http://www.frankcass@com/vm

Alfred Wiener and the Making of the Holocaust Library

Ben Barkow

This book combines the biography of Alfred Wiener and the history of the distinguished library and research institution he founded.

From 1919, when he joined Germany's largest Jewish civil rights organisation, Wiener worked against the rising tide of right-wing extremism. With the coming to power of Hitler in 1933 he fled with his family to Amsterdam. There he set up the Jewish Central Information Office, which collected, collated and disseminated detailed information about events in Nazi Germany on a scale matched by no other organisation anywhere in the world.

This volume offers a vivid portrait of the personalities and circumstances which have shaped the development of one of Britain's most remarkable research institutions.

1997 224 pages illus
0 85303 329 3   cloth £35.00/$47.50
0 85303 328 5 paper £17.50/$24.00
Parkes-Wiener Series on Jewish Studies

The Chosen People
The Story of the '222 Transport' from Bergen-Belsen to Palestine

A.N. Oppenheim

In the summer of 1944, as the Second World War was reaching its climax, a group of almost 300 emaciated and bedraggled Jews arrived by train from Bergen-Belsen. The Germans had put them on a train, which carried them across war-torn Europe to Istanbul, where – unknown to them – they were exchanged for a group of German civilian internees from Palestine. It was an extraordinary transfer and an extraordinary deliverance.

A clear and powerful depiction of this unique event and its background, this book will be of interest to the general reader as well as to students of the history of the Holocaust and the Second World War.

1996 200 pages
0 85303 323 4   cloth £25.00/$39.50
0 85303 330 7 paper £13.50/$19.50

Vallentine Mitchell

Newbury House, 900 Eastern Avenue, Newbury Park, Ilford, Essex IG2 7HH
Tel: +44 (0)181 599 8866 Fax: +44 (0)181 0984 E-mail: vminfo@frankcass.com

North America: Vallentine Mitchell, c/o ISBS, 5804 Hassalo Street, Portland OR 97213-3644
Tel: (800) 944 6190 Fax: (503) 280 8832 E-mail: orders@isbs.com

Website: http://www.frankcass@com/vm